TRANSNATIONAL THREATS

TRANSNATIONAL THREATS

Smuggling and Trafficking in Arms, Drugs, and Human Life

Edited by Kimberley L. Thachuk
Foreword by Spike Bowman

PRAEGER SECURITY INTERNATIONAL
Westport, Connecticut • London

Library of Congress Cataloging-in-Publication Data

Transnational threats : smuggling and trafficking in arms, drugs, and human life /
edited by Kimberley L. Thachuk ; foreword by Spike Bowman.
   p. cm.
  Includes bibliographical references and index.
  ISBN 978–0–275–99404–4 (alk. paper)
  1. Transnational crime. 2. Smuggling. 3. Illegal arms transfers. 4. Drug traffic.
  5. Human trafficking. 6. Organized crime. I. Thachuk, Kimberley.
 HV6252.T76   2007
 364.1′33–dc22   2007003032

British Library Cataloguing in Publication Data is available.

Library of Congress Catalog Card Number: 2007003032
ISBN-13: 978–0–275–99404–4
ISBN-10: 0–275–99404–X

First published in 2007

Praeger Security International, 88 Post Road West, Westport, CT 06881
An imprint of Greenwood Publishing Group, Inc.
www.praeger.com

Printed in the United States of America

The paper used in this book complies with the
Permanent Paper Standard issued by the National
Information Standards Organization (Z39.48–1984).

10 9 8 7 6 5 4 3 2 1

CONTENTS

FOREWORD

Transnational Threats is unique in that the threats described are measured against distinct yardsticks: both functional smuggling activities and techniques and country-specific harms. By using both functional and regional studies to illustrate the dangers posed to social order, the reader learns through real-life examples how international drug trafficking flouts the rule of law in ways that undermine social, economic, and political stability.

This book also illustrates how the drug trade supports and fosters other organized crime. One of the most poignant examples given is the purchase of a diesel submarine from the Russian mafia by South American drug dealers. The magnitude of such a transaction puts in perspective the enormity of the threat to world order. Simply put, the drug trade has become so immensely profitable that it can lavish money on criminal gangs, public officials, and even nations to buy whatever the organizers want.

In turn, this illuminates the inescapable fact that the drug trade is an international threat for more than the drug business. What we once considered to be only a law enforcement issue, and perhaps an educational problem as well, has become an issue of world order. The success of the drug trade and the many smuggling operations that spring from it now threaten international order because this illegal trade has successfully developed techniques that frustrate law enforcement and has purchased the complicit services of officials to such an extent that perfected techniques and corrupt officials can be used for many other purposes.

The reader will be easily persuaded that once the mechanisms are developed for smuggling drugs, many of the same techniques and routes can be used to smuggle other items, including people. Americans generally believe that human trafficking is a problem in the Third World, with a minor role for Europe and Asia where we often read about women forced into prostitution. But human trafficking into the United States itself is a reality—a reality with devastating consequences.

Perhaps the most important contribution of *Transnational Threats* is not so much what the individual authors convey directly, but what they collectively convey indirectly. Two necessary lessons are compelled from the collective wisdom of the authors, neither of which will be popular with authorities.

The first lesson is that there are few international controls to address threats such as smuggling. The contributors herein demonstrate the regional impact of the myriad smuggling operations that exist. That so much harm could be done by so many smuggling operations in so many regions simply begs the question as to why there are not more controls. One reason, of course, is money. Smuggling must have some "legitimate" elements to work with, and there is so much money involved that corruption of public officials is a major factor. However, money may not be the primary issue. Concepts of sovereignty centuries old may be a larger culprit.

For nearly four centuries, the world has been organized to respect borders as the paramount guarantee of sovereignty. The nature of international smuggling means that any effective international effort to thwart smuggling operations would necessarily include the ability by law enforcement authorities to cross borders expeditiously. The success of smuggling operations clearly illustrates that the sovereignty of nations does not yield an easy remedy to these operations. With only minor exceptions, the nations of the world have not found themselves willing to give up sovereignty to permit officials from either another nation or from an intergovernmental organization to cross their borders without explicit permission.

This has not gone unnoticed. On July 17, 2006, Canada's Attorney General, the Honourable Vic Toews, publicly stated that "Terrorists and drug smugglers know no borders and so neither should North American law enforcement agencies." Even with increasingly open borders everywhere, however, nations remain organized around a border—and that which is *within* the border remains for the sovereign *alone* to govern.

There are minor exceptions. Italy and Spain, for example, permit the other to search their flagged vessels at sea. The Hungarian National Police has agents from the Federal Bureau of Investigation working side by side with them in Budapest. But these are singular exceptions. Until the world finds a better way of enforcing order, effective transnational jurisdiction, collection, and preservation of evidence and locating and protecting witnesses will be a confounding problem.

The second lesson of this volume is the fact that, immediate harms aside, smuggling is such a direct challenge to world order that it has become a major destabilizing influence for nations and regions alike. The rewards for successful illicit smuggling are immense, and the result has been the availability of enormous sums of money for bribery and complicity of officials in the criminal enterprise.

By thwarting the rule of law and corrupting officials useful to their enterprises, criminals create a vacuum of law and order, causing citizens to lose confidence in the institutions intended to protect them. In this book, the reader will find illustrations of drug smuggling that fuels corruption. No large-scale criminal enterprise can exist long without some sort of legitimate cover, and the most effective cover stems from the public official who can open the border, decline to inspect, or provide a license when needed.

More than that, however, the success of smugglers and drug traffickers inspires an ever-expanding crop of nonstate actors to engage in similar activity. Drug traffickers and dealers in arms have been the most common of these, but, as of late, we see an increasing number of terrorist adherents, slavers, and pirates who are able to take advantage of loose borders, lax laws, and complicit officials. The only reasonable explanation for this is the lack of effective enforcement mechanisms for the rule of law on a global scale.

This volume also serves another important interest: Whether there is a bona fide nexus between terrorism and organized crime has been a hotly debated subject for at least a decade. This book puts to rest much of the conjecture, sometimes subtly, sometimes directly. Importantly, the chapters graphically illustrate the seamy nature of globalization that has permitted a deadly nexus between organized crime and terrorism to grow and flourish in multiple regions of the world. The threats described illustrate both the stranglehold that crime has on some nations and the increasingly diminishing spirit of cooperation that exists in a world filled with weak, failing, or failed states.

Trafficking in weapons is yet another highly disturbing focus of this book. Arms sales are a huge business in many nations, including the United States, but a half-million people die each year from gunshot wounds. Despite this fact, it is impossible to find an international regime designed to control the dispersal of weapons. Worse, there are thousands of tons of weapons and explosives left over from the Cold War, quietly rusting away and becoming increasingly unstable because the former Soviet client states cannot afford either to maintain or to disable them. Additionally, and perhaps even more concerning, are the thousands of man-portable air defense missiles that are missing from inventories of several nations. This is particularly disturbing in an era that has recorded numerous incidents of terrorists attempting to procure these weapons to bring down commercial airliners.

Less subtle, but no less important, is another conclusion to be drawn from this collection of writings. While this volume covers a broad gamut of smuggling activity, it becomes clear that the genesis of most smuggling lies in the success of the drug trade. It was the profitability of the drug trade that permitted elaborate operations to be mounted that, in turn, provided experience and techniques that could be used for other smuggling operations.

Taken together, the chapters herein convincingly demonstrate that smuggling represents a threat to both national and international security. Of course, we should already know this. In 1981, President Ronald Reagan authorized the "collection of information concerning, and the conduct of activities to protect against, intelligence activities directed against the United States, international terrorist and international narcotics activities, and other hostile activities directed against the United States by foreign powers, organizations, persons, and their agents." The effect of this Executive Order 12333 was to declare international terrorism and international drug trafficking national security threats. Nevertheless, until September 11, 2001, neither was treated as anything more than a criminal problem, and since then, only terrorism has gained the stature of an international menace of a quality that could threaten social order.

The question left hanging by *Transnational Threats*, and properly so, is why there has been no follow-through on the processes spawned by these two threats identified by President Reagan. This, in a world of nations that are increasingly interdependent, is a question that daily grows in importance. Even a casual read of this book will illustrate that organized crime, which depends for its existence on the ability to move people and materials across borders, is a threat to more than the pocketbook; it is a collection of enterprises that has the ability to destabilize economies, purchase the allegiance of officials, fuel terrorism and, in the end, defeat the rule of law in a way that could throw the entire globe into a state of chaos.

Organized criminal activities are no less a threat to national and global security than terrorism. Russia's Prosecutor General, Vladimir Ustinov, recently said that organized crime "penetrates into state and law enforcement agencies, which poses a serious threat to the country." Crime-based corruption not only undermines the rule of law but also destabilizes governmental institutions. Similarly, success in defeating border controls creates distrust between neighbors. Lax controls of weapons and radioactive materials are the raw material for indiscriminate threats by terrorists. In short, the reader should consider these chapters not just for what they expose, but for what the activities they describe mean for world order.

Spike Bowman

ACKNOWLEDGMENTS

Having spent much of my adult life with somewhat of a strange fascination for the underbelly of international relations, this book will come as no great surprise to those who know me. Indeed, many friends and colleagues who kindly contributed to this volume are among those scholars also best known for their views on the dark side of global life. That is not to say that we have criminal minds, but to be sure we arguably view crime and criminal life through a different lens than most. Hence, when I embarked on this project, the authors responded almost immediately and enthusiastically that they had a piece to add to the jigsaw puzzle that is global smuggling and trafficking. Fitting all the pieces together over a couple of years was rather aggravating at times, but the overall picture that emerged was well worth the effort.

I have many people to whom I owe a great debt of gratitude. First, my thanks go to the authors of these chapters. Without you, this book would have been impossible since global smuggling and trafficking is so nuanced and multidisciplinary, requiring such a variety of perspectives. Your scholarship, research, and insights are truly incredible, and I appreciate how much effort you put into your chapters. Because of you, this book provides a much clearer view of global smuggling and trafficking. The threats and challenges to international security that these activities pose can now be seen with much greater clarity, hopefully spurring policymakers into renewed action.

I have a number of friends who have encouraged and supported me throughout. My gratitude goes to you my friends, Gordon Adams, Charlotte Sullivan, Stephen Flanagan, Neyla Arnas, Stuart Johnson and Michael Gold-Biss.

If I have forgotten anyone, it is only because of old age, not because I do not cherish you. I must also thank my good friend Spike Bowman for his great ideas, insights, and wonderful sense of humor. You gave me some superb information and helped put a great deal of information into perspective. Moreover, you never seemed to mind (cheerfully) rereading things innumerable times. Spike, you have so many books in your head, and I cannot wait until we coauthor our own book, my friend.

I would like to thank my research assistants, Lindsay Jarboe and Courtney Richardson. Lindsay, I bet you never thought you would see the day that this book would be published. Thank you for all the amazing background work that you did. Courtney, you are truly a champion. Thank you for all your help with background and, more importantly, with the assistance you rendered in maintaining a steady course when it sometimes looked as though the ship might sink.

I must also thank Bob Silano who believed that this book is actually worth publishing and who promoted it to Praeger Security International. As always, Bob, your wry sense of humor seems to carry the day, and let's hope that this book will be published without anyone landing in jail.

Almost without saying, a special and overwhelming thanks goes to Jeffrey Smotherman, who, in my opinion, is the Prince of All Editors. Jeff, you are a true professional. You are able to turn good work into true scholarship because you have such a keen eye and an amazing talent for crafting words into works of art. I am truly humbled by your abilities. I thank you for taking a binder full of paper and turning it into a real book.

Finally, I wish to thank my family: my rather bewildered parents, Norman and Patricia, and sister, Shelley, who are still rather unsure as to why exactly I am so drawn to criminal life. I am only *studying* this you guys! Also to my two most adored and adoring fans, my husband Joe and my son John (Bee). Thank you, Joe, for being the patient and kind and loving person you are. What was the world before you? And to the Bee: Precious Angel, I promise you, this really is not the "crap" that you say it sounds like. I hope that one day you will read it and find it at least marginally interesting. If not, please write a book of your own!

PART I

Introduction

CHAPTER 1

An Introduction to Transnational Threats

Kimberley L. Thachuk

THE OPPORTUNITIES OF A NEW AGE

In recent years, an unfortunate but perhaps inevitable underbelly of globalization has emerged to reveal increasingly adaptive individuals and groups with malevolent associations and agendas.[1] While long the scourge of international society, a fresh crop of nonstate criminal actors such as terrorists, organized criminals, pirates, and valueless international entrepreneurs in the arms and slave trade are assaulting states the world over. Many, if not all, of these powerful groups are armed with new and improved technological advances and opportunities peculiar to this age. As a result, a conundrum has arisen for international civilized society: how to counteract these transnational, nonstate enemies and still remain cohesive and cooperative in the interests of international order.

At the heart of the problem, these menaces are increasingly weakening the relatively concordant spirit between states, while simultaneously strengthening their stranglehold on host nations. Meanwhile, states squabble over legal, political, and economic measures adequate to combat terrorists and criminals. One of the more sinister activities that nonstate criminal actors excel in is the smuggling and trafficking of any number of goods, services, and people. While much of this illicit trade brings great misery and sorrow to many, so too does it provide jobs and buoys up sagging economies, often blending seamlessly into busy commerce.

It is this problematic dichotomy that has led to nothing short of a strategic quandary for leaders of fledgling democracies. The so-called losers of globalization are finding it tricky to survive in an increasingly competitive and interconnected world. Leaders now have to respond to citizen demands for prosperity. When it comes to the *source* of critical revenues, if looking the other way means vast amounts of foreign exchange will flow into the country, even if the activities involved are criminal, governments may find themselves bending to their need for political survival first and international public opinion second.

Beyond this problem, the globalized world has become so complex that it may be impossible to distinguish between the various roles and relations of the actors. States may harbor terrorists, mafia bosses may govern states, terrorists may be voted into office, criminal enterprise may be funding terrorists, and terror tactics may be used by criminals. This situation could create an atmosphere of near global anarchy. It is hardly surprising that, along with every other nonstate actor, terrorists and organized crime groups have capitalized on this chaos to delve into myriad schemes for survival and prosperity.

Smuggling and trafficking, now more than ever, are booming industries. Left untended, the consequences will be long lasting and detrimental to both economic and political stability of entire regions. Borne of this realization, states have intensified cooperative multilateral and bilateral initiatives to become a unified force in the battle against international thugs and thieves. Yet there is still work to do. To cope effectively with these complex and dangerous threats, the United States needs to tackle six significant challenges:

- understand the true nature of the problem
- resolve bureaucratic inefficiencies
- deal more effectively with root causes
- improve intelligence and law enforcement sharing
- close the security gaps between military, law-enforcement, and intelligence authorities in situations where their competencies overlap
- engage in a more comprehensive threat assessment

It is the intent of this book to address this overall need and to connect the dots between seemingly disparate threats. Examining smuggling and trafficking gives a unique perspective of the underbelly of global commerce. It further provides a glimpse of the true challenges of this era.

For their part, policymakers would be well served to view national security as a continuum where there are gradations of threats that must be dealt with by all of the tools in the government's toolkit. This would mean taking new approaches to deal effectively with matters that no longer fall neatly into either the law enforcement or the defense domains exclusively. The challenge for the U.S. Government is to address threats such as smuggling and trafficking and to formulate working relationships among agencies that meet the new reality. The terrorist attacks of September 11 only underscore the urgency of this task. Few people would have been able to predict that— in a century in which technology dominates—terrorists would use some unconventional ideas combined with very simple means to wreak significant havoc. Nor would they have imagined the complexity of the criminal schemes and the extent of the power that organized criminal groups have developed. Combating such unpredictable behavior will require a revolutionary examination of how the world is viewed, combined with some unconventional and innovative means on the part of the U.S. Government to counteract these menaces.

THE NEW WORLD

With the end of the Cold War and the increasing globalization of the economy, many people expected an era of peace and sustained global well-being to be the hallmark of the twenty-first century. The new century, however, took an unexpected turn: greater disparity of wealth and opportunity around the globe, regional instability and conflict, and the threatened failure of many states all contributed to a surprising number of transnational threats to the security of many, if not most, nations. In the United States, as policymakers were muddling their way into the global century, they often gingerly sidestepped looming issues, such as those brewing in Afghanistan and Rwanda, preferring to remain at a careful distance from unsavory situations to avoid more disasters such as Mogadishu in 1992.

Arguably, this cautious detachment gradually developed into a "gap in understanding" and overall incomprehension of the magnitude of the problems that face the world. The extent to which the gap saturates the U.S. policy community and hampers the ability of many government agencies to analyze and address threats to national security correctly and adequately is a problem of immense proportions. Issues and threats tend to be analyzed and treated discretely, without seeing, or understanding, the connections between them and the fluid nature of the problems they pose.

Since September 11, a great deal of catch-up in this field has transpired. Indeed, a near avalanche of bewildering and often contradictory information on terrorists and their networks has emerged. Experts and hacks alike have sifted through and analyzed every available detail of terrorists' financial records, their modus operandi, childhood backgrounds, mental and emotional states of mind, religious upbringing, criminal lives, socioeconomic status, and so forth, looking for clues to answer a rather simple question: Why do they hate us?

While sociologists and psychiatrists continue to ponder the answer to this question, what is more important is to sweep aside the detritus of these studies and reveal what is being said about power and the way that has changed. That is, power has somehow morphed from something that was possessed and located within institutions to an ephemeral phenomenon wielded by individuals and arranged in rather confusing collectives of influences and pressures. These collectives appear in varying stages of organization but are most often manifested in quasi-hierarchical yet loosely coordinated clusters of relations between primarily nonstate actors.

That they have all seemingly materialized from thin air in a few short decades is nothing short of alarming to conventional warfighters and traditional brokers of influence and authority in Washington, London, Paris, and, presumably, Moscow—all of whom are accustomed to the rule-laden second strike nuclear chess game of the Cold War. Yet, despite this blizzard of new information on terrorism, foreign policy has since September 11 reflected a chronic reliance on outdated and misguided conceptions of the threats to national security, driving it inexorably off course to flounder on the rocks of any number of Third World states such as Iraq. Of course, for others who follow trends in organized crime and other transnational threats, these problems have been looming for generations and, to them, the fall of the Berlin Wall was the signal that every international villain with ambition and ability would soon be vying for power in the new global disorder.

Almost 5 years after September 11, the policy gaps that mirror these gaps in understanding are slowly being closed. From the perspective of U.S. policymakers, the attacks of September 11 were a nasty jolt that irrevocably altered the perception of what and who threatens global stability. Errant individuals of indeterminate origins, loosely knit gangs of determined killers, small bands of criminal clans with extensive international connections and numerous other combinations of nonstate actors, many of whom possess state-like capabilities, are proving to be elusive, sophisticated, and deadly enemies, not only in the war on terror but also for the stability of many sovereign states in a number of regions. The actions of these groups have generated a host of problems in the economic, political, and social realms in every region where they operate, hijacking entire governments through corruption and extortion campaigns, visiting violence and terror on local populations, and distorting local economies until they are dependent on, and monopolized by, criminal enterprise.

Power in the international arena has transformed from a tool of national influence (systematically applied and bounded by rules of engagement as it was during the Cold War) to a dispersed mechanism that borders on near anarchy in any number of areas and that falls beyond the grasp of states to manage. Much of this may be attributable to globalization, which has brought with it the good, the bad, and the ugly. Along with the rapid movements of people, money, and information have come the criminals, terrorists, and thugs who cross international frontiers undetected, who peddle human beings, who sell weapons intended for mass murder, who conduct illicit monetary transactions in mere minutes, and who may carry disease and death in a suitcase.

By exporting capitalism and democracy to the world, the West did not envision that free trade would be twisted by rogues who understand that the new world order is less orderly and more anarchical than before. Indeed, the anarchy that is perpetuated by the international free market has afforded villains more opportunity and maneuverability than at almost any time since the Treaties of Westphalia. Today, prowess is measured by guile and stealth, the ability to suborn and to distort, and the ability to buy and sell any merchandise for which there is a market.

No longer can domestic security, or even law and order, be conceptualized as something distinct from national security and international armed conflict. There has been a fundamental shift in the international strategic environment, and criminal actors with ideological purpose now threaten the national security of states. Meeting this challenge will require changing the approaches of both law enforcement and the national security establishment. Both currently sit at opposite ends of the security continuum in many countries. Closing the gap between them must occur if global terrorism and organized criminal activity is to be successfully combated.

TRANSNATIONAL THREATS

For U.S. policymakers, the attacks of September 11 were shocking in terms of their source and the power behind, as well as for what the attacks meant for the victory of democratic values over communism. That the end of Cold War competition did *not* bring the desired peace and prosperity to the world was a stunning blow to those who had built careers on this ideal. To their credit, critical thinkers in Washington realized the need for a broader and more comprehensive definition of national and international security, one which transcends the simple presence or absence of military conflict.

Nevertheless, that it took a major terrorist attack on the U.S. homeland to occur for transnational threats to be addressed as serious menaces has made serious analysts reexamine many long held assumptions about what exactly is meant by "threats to national security." Indeed, the events of September 11 only underscored the need for a new understanding of a security spectrum along which are found more human-centric issues than simply the absence of war. Issues of the environment, development, social justice, democratization, universal health care, disarmament, justice, and the rule of law must now be incorporated into the concept of security.

One salient characteristic of many contemporary transnational threats that distinguishes them from those of the past is that individuals (or clusters of individuals) rather than states are the primary drivers. Historically, because problems have been addressed in some form of state-to-state relations and because the world continues to define and divide itself into sovereign states, solutions to these threats are still slow to develop; solutions have to be international in scope, but most states are unwilling to surrender their sovereign power to a global common for fear of losing an unforeseen future advantage.

Threats range from terrorism, to widespread international crime, to the rapid transfer of privately held armaments technologies, to international narcotics trafficking, to money laundering and corruption, to cyberwar and cybercrimes, to mass migration and human trafficking, to the movement of infectious diseases, to environmental degradation, to the dissemination of ethnic and religious hatred. Indeed, citizens are facing a broader and more interrelated series of security challenges than in any previous era.

Such threats have an understated profile in global security considerations when compared with big-power geopolitics, regional wars, and weapons of mass destruction (WMD) proliferation. Furthermore, some transnational issues are not viewed as direct threats to national security but rather as threats to the economy and quality of life of citizens. Others are treated as matters of domestic security, more properly addressed with a law enforcement response. Yet the combined effect of transnational threats will have damaging long-term consequences to global political and economic stability—and thus to security interests.

Most transnational threats cut across national borders (sometimes many of them) and, therefore, are frequently beyond the control of national governments. They emerge from, and are amplified by, three major trends in the global system. First is the globalization of economic activity and communications, which has brought both disparity of opportunity and economic standing, as well as a greater awareness of the technologies that make such threats truly global. Second, there is a growing imbalance in governance between a number of relatively stable, healthy democracies and a far larger number of states, especially in sub-Saharan Africa and the unstable region from North Africa, through the Middle East, South Asia, Central Asia, into Southeast Asia. Third, overlapping substantially with the other two, is a widespread increase in ethnic and religious hatred that fuels terrorism, civil strife, and international conflict.

Many of these threats are overlooked as matters of domestic security or as outside the purview of structures more traditionally devoted to national security. Yet, for instance, if environmental threats are considered, a far different picture begins to emerge. Environmental problems such as global warming were not viewed as significant to anyone but environmentalists and scientists until very recently, and even now only a few national leaders take the situation seriously so as to consider the subject grave enough for national debate. Climate change has not only led to droughts and famines in regions such as sub-Saharan Africa but also contributed to massive migrations and genocides, such as those currently in the Darfur region.[2] While this does not pose a direct threat to U.S. national security, the incessant destabilization of the region has acted as a magnet for organized crime and terrorist groups who have found fertile ground to plan operations free of interference by any form of state authority.

Compounding the inherent issues of any transnational threat are the facts that these threats are varied in nature and scope and that they overlap in curious and obscure ways. Transnational threats clearly have an understated and underappreciated profile in global security considerations compared to big-power geopolitics, regional wars, and WMD proliferation, in part because policymakers tend to be largely *reactionary*. Terrorism is the most poignant example.

Terrorism came to the forefront of U.S. policy considerations only after a significant loss of life and treasure on the American homeland. While some transnational threats are perhaps better characterized as threats to the economy, and quality of life of citizens, and therefore threats to national interests rather than national security, the combined effect of drug, weapons, and human trafficking, piracy, acts of terrorism, along with their critical enablers, cannot be overlooked merely because they do not fit into the more traditional, and perhaps more *comfortable* notions of what constitutes a threat to national security.

Understanding the nature of the threat, the environment that spawns it, the special challenges involved in combating it, and developing broad guiding principles for coping with an altered global reality have been as difficult as confronting the immediate challenges of transnational threats. For many, September 11 represented a watershed in terms of threats to U.S. national security; the attacks laid bare the reality of a world that had already come into existence but which had barely been acknowledged. Today, nonstate actors are as significant to national security as state aggressors; technology has permitted the actions of even small groups to be as lethal as those of nation-states in older and more comfortable times. No longer can the use of military force as a predominant instrument of foreign policy successfully counter small cells of highly mobile, often fanatical individuals.

A new and broader view of global security is needed, along with a "new security packaging,"[3] that will allow the United States, other nations, international organizations, nongovernmental organizations, and the private sector to formulate effective long-term strategies, rather than remain mired in a reactive posture. Developing such a strategy requires a better understanding of how transnational forces threaten the security of humanity, how they are linked, and how they are likely to mutate and grow in the future.

CORRUPTION AND MONEY LAUNDERING

In recent years, there has been a growing reliance by criminals and terrorist groups on weak states with regimes that can be suborned and manipulated in order to provide safe havens for terrorists and outlaws. Weak states are bases from which smuggling operations can be run, havens where money can be laundered, and launching pads for secure transit zones that permit illicit goods and people to be trafficked. Most recently, an even more alarming trend has been seen in which the financial and legal systems of strong states begin to fall victim to criminal manipulations.

The war on terror has exposed a number of critical weaknesses and vulnerabilities in the international system. While it has long been understood that terrorists and organized criminals use sovereign states as havens from which to conduct operations, it was unclear until recently to what extent these groups had insinuated themselves into a number of regions and how they did it. A significant key to unraveling this mystery lies in one word: *money*. Terrorists and criminal groups simply cannot function without ready access to money and the ability to maneuver it quickly and secretly across borders. Yet these groups also need impunity from detection and prosecution in the states where they operate. They have therefore used large amounts of money to breach vulnerable jurisdictions and then mold them into "states of convenience" for themselves by duping, suborning, and extorting individuals in governments.

Smuggling and trafficking activity distorts local economies and helps outlaws build semifeudal fiefdoms from which they control parts of states into which government authorities are often afraid to enter. Citizens are lured into these illicit trades, either by the vast amounts of money involved or through extortion by the criminal bosses who run them. In any number of states, ranging from Colombia to Angola to Afghanistan, official state justice has been displaced by parastate or vendetta justice that casts doubt on the government's ability to guarantee even the most basic elements of sovereignty. In that sort of environment, criminal entrepreneurs have eroded the legitimacy of government institutions through the subornation and extortion of public officials to such an extent that the state is unable to guarantee even the most basic order for citizens. Indeed, coupled with the use of extreme violence, this has not only led to a crisis of legitimacy for many governments but also allowed many individuals to operate with relative impunity for long periods of time.

As a result of years of lost legitimacy and quasi-rule, military and police forces are demoralized, justice systems barely function, and governments increasingly resort to ineffective crisis-driven policy. Meanwhile, citizens alternate between indifference and skepticism that anything will change to outrage that the government is incapable of maintaining even the most basic order in the country.

Increasingly, such crises in governance have generated the perfect ecosystems for private power brokers. It is much easier to conduct illicit commerce, plan conspiracies, recruit and train terrorists, and bypass a system when order is lacking and public institutions are rife with patronage and graft. If criminal bosses manage to wrest control from state authorities, entire communities become subject to a range of arbitrary and personally motivated interests, most often bolstered by extreme use of violence and fear. In some regions a quasi-government can emerge in which groups provide "public services," such as housing, education, and even rough justice to the people, effectively replacing the state as the governing authority in certain sectors.

However magnanimous these deeds may appear to the recipients, these self-appointed leaders were not democratically chosen by the people, and they perform these acts with corrupt motives. They insinuate themselves into the culture using large amounts of money, coupled with some ideology and appeals to the disaffected, to breach vulnerable jurisdictions and then mold them into states of convenience for themselves. An additional and inescapable fact is that these conditions only serve as a breeding ground for those who are liable to take advantage of feelings of alienation and despair as has been demonstrated in Afghanistan and Somalia.

Corruption serves as a pillar of support for smuggling groups. It is a critical enabler that guarantees impunity for criminal and terrorist groups who must be able to safeguard the immunity from detection and prosecution of their members and maintain increasingly complex international operations free from interference by the authorities. Organized criminals and terrorists successfully target weak and corrupt states to become safe havens. Once situated, these groups continue to work the system by assembling an extensive web of compliant officials whom they suborn to be left alone, to facilitate their operations and financial transactions, to supply them with information on government plans, and to provide protection. In this manner, they slowly erode whatever legitimacy is left of institutions, corrode the rule of law, and undermine the ability of central governments to cooperate on global agenda items, such as the exploitation of global financial systems. The fact that terrorists and international criminal groups strategically use money to corrupt individuals, business sectors, and governments means that this is no longer simply an internal state problem.

Indeed, official corruption will be the key determinant of whether organized crime thrives or withers in emerging powers such as China. That this will have great impact for the rest of the world cannot be overlooked. Hence, not only does corruption minimize the opportunities for state control over the activities of criminals, it inevitably defeats the fundamental basis of state sovereignty and by extension international order at some level. At a minimum, to operate fluidly across the frontiers of multiple states simultaneously, secret networks must have reasonable assurance of impunity from detection and apprehension. The subornation of public officials and political leaders through the use of bribery, graft, collusion and/or extortion is the vehicle by which to secure that assurance.

The ability to launder or manipulate the proceeds of smuggling and trafficking activity are critical to illicit activities. Without this ability, these industries would dry up overnight. For international terrorists and criminals, the ability to move, manipulate, and launder money is crucial to successful operations.[4] Such money maneuvers can ripple across entire regions, embroiling global markets and threatening vital economic interests, as well as destabilizing countries politically. Large amounts of money can be shifted rapidly and anonymously across the globe, using wire transfers, faxes, and Internet connections. Sometimes such technology is exchanged for, or used in conjunction with, centuries-old practices. Such fluid and interchangeable combinations for manipulating money undoubtedly give terrorist and criminal networks a strategic advantage over many states.

The facilitators for these transactions are corrupt individuals. Indeed, the reliance on personal connections cannot be overstated. From the perspective of organized crime and terrorist groups, governments that willingly acquiesce or actively facilitate criminal transactions are ideal sovereigns. Hence, organized crime and terrorist groups are found on the darker side of the system of vested interests and factional struggle.

Traditionally, illicit money movements involved black market currency exchanges and parallel remittances. In the case of black market money exchanges, the proceeds of criminal activity would be generated in one currency, sold to a currency broker, and then exchanged for a different currency. The so-called *hawala* (or "trust") system is one method by which Islamic terrorists and organized crime groups have managed to distribute money more easily and quickly. The system works on an honor scheme, with transaction records being kept only until the money is delivered and subsequently destroyed. Anyone can go to a *hawala* dealer in thousands of cities around the world and have any quantity of cash transferred anywhere in a matter of hours. No cash moves across a border or through an electronic or sanctioned financial transfer system. If practiced on a large scale, such money maneuvers could destabilize global markets, undercut vital economic interests, and destabilize the political hegemony of entire nations.

SMUGGLING AND TRAFFICKING AS SECURITY THREATS

Most smuggling activities may not appear as overly menacing in relation to wars, genocide, and other atrocities that the world continues to witness. Indeed, if one were to consider the intrastate smuggling of cigarettes within the United States, it might appear to deprive state authorities of tax revenue, which people often find amusing. What is not amusing is that even cigarette smuggling has a sinister side. For example, Hezbollah ran a complex cigarette-smuggling scheme in North Carolina from 1996 until the summer of 2000, when 18 members of the ring were apprehended.[5] Among other things, proceeds from this scheme purchased night-vision goggles, cameras and scopes, surveying equipment, global positioning systems, mine and metal detection equipment, video equipment, advanced aircraft analysis and design software, laptop computers, stun guns, radios, mining, drilling and blasting equipment, radars, ultrasonic dog repellers, and laser range finders.

Other forms of smuggling and trafficking are more egregious still. Human trafficking, which often means slavery, has long been considered a legacy banished centuries ago. However, today both of these anachronisms have managed to reappear and flourish. Trafficking in human life not only is increasing in frequency but also continues to exact a terrible toll on its victims, stripping them of liberty and visiting upon them humiliation, suffering, torture, and other outrageous violations of human rights. It is the fastest growing criminal enterprise in the world, which only shows how dispensable human life remains in an era of globalization and democratization.

In almost every region of the world, human trafficking has become a more attractive business prospect than other forms of smuggling and trafficking because it does not require technical expertise or a distribution network as do other highly profitable enterprises, such as narcotics and smuggling of military hardware. Furthermore, in many countries, the penalties for trafficking in persons are significantly lower than they are for narcotics. Malaysia, for example, provides the death penalty for drug trafficking—but has a maximum penalty of 15 years for human trafficking. Much of this trade involves the abduction or fraudulent recruitment of women and children for the purposes of the sex industry, domestic servitude, and sweatshop labor. This tends to raise a plethora of gender issues, making it a problem that is almost taboo for some cultures to tackle and one to which others pay too little attention because of gender stereotyping.

The traffic in illicit drugs is also a grave threat to international security. The illegal narcotics business is estimated to be the second largest industry in the world, meeting the demand of between 3 and 4 percent of the world's population.[6] The obscene profits that flow from the illicit drug trade rival the gross national product of many countries. Moreover, these profits are sufficient to undermine legitimate commerce and a nation's balance of payments and monetary system, as well as to jeopardize international bank cooperation. The drugs that end up on the streets undermine social order, contribute to diseases, spark poverty for many, and often lead to the breakdown of justice systems. The profits from the traffic of illicit narcotics have enabled drug traffickers to become increasingly adept at suborning, undermining, and threatening entire governments and, thereby, not only elude law enforcement efforts but also conduct their activities with relative impunity. Moreover, drug trafficking activity is more than ever what former U.S. Drug Czar William Bennett termed a "clear and present danger to the national security of the United States," if not the world. This danger increases exponentially as many of the most powerful terrorist groups are now engaging in drug trafficking to fund terrorist operations.

Meanwhile, the traffic in small arms amounts to somewhere between $1 billion and $4 billion per year and contributes to seemingly intractable and bloody conflicts that have continued unchecked for decades. The spread of arms is a catalyst for further and more intense conflict in regions such as sub-Saharan Africa where protracted ethnic strife has spread from within single states to inundate entire regions in genocidal rampages. The arms are often circulated from one war zone to another, stoking conflicts wherever they arise. With mass killing comes stymied economic growth, the spread of disease, mass starvation, mass migrations, and the use of child soldiers. The tragedy in Darfur is only the latest in generations of wars fueled by small arms trafficking.[7]

The trafficking in higher-end arms, such as nuclear, biological, or chemical weapons, has far-reaching and nightmarish consequences. In terms of nuclear smuggling, *availability* of materials and the *intentions* of the end user dictate the nature of the threat. While great fear is generated by the chance that a nuclear weapon will be smuggled into the wrong hands, the probability is low. More probable scenarios are the smuggling of nuclear materials or components used to make weapons. In 2003, the smuggling network of the infamous "godfather" of Pakistan's nuclear weapon's program, A.Q. Khan, was revealed to have been selling nuclear components to Libya, which led to speculation of other similar marketplaces such as North Korea, Iran, Iraq, and Syria.[8] Whether all the components were to land in the hands of state authorities is another question altogether.

Biological weapons contain living or viral organisms, or the toxins produced by them, to kill or incapacitate. Some toxins cause death within minutes or hours, while bacteria and viruses usually require an incubation period of at least 24 hours before symptoms appear. Chemical weapons include nerve and cyanide gases and more plebian toxic industrial chemicals such as chlorine. The proliferation of both chemical and biological weapons has increased since the termination of chemical/biological programs in a number of countries, most significantly in some of the client states of the former Soviet Union. It is unknown precisely what chemical or biological agents terrorist groups may have in their possession. The al Qaeda videotapes documenting the testing of poison gas on three dogs confirmed that the group had been experimenting with chemical weapons.[9] The use of sarin gas in the Tokyo subway in 1995 by Aum Shinrikyo, killing twelve and leaving approximately 5,000 with damaged health, demonstrates that this kind of attack could be easily repeated in virtually any major city.

The traffic in other commodities (for example, cigarettes, gold, diamonds, and counterfeit items) represent large criminal enterprises the world over. The trade in the now notorious "blood diamonds" has been well documented as a funding source for such deliberate bloodbaths in places as Sierra Leone, Liberia, Angola, Guinea, and the Democratic Republic of Congo. In Sierra Leone, the country's 10-year civil war was significantly fueled by the smuggling of diamonds. In a bid for control of the country's rich diamond fields, the Revolutionary United Front rebel group waged a brutal campaign against the government. Employing a combination of guerrilla, criminal, and terror tactics, they systematically murdered, tortured, and mutilated tens of thousands of civilians to win the advantage. To fund their campaign, the rebels traded in illegally mined diamonds, often dumping them below fair market value. The diamonds were subsequently smuggled to international diamond markets in places such as Antwerp, Belgium, to be sold at unseemly profits.

Al Qaeda has also been involved in smuggling diamonds as a way of moving money to fund operations around the world.[10] Along with gold, which can be melted down, diamonds are practically untraceable and can be readily sold for cash just about anywhere. Moreover, due to the increasingly successful interdiction of illegal monetary transactions by law enforcement, terrorists and criminal groups have been driven further underground or toward more sophisticated methods for moving their money. The underground money exchange system in South Asia has been used extensively, as have other alternate specie such as gold and diamonds. Gems are easy to hide, generally maintain their value, and are untraceable for the most part. Gold is often used by *hawaladars* to balance accounts. Its origins are also untraceable because it can be smelted, made into jewelry, and reconstituted in a variety of forms. Gold is probably more easily manipulated than are gems because it can be deposited on account without a transaction report.

There has always been incentive for just about everyone in society to be complicit in such illegal trade: from consumers who prefer the better/lower priced goods, to smugglers who make a large profit, to middlemen and authorities with their propensity for bribery and corruption. Even in countries such as the United Kingdom and the United States, consumers save money when and where they can. In the United Kingdom, it is estimated that approximately one-third of the cigarettes smoked are imported illegally.[11]

Smuggling in counterfeit goods has exploded in recent years. In June 2006, trade representatives from the European Union met with U.S. trade representatives to intensify efforts across the Atlantic to stop counterfeit goods trafficking. The overwhelming majority of these goods are consumer luxury items, such as Gucci handbags, Rolex watches, and Louis Vuitton luggage.

A sobering statistic is that along with the seemingly harmless counterfeiting of luxury items there has been an egregious global trade in counterfeit pharmaceuticals: an estimated 10 percent of all the medicines traded globally are counterfeit.[12] For instance, criminal groups have exploited the market for a drug based on the Chinese plant Artemesinin. It is the only drug left available that resists the malaria parasite. To realize windfall profits, criminals have diluted the drug to the point that it is inevitable that the parasite will soon be able to resist Artemesinin. In a world where malaria accounts for some 350 to 500 million malaria illnesses annually—of which more than a million end in death—this is not simply a trade in counterfeit snake-oil remedies; it is trade in human misery and poses a potential catastrophic transnational health threat.[13]

THE NEXUS BETWEEN ORGANIZED CRIME
AND TERRORISM

Another piece of the smuggling puzzle is the material support that organized criminal activity provides for terrorism. In recent years, as state sponsorship for terrorist groups has steadily declined, terrorists have resorted to a variety of schemes that include myriad criminal conspiracies previously considered the sole domain of organized crime groups. The most lucrative profit makers involve a range of smuggling and trafficking ventures. There are at least four main criminal activities traditionally thought of as the domain of organized crime and which now constitute money-generating activity of terrorist groups: narcotic trafficking, arms trafficking, human smuggling and trafficking, and smuggling of WMD. Moreover, these activities include any number of lesser crimes such as extortion, kidnapping, gambling, shakedowns, document forgery, bank robbery, identity theft, credit card fraud, and so forth.[14]

What continues to be one of the greatest errors in the campaign to defeat terrorist groups is the tendency to downplay their criminal activity or the key members of these groups who engage in criminal conspiracies to raise needed cash to sustain the operational elements of terrorism. In particular, the effort to combat these threats is based on a rather myopic view of terrorism that often overlooks its connection to international criminal activity and its proceeds to finance terrorism. As a result, these two phenomena are treated separately by policymakers, which is not conducive to understanding the multifaceted nature of either. In fact, it is precisely the fluid and often overlapping nature of both types of transnational actors that is frequently misunderstood.

One need only look at drug trafficking to draw the connection between organized criminal enterprise and terrorism. Nor is the motive for engaging in this illicit trade solely profit-driven. Indeed, terrorist groups benefit from dealing with narcotics smugglers who, through the years, have established reliable underground networks that enable the almost seamless movement of money, goods, and people quickly and reliably. According to the U.S. State Department, at least a dozen of the world's 25 largest terrorist groups have ties to drug traffickers around the world.[15] Some of these terrorist groups include the Revolutionary Armed Forces of Colombia, the United Self-Defense Groups of Colombia, the National Liberation Army, the Shining Path, the Palestinian Islamic Jihad, al Qaeda, the Islamic Movement of Uzbekistan, Hezbollah, the Kurdistan Worker's Party, the Basque Fatherland and Liberty, the Liberation Tigers of Tamil Eelam, and Abu Sayyaf.

Many of the transactions demonstrate the sinister outcome of smuggling and trafficking. For example, in November 2002, the Federal Bureau of Investigation helped to halt two major drugs-for-arms deals. In the first case, an American and two Pakistanis attempted to trade 5 metric tons of hashish and 600 kilograms of heroin for 4 Stinger antiaircraft missiles, which they planned to send to al Qaeda operatives. In the second case, four members of the paramilitary organization, the United Self-Defense Forces of Colombia, planned to trade $25 million in cash and cocaine for 5 containers of Warsaw Pact weapons.[16]

To raise capital terrorist groups, besides drug trafficking, engage in a variety of intricate and sometimes convoluted schemes involving numerous countries. The perpetrators are just as complex to follow as their machinations. For instance, in June 2003, Italian financial police targeted some 40 sites in and around Milan, arresting five Tunisians and a Moroccan. The suspects, an *imam* among them, were accused of providing financial and logistical support to the Algerian Salafist Group for Preaching and Combat. Charges ranged from false accounting, engaging in illegal immigration, receiving counterfeit documents, abetting and financing a terrorist organization, and trafficking in stolen cars. They are also believed to have been running legitimate businesses as fronts to raise money for terrorist purposes.

Along with other counterfeit criminal operations that pirate everyday goods, al Qaeda has been linked to a scheme in which counterfeit Vaseline is smuggled from Dubai to Britain.[17] According to the Organisation for Economic Co-operation and Development, counterfeiting and the traffic in such luxury items accounts for approximately 7 percent of world commerce.

Indeed, Great Britain's Organized Crime Task Force reports that the so-called victimless crime of the counterfeiting and smuggling trade in Northern Ireland, which nets approximately £9 billion annually, generates a loss to the national treasury of £1.5 billion per year in unpaid taxes.[18] One of the benefits for criminals has been that, to date, the penalties for being caught are less serious than for drug trafficking. Hence, while Irish paramilitaries have smuggled shipments of heroin from suppliers in southern Spain and elsewhere, counterfeit tobacco products from eastern Europe have netted similar profits but with less risk. In the case of the Provisional Irish Republican Army (PIRA), it is estimated that between $1 million and $15 million is needed to sustain their terrorist campaigns. The PIRA's estimated fundraising capacity from smuggling counterfeit goods and contraband is between $7.7 and $12.3 million.[19]

UNDERSTANDING A COMPLEX THREAT

Far from being local law-enforcement problems, many smuggling and trafficking operations are threats to international security and world stability. While it is impossible to know for certain the amount of money laundered annually, it is estimated to be somewhere around $1 trillion.[20] This mirrors not only the scale of the illicit economic activity from which this money flows but also the violence, extortion, corruption, and devastating social consequences for all the regions and peoples affected by these activities.

Furthermore, sums of money this vast yield great power and strategic lever-age, especially when compared to the global licit economy, which generates somewhere between $5 and $10 trillion per year. Additionally, criminal en-trepreneurs have learned that diversity in crime translates to diversification of power, and over time, a few groups have come to rival, if not surpass, the influence of some sovereign states.

Many governments are unable to stop such entrepreneurial outlaws from hijacking strategic pieces of their sovereign influence and even of their sovereign territory. From these virtual states of convenience, criminals and terrorists can successfully prosecute conspiracies on a global scale and threaten international stability and security with relative impunity. Fight-ing the activities of terrorist and organized crime groups is often a losing proposition for a developing/democratizing state that has dire need of both foreign exchange and the time necessary to allow its new governmental insti-tutions to take hold. Governments would have to divert significant resources to bring these groups to justice, but in some cases illicit capital from criminal enterprise exceeds and becomes more important than that of the nation's principal foreign exchange earners. The result is that this much-needed for-eign exchange could be forfeited if the illicit income were sacrificed. In newly minted democracies, the people have little time for leaders who cannot de-liver on campaign promises and bring prosperity to countries that have languished economically and politically under authoritarian rule.

What is increasingly evident is that criminals and terrorists are more adroit than many states at adapting to the realities of a globalizing world. Governments must not only catch up to the methods being employed by such groups but also surpass the groups by responding creatively, consistently, and quickly to the security challenges of this new century. In an era of emerging technologies and criminal actors far more agile than nation-states, catching up is possible, surpassing may not be.

NOTES

1. Kimberley L. Thachuk, "Globalization's Sinister Underbelly: Organized Crime and Terrorism," in *The Global Century: Globalization and National Security*, vol. 2, ed. Richard L. Kugler and Ellen L. Frost (Washington, DC: National Defense University Press, 2002), 743–760.

2. Environmental insecurity is a central long-term cause to the Darfur crisis. Drought and desertification exacerbated land disputes between sedentary agricul-turalists and seminomadic herders for decades. Competition for arable land became more intense after the 1980s when the Sahel region underwent longer periods of drought and when the land disputes became politicized. For more detail on the role of the environment as a long-term cause to the Darfur genocide, see Scott Strauss, "Darfur and the Genocide Debate," *Foreign Affairs* 84, no. 1, January–February 2005. See also BBC News, *Q & A: Sudan's Darfur Project*, available at http://news.

bbc.co.uk/2/hi/africa/3496731.stm; and Human Rights Watch, *Darfur in Flames: Atrocities in Western Sudan* 16, no 5, April 2004, 7, available at www.hrw.org/reports/2004/sudan0404/sudan0404.pdf#search=%22causes%20of%20darfur%20conflict%22; I am indebted to Courtney Richardson for the sections on Darfur in this chapter.

3. Julian Lindley-French, "Towards a New Security Package?" Presentation at *The Security Gap between the Military and Law Enforcement in Counter Terrorism*, National Defense University, Washington, DC, October 23–24, 2002.

4. *Money manipulation* connotes the ability to move and maneuver sums of money without detection, while *money laundering* is the steps by which the proceeds of a crime must be obscured and reintroduced into the financial system.

5. "18 Accused of Cigarette Smuggling to Help Hezbollah," *USA Today*, July 22, 2000. The smuggling operation exploited the tax differential between North Carolina, which has low cigarette taxes at 5 cents per pack, and Michigan, with high taxes at 75 cents per pack. Another group of 18 people were indicted in March 2006 in Michigan for helping to fund Hezbollah with profits from bootlegged cigarettes, counterfeit tax stamps, fake Viagra tablets, and hijacked toilet paper. See Joe Swickard, "Feds Say Smuggling Ring Helped Fund Hezbollah," Associated Press, March 29, 2006.

6. For recent trends, see United Nations (UN) Office for Drug Control and Crime Prevention, *Global Illicit Drug Trends 2003* (New York: UN International Drug Control Programme, 2003).

7. In recognition that the small arms trade is in part fueling the Darfur genocide, UN Security Council Resolution 1556 of July 30, 2004, called for an arms embargo on nongovernmental entities and individuals operating in Sudan. The 2005 expert panel, appointed by UN Secretary General Kofi Anan to monitor the arms embargo, found that the arms were most likely of Chinese origin and that weapons sold by Beijing to Khartoum were likely to be used in Darfur. However, highlighting the circuitous nature of small arms trafficking, the panel was unable to state definitively that the arms were of Chinese origin and found no evidence that Beijing was overriding the embargo. For more details, see Sudan Tribune, "Chinese Arms in Darfur: The Twisted Trail of Weapons," *Sudan Tribune*, June 19, 2006, available at www.sudantribune.com/spip.php?article16264. See also Dianne E. Rennack, *Sudan: Economic Sanctions*, CRS Report for Congress, RL32606 (Washington, DC: Congressional Research Service, October 2005). For a discussion of possible responses to mass killing, see David C. Gompert, Courtney Richardson, Richard L. Kugler, and Clifford H. Bernath, *Learning from Darfur: Building a Net-Capable African Force to Stop Mass Killing*, Defense and Technology Paper 15 (Washington, DC: Center for Technology and National Security Policy, July 2005).

8. Charles D Lutes, "New Players on the Scene: A.Q. Khan and the Nuclear Black Market," *eJournal USA: Foreign Policy Agenda* 10, no. 1, March 2005.

9. Judith Miller, "Al Qaeda Videos Seem to Show Chemical Tests," *The New York Times*, August 19, 2002.

10. See, for example, Lucy Jones, "Al Qaeda Traded Blood Diamonds," BBC News, February 20, 2003.

11. "UK is Tobacco Smuggling Hotspot," BBC News, February 13, 2001.

12. "Action on Fake Drugs Urged by WHO," BBC News, February 16, 2006.

13. World Health Organization and the United Nations Children's Fund, "World Malaria Report 2005," i, available at www.rbm.who.int/wmr2005/.

14. Financial Action Task Force on Money Laundering, "Report on Money Laundering Typologies 2001," 19.

15. For recent trends, see, for example, UN Office for Drug Control and Crime Prevention, *World Drug Report 2005*, 2 vols. (New York: UN Office on Drugs and Crime, 2005).

16. "Feds Break Up Drug Smuggling Linked to Terrorist Groups," *New York Times*, November 6, 2002. The weapons cache included 9,000 assault rifles, 300 pistols, 53 million rounds of ammunition, 300,000 grenades, and some rocket-propelled grenade launchers.

17. These include condoms, repackaged medicines such as Viagra with expired shelf-lives, toiletries such as Armani and Chanel perfumes, Head and Shoulders shampoo and Oil of Olay cream, chocolates and other food products, spare car parts, and compact discs. See "Massive Haul of Counterfeit Goods," BBC News, July 26, 2002.

18. The Organised Crime Task Force, *Threat Assessment 2003: Serious and Organised Crime in Northern Ireland* (Belfast: Northern Ireland Organised Crime Task Force, 2003), 12, available at www.nio.gov.uk/octf_threat_assessment_2003.pdf. On July 28, 2005, the Provisional Irish Republican Army (PIRA) released a statement announcing a cessation of all illegal activities. However, it is the belief of the UK Organized Crime Task Force that some members of the PIRA, as well as dissident elements of the Continuity IRA (CIRA) and Real IRA (RIRA), continue to be heavily involved in contraband smuggling, extortion, fraud, robberies, and intellectual property crime. See Organized Crime Task Force, *Annual Report and Threat Assessment 2006: Organized Crime in Northern Ireland*, 29, available at www.octf. gov.uk/publications/PDF/OCTF%20Annual%20Report %20 and %20Threat % 20Assessment%202006.pdf.

19. National Criminal Intelligence Service, *UK Threat Assessment of Serious and Organised Crime 2002*, July 2, 2003.

20. *Anti Money Laundering and the Financing of Terrorism*, World Bank and IMF Global Dialogue Series, 2002, vii.

PART II

Functional Areas

CHAPTER 2

Narcoterrorism: A Definitional and Operational Transnational Challenge

André D. Hollis

On a quiet Sunday morning in Colombia, a Catholic priest delivers a sermon to a congregation in a small church. As he does so, members of the Fuerzas Armadas Revolucionarias de Colombia (FARC) surround the church, enter it, and lock the doors. FARC members kill the priest by cutting his throat. Moreover, they cut out the 6-month-old fetus from a young woman, killing both. They videotape this massacre and leave the tape as a warning to residents not to cooperate with government efforts to combat coca cultivation—a source of hundreds of millions of dollars to the FARC who tax cultivation, processing, and transport as a means of financing their terror operations.

In Afghanistan, a senior narcotics trafficker named Haji Bashir Noorzai similarly taxed opium production. He generated millions of dollars in profit and used a portion of his profits to purchase weapons, improvised explosive devices, and other materials that he provided to representatives of the Taliban, al Qaeda, and other terrorists. Congressional testimony revealed that Noorzai provided a least $28 million directly to al Qaeda in 2003.

Over the past several years, Colombian-based groups such as the FARC, the Autodefensas Unidas de Colombia, and Ejército de Liberación Nacional have waged a brutal campaign of terror against the Colombian people by financing their efforts through taxation of coca cultivation. Individuals and groups in Afghanistan, Southeast Asia, and Russia similarly tax the growth, processing, transport, and sale of illicit drugs to finance terror, criminal, and other covert activities. The profits are used to purchase weapons, safe houses, transportation, and information. Most ominously, terrorists and other criminal organizations increasingly rely upon the methods of moving drugs across national and regional boundaries as a means to move individuals, weapons, and precursors.

Narcoterrorism exists in two forms: First, it exists *wherever* the profits from drug trafficking—its cultivation, processing, transport, or eventual sale and use—are used to pay for politically motivated terrorist activity; and second, it exists *whenever* drug traffickers use terrorist acts, such as assassination, bombing, extortion, and other threats, to hinder or otherwise contest acts of sovereignty, including law enforcement. Most often, narcoterrorism thrives in parts of the world where the state is either ineffective or nonexistent.

For example, narcoterrorism thrived in Colombia until that country's government, with the support of the United States and other nations, began efforts to establish sovereignty and combat drug trafficking. In response to these efforts, these criminal groups threatened coca farmers with death, kidnapping, and extortion if they did not continue to produce coca for processing and shipment. Colombian officials who oppose their efforts are also threatened, killed, or otherwise intimidated.

In the Balkans and central Asia, criminal and terrorist groups use drug trafficking tactics, techniques, and procedures (often with the active, paid assistance of drug trafficking organizations) to move weapons, people, money, and information throughout the regions. As a result, groups are able to pay volunteers and move weapons, people, and other material throughout the region (weapons and terrorist transport to and from Georgia's Pankisi Gorge is an example) via routes and established methods that are clandestine and time-proven.

In Southeast Asia, groups have encouraged drug cultivation and trafficking to generate profits to pay for terrorist activity. Jemaah Islamiah, for example, derives significant proceeds from heroin and methamphetamine consumption by U.S., Australian, and other Western citizens. These proceeds are used, in part, to fund its activities in Southeast Asia and support terrorist organizations there.

Finally, and perhaps of most concern to U.S. policymakers, drug trafficking organizations in Mexico, the Caribbean, and other Latin American countries are known to provide transport, for a price, to non-Latins seeking illegal entry into the United States. Many of these individuals seek entry for criminal or, potentially, terrorist activity. The existence of time-proven, clandestine access into the United States is a continuing threat to homeland defense and security since these access providers seek to kill or injure American citizens (through drug trafficking) and will provide support for the right price.

International and governmental responses to these worldwide threats have been tepid for several reasons. First, many do not understand the nature of the threat. Traditional threats to national sovereignty and regional stability have been viewed as state action (that is, state-on-state aggression). This traditional view considers narcotics-related activity as exclusively criminal in nature. Second, some view the threat of narcotics-funded terrorism as someone else's problem. These views ignore the fact that this threat is a multinational or transnational one. Third, many governmental and international bodies lack the will to confront this threat individually or as a collective group. Thus, the narcotics-funded terrorist threat to Colombia is seen as a *Colombian* problem, rather than a regional or hemispheric one. Finally, some governments lack the capability to address the threat even when they recognize the danger. In these cases, they either ignore the challenge or seek, unsuccessfully, regional or international assistance.

Narcoterrorism, however, is starting to receive attention from U.S. officials and the international community. Prior to September 11, 2001, conventional wisdom failed to appreciate not only the nature and danger of transnational threats such as terrorism but also the need to identify and combat the lifeblood of these threats: the money that finances it. Narcotics trafficking was viewed as a purely criminal and social problem, not as a source of funding and method of covert movement for terrorist activity.

Soon after 9/11, U.S. leaders began to call for increased attention and effort to combat terrorist financing, including drug trafficking. For example, former U.S. Drug Enforcement Agency (DEA) Administrator Asa Hutchinson called on the U.S. Government to combat drug trafficking since it funded the Taliban. Soon after, President George W. Bush similarly drew attention to the need to combat narcoterrorism as a part of the larger war on terror. While many outside the Department of Defense (DOD) have opined on this issue, few understand the nature and potential of the threat. As a result, U.S. policies, and the necessary coordination with U.S. agencies, are not as effective as possible. For instance, U.S. Southern Command, the DOD component with the most experience in fighting transnational threats such as narcoterrorism, has not been called upon to provide guidance or other assistance to U.S. Central Command, whose area of responsibility includes states in Central Asia. As a result, understanding of the nature of the threat is limited and the ability to work closely with other U.S. and international agencies to combat narcoterrorism is minimal at best.

As a preliminary matter, however, one must identify terms and assumptions in order to assess the ability of U.S. agencies to combat the problem. What *is* narcoterrorism and why should it be of concern? This chapter identifies what narcoterrorism is, differentiates it from purely criminal narcotics trafficking and terrorism, and discusses the potential that it has to support terrorism and the proliferation of weapons of mass destruction (WMD).

NARCOTERRORISM AS AN ISSUE OF U.S. POLICY

Narcoterrorism is not a novel concept or issue. For decades, many have referred to it, but U.S. leaders began to use the term only after September 11,

2001. Narcoterrorism, commentators conclude, was first coined as a term of art in 1983 by former Peruvian President Belaúnde Terry to describe attacks by Sendero Luminoso and others upon Peruvian counternarcotics police. Since 9/11, U.S. leaders now describe narcoterrorism as acts that support terrorist activity and provide financing and other support to terrorist organizations.

Part of the problem lies in the fact that some U.S. agencies—with the authority and resources to combat potential domestic and international narcoterrorism—either define the term in limited ways or fail to identify it at all. Thus, the United States will continue to face difficult obstacles in delineating and defeating this threat because responsible agencies lack even a common concept of the problem, much less a coordinated strategy.

The DEA, for example, defines *narcoterrorism* as:

> [A] subset of terrorism, in which terrorist groups, or associated individuals, participate directly or indirectly in the cultivation, manufacture, transporta-tion, or distribution of controlled substances and the monies derived from these activities. Further, narco-terrorism may be characterized by the participation of groups or associated individuals in taxing, providing security for, otherwise aiding and abetting drug trafficking endeavors in an effort to further, or fund, terrorist activities.[1]

This definition, however, is largely limited to the context of drug law enforce-ment. It fails to identify the diplomatic, commercial (particularly maritime), intelligence, military, and other equities needed to combat the threat. More-over, this definition is perhaps the broadest among U.S. agencies and fails to address key parts that other responsible agencies' efforts are required.

On the other hand, DOD defines narcoterrorism in an even more lim-ited (and, from an operational perspective, limiting) manner. According to Joint Publication 1–02, *DOD Dictionary of Military and Associated Terms*, narcoterrorism is:

> Terrorism conducted to further the aims of drug traffickers. It may include as-sassinations, extortion, hijackings, bombings and kidnappings directed against judges, prosecutors, elected officials, or law enforcement agents, and gen-eral disruption of a legitimate government to divert attention from drug operations.[2]

Clearly, this definition maintains the distinction between violence-related drug trafficking and other transnational threats, including narcoterrorism. It fails to acknowledge, though, the past, present, and future ability of the drug trade, first, to finance operations by those not necessarily involved in drug trafficking (that is, those who tax the cultivation, processing, shipment, or sale of drugs); and second, most glaringly, to transport terrorists, arms, money, and WMD through established, covert logistical networks.

For the purposes of this chapter, therefore, basic principles of economics are instructive. Assume that if one can transport a product—radios, cars, food, or other commerce—from point *A* to point *B*, then that capability is of value. Americans spend millions (if not billions) of dollars each year for the delivery of food, personal services, and other items. This assumption is axiomatic.

Further assume that if one can transport a product covertly (across borders and without notice to law enforcement, security, or regulatory authorities), then that capability increases in value. Again, this principle is axiomatic. The ability to move drugs covertly and across local, national, regional, and international borders has been a lucrative commodity. The better the track record of undetected movement, the more is the value of that service. Thus, the international drug transport industry presents an additional threat to U.S. domestic and international security. The industry is a logistical system that moves drugs, arms, terrorists, and WMD at any time.

This is not just a potential capability. In fact, many nations are encountering this development. In early 2004, for example, European law enforcement, while reviewing entry documents for passengers on board a train leaving Russia and traveling west, found an individual carrying a large container marked "radioactive," which contained weapons-grade uranium. The individual was carrying the uranium on orders from a Russian drug trafficker who was paid to transport the uranium into Europe. The Colombian navy has interdicted numerous diesel-fueled submarines carrying hundreds of millions of dollars of cocaine to the United States. The traffickers purchased at least one submarine, investigations found, from members of the Russian mafia. Afghan, Tajik, and other southwest Asian drug traffickers who deliver Afghan-produced opium to Russia have increased their profits by offering their capability to those who wish to move things and people out of Russia. The traffickers either offer new contracts for this return delivery service or, if they themselves want a Russian product, barter or sell the drugs in exchange. Items transported out of Russia and south toward Afghanistan have included arms, individuals, money, and WMD precursors.

Thus, it would be accurate to describe narcoterrorism as more than just a means to generate funds for terror and a description of the violence committed by drug traffickers. A discussion of narcoterrorism must also recognize and address its logistical network. Perhaps the following definition, then, is appropriate: Narcoterrorism refers to the transnational threat that:

- generates revenue for terrorist activity by taxing all facets of the drug trade (cultivation, processing, shipment, or sale)
- challenges national and international sovereignty through acts of violence, corruption, and intimidation to create or maintain ungoverned space within which drug trafficking and other illicit activity may flourish
- moves any illicit product from one point to another.

DEPARTMENT OF STATE

The U.S. Department of State serves as the lead Federal agency for the conduct of foreign policy. Among other issues, the State Department is charged with the primary implementation of counternarcotics, counterterror, and counterproliferation (arms and WMD) policies. It should grasp and articulate U.S. policy and programs with respect to the issue of counternarcoterrorism.

The State Department has not yet evinced a full understanding or efforts to combat this problem. The bureau within the State Department that executes the authorities and resources that could address this problem is the Bureau of International Narcotics and Law Enforcement (INL). INL, as its Web site touts, "advises the President, Secretary of State, other bureaus in the Department of State, and other departments and agencies within the U.S. Government on the development of policies and programs to combat international narcotics and crime."[3] While State sought and received similar authorities as granted to the Department of Defense and Central Intelligence Agency (CIA) to use its Colombia-oriented resources to combat a unified campaign against drugs and terror, the State Department and INL have not requested similar authorities to combat transnational threats in Afghanistan, Pakistan, Uzbekistan, Africa, or Southeast Asia. In addition, State has not formulated a policy specific to the threat of narcoterrorism.

INL is authorized to execute programs worldwide against transnational threats, such as drugs and crime. INL conducts bilateral and regional counterdrug programs, such as illicit crop eradication, education, training, and intelligence collection. INL also oversees efforts to build law enforcement capacity and anticorruption initiatives. These efforts, if focused to complement counterterrorism efforts within the State Department and other agencies, could prove effective tools against a wide range of transnational threats.

To meet these challenges, the President has placed the fight against terrorism, international narcotics, and transnational organized crime high on the national security and foreign policy agendas. The State Department and INL play a key role in carrying out the President's agenda by leading the development and coordination of U.S. international drug and crime policies and programs. To deal with the increasing linkage and overlap among terrorist, drug, and crime groups, INL has begun shifting from separate programs for counternarcotics and anticrime to a broader and more integrated law enforcement effort to combat the full range of criminal, drug, and terrorist threats.

It remains to be seen, however, whether this comprehensive statement will translate into effective action. INL's fiscal year 2004 budget request was heavily oriented to programs designed, prior to 9/11, to assist Colombia with counterdrug programs. INL requested only $40 million for counternarcoterrorism efforts in Afghanistan, $38 million for anticrime and corruption programs in Pakistan, and $7 million for the entire African continent.

DEPARTMENT OF HOMELAND SECURITY

The Department of Homeland Security (DHS) is so overburdened with priority missions such as securing U.S. air transport, borders, and providing support to first responders that it has not had the time, resources, or staffing to consider and implement policy designed to detect and defeat narcoterrorist threats to the United States. Recognizing that challenge, however, does not excuse the lack of any central guidance for an agency that controls over 80 percent of the U.S. law enforcement resources whose primary mission is to protect our borders from covert entry.[4]

The Homeland Security Act of 2002, which created DHS, unsuccessfully tried to place all Federal law enforcement agencies responsible for securing U.S. borders from covert entry into one department. Congress also suggested (rather than required) that DHS pool its operational and intelligence collection assets with other U.S. assets into a Joint Interagency Task Force for Homeland Security.[5] Unfortunately, the Congress failed to create a department office responsible for DHS-wide policy development. As a result, Homeland Security has not promulgated policy, including common definitional policy, that would align the policies, programs, and budgets of the respective components.

Congress also created the DHS Office of Counternarcotics. Unfortunately, the official named to lead this office is also tasked with responsibilities within the Office of National Drug Control Policy, serves as the U.S. Interdiction Coordinator, and maintains no staff. The position, as currently authorized and organized, lacks the ability to institute meaningful change.

DEPARTMENT OF JUSTICE

The Department of Justice is the Federal agency with lead responsibility for the investigation and prosecution of crimes committed in the United States and against U.S. interests overseas. By its very charter, therefore, it is limited in its ability to identify and combat transnational threats, such as narcoterrorism, which defy borders, national and international law, and conventional criminal investigation.

Department of Justice resources, furthermore, have been shifted away from more mundane issues of crime and investigation to investigating and prosecuting acts of terror. Since 9/11, resources, including agents of the Federal Bureau of Investigation and the associated funding, have been focused on counterterrorism prevention (when possible) and prosecution. To the extent that Justice focuses on national issues, such as counternarcotics, it continues to execute pre-9/11 programs intended to strengthen international agency capabilities to investigate and prosecute traditional crime.

DEA, the lead agency within the Department of Justice, has been on the forefront of U.S. policy transformation with regard to the need to combat narcoterrorism. Partially due to its historical mission of narcotics law enforcement, DEA is experienced in using law enforcement and intelligence tools to defeat organizations and individuals who seek to move people and products covertly into the United States.

In addition, DEA leaders, including former Administrator Asa Hutchinson and current Administrator Karen Tandy, have been among the few senior U.S. leaders who have identified the narcoterrorist threat and called for action. DEA, to its credit, formulated the necessary policy understanding needed to focus resources.[6] What the agency maintains in terms of understanding the problem, however, is limited by its lack of resources and inability to participate at senior levels in executive branch coordination of war on terror objectives.

CENTRAL INTELLIGENCE AGENCY

The CIA lacks a definitional understanding of narcoterrorism and, therefore, has not issued policy or executed programs designed to combat the threat. The institutional weaknesses identified during the national discussion of the 9/11 Commission Report are replicated within the CIA offices charged with dealing with drug trafficking and other transnational threats. Officials with responsibility for counterdrug intelligence collection and analysis lack working relationships with operational bureaus (except for the office responsible for Central and South American issues). This weakness is most glaring in terms of the offices responsible for intelligence collection and analysis and operations for southwest Asia.

The southwest Asia operational and intelligence offices do not interact with the office responsible for counterdrug intelligence collection and analysis. In fact, after 9/11, most of the officers in the counterdrug intelligence office were detailed to assist the southwest Asia offices. They were unsuccessful, however, in pointing out the need to collect and analyze information relating the links between drugs and al Qaeda, the Taliban, the Islamic Movement of Uzbekistan, and other terrorist groups in the region. Hence, it should be of no surprise that the 9/11 Commission found no information indicating that al Qaeda relied upon any facet of the Afghan narcotics trade for revenue, logistics, or other support. Since no one had asked the question, no one could provide an answer.

Similarly, the office responsible for counterdrug intelligence collection and analysis does not interact with other non-Latin American offices. As a result, the CIA lacks the information to assess to what extent:

- other international and regional terrorist organizations are generating revenue from some facet of the international drug trade
- other drug trafficking organizations are using violence and other means to create or maintain ungoverned space useful for drug trafficking and other activity
- the international logistical network that moves drugs is used to move terrorists, money for terrorism, or WMD.

On a positive note, the Bush administration, CIA, and Congress have recognized that the CIA's ability to coordinate drug intelligence collection and analysis with its operations in support of Colombia require the agency to support more than counterdrug activities. The Intelligence Authorization Act of 2004 and Intelligence Authorization Bill for Fiscal Year 2005 both include language allowing the CIA to support Colombian counternarcoterrorist, rather than just counterdrug, efforts.

DEPARTMENT OF DEFENSE

For years, DOD resisted any involvement in activity, whether foreign or domestic, that countered transnational threats such as narcoterrorism. This cultural and institutional resistance is based on legitimate concerns and an ignorance of these threats to international, as well as U.S. national and domestic security.

Counterterrorism has never been a concept that the conventional U.S. military has understood, fully accepted as a "military mission," trained for, or practiced. The Armed Forces fought the creation of Special Forces and other unconventional, special, or low-intensity conflict that the world now faces. Indeed, DOD opposed efforts to create an organization within the Office of the Secretary of Defense that would advise him on all matters (for example, special operations, counterterrorism, counternarcotics, U.S. territorial security, stability, and information operations) until Congress forced its creation as part of the Goldwater Nichols DOD Reorganization Act of 1986. The Assistant Secretary of Defense for Special Operations and Low Intensity Conflict, the official in charge of that office and principal advisor to the Secretary on those issues, however, remained vacant until the summer of 2003—almost 2 years after 9/11.

Again, some of the resistance within DOD to address counternarcoterrorism and other transnational threats is valid. In a democratic society, the military should not have a significant role in domestic issues such as illegal drug use, domestic terrorism, and immigration control. As far back as the nineteenth century, U.S. law has prohibited military involvement in domestic law enforcement. While notable exceptions do exist, such as for providing limited support to domestic counterdrug law enforcement, domestic nuclear terrorism, and specific support for national security events such as the Super Bowl and political conventions, the U.S. military continues to perform strictly limited domestic missions, even after 9/11.

The resistance lacks validity, however, in terms of supporting U.S. and international partners in combating transnational threats. Partner nation intelligence and military forces and international and U.S. law enforcement agencies lack the necessary resources, training, and, most notably, command, control, communication, and intelligence, which are so necessary to prevent and defeat narcoterrorism and other transnational threats to our friends and the U.S. homeland. Thus, DOD is called upon to use its unique resources and capabilities to address this problem in a holistic manner. Changes to DOD policies and authorities since 9/11 reflect the beginning, hopefully, of this change and recognition that the U.S. military must identify and defeat the narcoterrorist threat to defend the homeland from a variety of dangers that will utilize the logistical network to gain entry to the United States.

In 2003,[7] the Bush administration requested congressional authority to expand its support to Colombia from the limited counterdrug support that it provided pursuant to Colombia's Plan Colombia.[8] The administration requested the authority to use counterdrug resources, mainly provided by the Departments of State and Defense, to assist Colombian efforts to fight narcoterrorism, rather than the limited counterdrug role originally intended. The administration requested and received authorization and appropriations to continue support, through DOD, State, and the CIA, for Colombian counternarcoterrorism until 2006.

On October 3, 2003, DOD Deputy Secretary Paul Wolfowitz instituted a long-awaited policy that attempted to address the transnational threat of narcoterrorism.[9] It also recognized the danger to the United States by the threat's logistical network. While it is directed to all parts of DOD, including its regional (for example, U.S. Central Command) and functional (for example, U.S Special Operations Command) commands and intelligence organs, including the National Security Agency and Defense Intelligence Agency, passive resistance to the policy shift remains.

First, the DOD policy expressly recognizes the links between drug trafficking and terrorism and recognition that activities traditionally separated from military missions should cross jurisdictions when appropriate. Moreover, the policy's most important, and perhaps most subtle, shift was to define DOD *counterdrug activities*.[10] The term is consistent with the purpose of congressional appropriation and provides the necessary flexibility to address narcoterrorist and other transnational threats in a timely, efficient, and coordinated manner:

> [t]he term "counterdrug activities" includes those measures taken to detect, interdict, disrupt, or curtail *any* activity that is reasonably *related to narcotics trafficking*. This includes, *but is not limited to*, measures taken to detect, interdict, disrupt or curtail activities related to substances, materiel, weapons, or resources used to finance, support, secure, cultivate, process or *transport* illegal drugs.[11]

Thus, as a matter of policy, DOD recognized all three prongs of narcoterrorism: the act of funding terror; the use of violence to create instability necessary to support drug trafficking; and the logistical network that moves drugs and other things across U.S. and international borders.

THE NEED FOR CROSS-INSTITUTIONAL SOLUTIONS

As the summary of individual agency authorities and policies indicates, the executive branch varies in its understanding and capability to combat narcoterrorism across the spectra—with all U.S. legal, intelligence, political, and military tools. This inability is due to the institutional weaknesses that continue to prevent the U.S. Government—executive and legislative—from coordinating all resources and authorities across agencies in a manner that has never been used in our history.

The current debate over the role of intelligence that resulted in 9/11 is indicative of this problem. Organizations and individuals possessing the authorities and resources to identify and prevent the 9/11 attacks were unable—either by statute or custom—to work together or cede the lead responsibility and credit to other agencies. CIA representatives possessed information about some of the hijackers but could (or would) not pass that information to domestic law enforcement agencies. Agents of one part of the Federal Bureau of Investigation with information about the hijackers could not pass that information to others due to policy obstacles within the Department of Justice.

Similar weaknesses also limit the ability of the United States to combat narcoterrorism. First, narcoterrorism is a newly identified concept that not all agencies understand or accept as a priority. Second, certain agencies, notably the Departments of State and Justice, as well as the CIA, have not pooled resources across disparate internal jurisdictions or sought broader use of their existing authorities to combat narcoterrorism. Third, parts of the Department of Defense oppose a greater role for the military in combating narcoterrorism, due to an institutional fear of "fighting drugs," even though the profits and methods of shipment associated with the drug trade do, in fact, benefit terrorists and those who seek to move WMD without detection.

What, then, is the solution? First, senior U.S. leadership must be educated on the nature and potential of the threat and demand new statutes and policies that pool authorities and resources traditionally "stovepiped" within distinct agencies. Some leaders recognize the threat and have called for action, but their suggestions have not galvanized the respective bureaucracies and Congress. At the President's direction, the National Security Council staff should formulate interagency policy and plans designed to address the threat. These policies should reflect the following realities:

- Narcoterrorism constitutes a dual threat to U.S. interests since it both funds terrorist activity and provides critical logistical support worldwide, not just in the Western hemisphere.
- International cooperation is required in the form of information-sharing, international standards with respect to maritime and aviation transportation of cargo, operational coordination, and the uniform implementation of existing (and additional) legal tools.

- Military and contractor-supplies trainers, advisors, and other support outside the traditional areas in the Western hemisphere are useful for not only combating narcoterrorism but also assisting other nations in the development of tools that will establish sovereignty over ungoverned space.
- The traditional reluctance of agencies to use existing narcotics-related tools and resources for areas other than the Western hemisphere (particularly in the Middle East, southwest Asia, and central Europe) must end. The lessons learned from U.S. support to countries such as Colombia and Thailand should be reviewed and replicated in other appropriate areas that face threats of terrorism and weapons proliferation.

Second, Congress, in cooperation with the executive branch, should review existing authorities and resource allocation to ensure that the fight against narcoterrorism incorporates the distinct capabilities of all appropriate agencies. Congress should provide agencies that possess unique capabilities and access in other parts of the world with the requisite authority and resources to contribute to global counternarcoterrorist efforts. For example, the challenges to sovereignty, stability, and weapons control are particularly acute in Central Asia and Europe. Agencies such as the DEA, which have unique relationships with host nation counterparts in these nations, should be re-sourced and directed to leverage those relationships in coordination with agencies such as the Departments of State and Defense and CIA to provide training, access, and information useful to combat narco- and other forms of terrorism and weapons proliferation. Where necessary, the lead agency role should be shifted if doing so would enhance access, training, cooperation, and effectiveness. Congress possesses a unique ability to induce cooperation between U.S. agencies or host nations by providing—or reducing—funding based upon their levels of cooperation and success.

Finally, U.S. leaders should encourage allies and international institutions to recognize this threat and pool resources, including information and training. Support for bilateral or multilateral operations and exercises can generate significant benefit for U.S. and international objectives, security, and stability.

Narcoterrorism is not necessarily a new concept. The attendant crime, violence, and terror associated with drug trafficking have existed for hundreds of years. Its potential as a funding source, logistical support, and access for international terror and weapons proliferation, however, has become a real threat in our post-9/11 world.

NOTES

1. See Asa Hutchinson, Drug Enforcement Agency (DEA) Administrator, "International Drug Trafficking and Terrorism," testimony before the Senate Judiciary Committee Subcommittee on Technology, Terrorism, and Government Information,

Washington, DC, March 13, 2002, available at www.state.gov/p/inl/rls/rm/2002/9239.htm.

2. Joint Publication 1–02, *Department of Defense Dictionary of Military and Associated Terms* (Washington, DC: Department of Defense, April 12, 2001).

3. See www.state.gov/g/inl/.

4. The Department of Homeland Security (DHS) includes the U.S. Coast Guard, the primary maritime law enforcement agency, U.S. Customs and Border Patrol, Immigration and Naturalization Service, Transportation Security Administration, and others.

5. The Joint Interagency Task Force (JIATF) concept is proven and well known to DHS career and political leaders. DOD funds JIATF–South, based in Key West, Florida, and JIATF–West, based in Hawaii. Both existing JIATFs collect, analyze, and disseminate information (relating to drug and other traffic toward the United States) that it receives from all Federal law enforcement agencies, the Intelligence Community, Department of Defense, and over a dozen other countries. See www.jiatfs.southcom.mil and www.pacom.mil/staff/jiatfwest/index.shtml.

6. For example, see statement by DEA Administrator Asa Hutchinson before the House Government Reform Committee, Subcommittee on Criminal Justice, Drug Policy, and Human Resources, October 3, 2001, available at www.dea.gov/pubs/cngrtest/ct100301.html; and statement by Hutchinson before the Heritage Foundation's Kathryn and Shelby Cullom Davis Institute for International Studies, April 2, 2002, available at www.dea.gov/speeches/s040202.html.

7. In 2002, the Bush administration asked for and received permission to use fiscal year 2003 *appropriations* to assist the government of Colombia in its counternarcoterrorism efforts. Due to scheduling limitations, it did not ask the Congress for the *authorization* to use fiscal year 2004 funds to assist Colombia until congressional consideration (and enactment) of the National Defense Authorization Act of 2004.

8. Many mistakenly believe that Plan Colombia is a U.S. plan. It is not. Plan Colombia is the effort initiated by former Colombian President Andrés Pastrana to convince European and U.S. governments to contribute to Colombian efforts to combat its narco-terrorism problem. European governments promised to provide billions in support. To date, Colombia has received only a few million dollars (to assist displaced persons) and other "soft" support. The United States provided the bulk of the international support to Colombia. The government of Colombia provided most of the overall funding.

9. See Paul D. Wolfowitz, Deputy Secretary of Defense, "Department of Defense International Counternarcotics Policy," appendix A, October 3, 2003.

10. Each year, the U.S. Congress appropriates over $1 billion for DOD "counterdrug activities," including operations, maintenance, intelligence, and other support. No statute, policy, or regulation, however, defined the term *counterdrug activities*. This lack of common definitional understanding resulted in differing priorities, uncoordinated effort, and increased barriers to cross-jurisdictional cooperation among the military commands, agencies, and with the U.S. National Guard.

11. Wolfowitz, emphasis added.

CHAPTER 3

International Human Trafficking

Francis T. Miko

Trafficking in persons is considered a significant criminal enterprise, affecting most countries around the world.[1] While trafficking and slavery are not new phenomena, in the past several years, governments and civil society groups have taken serious, concerted actions to combat them. Some have suggested that there may be a shift by criminal organizations away from other activities, such as trafficking in arms, drugs, and tobacco, toward trade in humans, thanks to high profits, lower risk of punishment, and the fact that trafficked humans can provide a continuing flow of profits.[2] Since 2000, the United States has worked closely with foreign governments and international organizations to curb human trafficking. The fact that there is a perceived growing connection among international organized crime groups engaged in trafficking, drug cartels, arms smugglers, and perhaps even terrorist organizations has given greater urgency to addressing this issue.

The United Nations defines *human trafficking* as the:

> recruitment, transportation, transfer, harboring, or receipt of persons, by means of the threat or use of force or other forms of coercion, of abduction, of fraud or deception, of the abuse of power or of a position of vulnerability or of the giving or receiving of payments or benefits to achieve the consent of a person having control over another person, for the purpose of exploitation. Exploitation includes, at a minimum, the exploitation of the prostitution of others or other forms of sexual exploitation, forced labor or services, slavery, servitude, or the removal of organs.[3]

U.S. law defines *severe forms of trafficking in persons* as:

> sex trafficking in which a commercial sex act is induced by force, fraud, or
> coercion, or in which the person induced to perform such act has not attained
> 18 years of age; or ... the recruitment, harboring, transportation, provision,
> or obtaining of a person for labor or services, through the use of force, fraud,
> or coercion for the purpose of subjection to involuntary servitude, peonage,
> debt bondage, or slavery.[4]

Others have put forward slightly different definitions. In the case of minors,
the trafficking term is generally applied whether a child is taken forcibly or
voluntarily.

While the trafficking in people is a costly tragedy in its own right, its
consequences reach much further. While there is no single victim stereotype,
a majority of people trafficked are thought to be women under the age of
25, with many in their mid to late teens. The fear of infection with Human
Immunodeficiency Virus (HIV) and Acquired Immune Deficiency Syndrome
(AIDS) among customers has driven traffickers to recruit younger women
and girls, some as young as 7 years, who are erroneously perceived by customers as too young for infection. Trafficking victims are often subjected
to cruel mental and physical abuse to keep them in servitude, including
beating, rape, starvation, forced drug use, confinement, and seclusion. Once
victims are brought into destination countries, their passports are confiscated. Victims are forced to have sex, often unprotected, with large numbers
of partners, and to work unsustainably long hours. Many victims suffer
mental breakdowns and are exposed to sexually transmitted diseases, including HIV and AIDS, at much higher rates than the general population.
They are often denied medical care, and those who become ill are sometimes
discarded or even killed.

A source of controversy is the relationship between human trafficking
and prostitution. Some politicians, religious groups, and feminist organizations argue for broadening the definition of trafficking to include all forms
of prostitution, whether forced or voluntary, on grounds that prostitution
is rarely truly voluntary and that traffickers will simply force their victims
to claim voluntary action. However, others oppose this broadened definition and warn that pushing it will impede the capacity of the international
community to achieve consensus and act decisively against major traffickers, given the differences in outlook about the sex trade. In a number of
countries, human trafficking is illegal and actively prosecuted, but prostitution is legal and regulated. Supporters of legalized prostitution argue that
legal sex workers can have access to medical care, counseling, and legal and
law enforcement protection. They argue that since prostitution exists everywhere and cannot be stamped out, it is better to regulate it than to drive it
underground.

THE RISE IN HUMAN TRAFFICKING

Human trafficking is one of the oldest crimes and can be traced to early human history. However, the problem is seen as having taken on new dimensions in recent years. Governments and international organizations have begun to address the problem with greater urgency in the belief that the crime has increased exponentially since the 1990s.

Present-day human trafficking has been fueled by a number of factors. With globalization has come the increased movement of people across borders, especially from poorer to wealthier countries. In general, the criminal business feeds on poverty, despair, war, crisis, and ignorance. Another factor is the continuing subordination of women in many societies, as reflected in economic, educational, and work opportunity disparities between men and women. Many societies still favor sons and view girls as an economic burden. In the worst cases, some desperate families in some of the most impoverished countries sell their daughters to brothels or traffickers for the immediate payoff and to avoid having to pay the dowry to marry off daughters.

Also playing a role are the hardships and economic dislocations caused by the transition following the collapse of communism in the former Soviet Union and Eastern Europe, creating an environment in which human trafficking could flourish. The lack of opportunity and the eagerness for a better life abroad have made many women and girls especially vulnerable to entrapment by traffickers. With the weakening of law enforcement in postcommunist societies, criminal organizations have grown and established themselves in the lucrative business of international trafficking.

Traffickers are known to exploit wars, turmoil, and natural disasters to target and enslave victims, especially women and children. Wars in the former Yugoslavia, Africa, and elsewhere have been a magnet for human traffickers taking advantage of the associated chaos and misery. Even international stabilization and peacekeeping forces have been implicated both as a source of demand for sex workers and, in some cases, as traffickers themselves. The international community has recognized the need for greater vigilance against human trafficking in the aftermath of natural disasters. Traffickers might be tempted especially to target children orphaned or separated from their families in such disasters. Such concerns grew after the December 26, 2004, Indian Ocean tsunami devastated a number of countries.

Trafficking victims often find it difficult to get help and protection in their destination countries. Even in the United States, effective protection is fairly recent and limited to victims of "severe forms of trafficking." Victims must prove that they are in the United States as a direct result of trafficking and that they have a well-founded fear of retribution if they are returned to their country of origin. They must be willing to help identify and prosecute their traffickers. Some critics argue that the standards are too high to help many deserving victims. Critics also argue that it may be difficult to draw a clear line between "pure" victims and those who have a degree of complicity in their plight. Such distinctions, they argue, will leave some victims unprotected. Children who have been trafficked may have special needs that are not always addressed. These include the need for reuniting children quickly with families, in some cases relocation of families, and providing care and education arrangements for child victims who cannot be returned to their families.

ROLE OF ORGANIZED CRIME

International criminal organizations have taken advantage of the freer flow of people, money, goods, and services to extend their own international activities in a number of areas. Human trafficking has been seen by many criminal gangs as more lucrative and less risky than many other criminal activities. There is a high demand, worldwide, not only for trafficked women and children but also for men as sex workers, cheap sweatshop labor, and domestic workers. Traffickers are encouraged by large tax-free profits and continuing income from the same victims. When authorities do crack down, it is often against victims themselves for prostitution or illegal entry into the country. Penalties for trafficking humans for sexual exploitation are often relatively minor compared with those for other criminal activities, such as drug and gun trafficking. Human trafficking is believed to generate billions of dollars annually for organized crime, estimated at some $9.5 billion per year by the Federal Bureau of Investigation (FBI).[5]

Chinese, Asian, Mexican, Central American, Russian, and other former Soviet Union gangs are among the major traffickers of people. Chinese and Vietnamese Triads, the Japanese *yakuza*, South American drug cartels, the Italian mafia, and Russian gangs increasingly interact with local networks to provide transportation, safe houses, local contacts, and documentation. As criminal organizations have grown, especially in Russia, they have gravitated to this lucrative business.[6] Russian organizations now play a dominant role not only in the trafficking of Russian women but also women from Eastern Europe. Russian organized crime groups and others, including Albanian, Estonian, Chechen, Serb, and Italian gangs, are involved in human trafficking throughout Europe. Furthermore, Russian organized crime is allegedly involved in the sex industry in a number of Western European countries.

Traffickers acquire their victims in a number of ways. Sometimes women are kidnapped outright in one country and taken forcibly to another. In other cases, victims are lured with phony job offers. Traffickers entice victims to migrate voluntarily with false promises of well-paid jobs in foreign countries as au pairs, models, dancers, domestic workers, and so forth. Traffickers advertise these "jobs," as well as marriage opportunities abroad, in local newspapers. Russian crime gangs reportedly use marriage agency databases and matchmaking parties to find victims. In some cases, traffickers approach women or their families directly with offers of lucrative jobs elsewhere. After providing transportation and false documents to get victims to their destination, they subsequently charge exorbitant fees for those services, often creating lifetime debt bondage. In some cases, police and other governmental authorities accept bribes and collude with traffickers by selling fake documentation. In addition, local police often fear reprisals from criminal gangs, so they find it easier to deny knowledge of trafficking.

GLOBAL TRENDS

Trafficking is a problem that affects almost every country in the world. Generally, the flow of trafficking is from less developed countries to industrialized nations or toward neighboring countries with marginally higher standards of living. Internal trafficking within countries is often from rural to urban areas or to tourist resorts. Since human trafficking is a hidden criminal enterprise, there are no precise statistics on the extent of the problem, and estimates are not reliable.

The U.S. Government estimates that between 600,000 and 800,000 people are trafficked across borders each year. If trafficking within countries is included in the total world figures, official U.S. estimates are that 2 to 4 million people are trafficked annually. However, there are even higher estimates ranging 4 to 27 million, including forced or bonded laborers. The International Labor Office estimates that there are some 12.3 million victims of forced labor at any given time. Of these victims, 80 percent are women and some 50 percent are under 18 years old. The U.S. Government Accountability Office (GAO), however, released a report in 2006, casting doubt on the methodology and reliability of the official U.S. Government figures. It concluded that the "U.S. government has not yet established an effective mechanism for estimating the number of victims or for conducting ongoing analysis of trafficking related data that resides within various government agencies."[7] Figures provided by other governments and international organizations are unlikely to be any more accurate.

MAJOR SOURCE, TRANSIT, AND DESTINATION COUNTRIES[8]

The largest number of victims trafficked internationally are believed to come from Asia. The former Soviet Union and southeastern Europe are growing sources of trafficking for prostitution and the sex industry. Many people are also trafficked to Eastern Europe. Other main source regions include Latin America, the Caribbean, and Africa. Most victims are sent to Asia, the Middle East, Western Europe, and North America. They usually end up in large cities, vacation and tourist areas, or near military bases, where the demand is highest.

Asia remains a major source and destination region for victims of trafficking. Among the major countries of origin are China, Thailand, Bangladesh, Cambodia, India, Laos, Burma, Nepal, Pakistan, the Philippines, and Vietnam. Thailand is both a major source and destination country. Japan, Israel, and Turkey are significant destination countries for victims trafficked from Southeast Asia and the Commonwealth of Independent States.[9]

The largest source region of trafficking victims is Southeast Asia, according to the Department of State. The growth of sex tourism in this region is one of the main contributing factors. Large-scale child prostitution occurs in many countries. Thailand, Cambodia, and the Philippines are popular travel destinations for "sex tourists" from Europe, North America, Japan, and Australia. Japan is considered the largest market for Asian women trafficked for sex. Victims are believed to come mainly from the Philippines and Southeast Asia. Victims are also trafficked to Taiwan, Malaysia, Hong Kong, and Thailand. Cross-border trafficking is prevalent in the Mekong region of Thailand, Burma, Laos, Cambodia, Vietnam, and the Southern Yunan province of China. Vietnamese women are trafficked to China and Cambodia. According to various sources, hundreds of thousands of foreign women and children have been sold into the Thai sex industry since 1990, with most coming from Burma, southern China, Laos, and Vietnam. East Asia, especially Japan, is a destination for trafficked women from Russia and Eastern Europe. Victims from Southeast Asia, especially China, Burma, the Philippines, Thailand, Cambodia, and Vietnam, are also sent to Western Europe, the United States, Australia, and the Middle East.

South Asia is also a primary source region for trafficking victims according to the State Department. The low status of women in some societies and the growth of sex tourism contribute significantly to trafficking in this region. Sri Lanka and India are among the favored destinations of sex tourists from other parts of the world. Bangladesh and Nepal, the poorest countries in the region, are the main source countries. India and Pakistan are key destination countries. The total number of Nepalese working as prostitutes in India is believed to be in the tens of thousands. Thousands of women and children from Bangladesh are trafficked to Pakistan each year. Also, according to Amnesty International, Afghan women have been sold into prostitution in Pakistan. Thousands of Nepalese women and children are believed to be trafficked for prostitution to the Asia Pacific region, especially Hong Kong. Bangladeshi women and children have been trafficked to the Middle East in large numbers over the last 20 years. India is a source, transit, and destination country, receiving women and children from Bangladesh, Nepal, Bhutan, Sri Lanka, and Pakistan and sending victims to Europe and the Middle East.

Australia has been a prime source of sex tourists in Asia but is also one of the countries that have done most to end the practice. The Australian government has developed stringent laws that give authorities extraterritorial jurisdiction over crimes committed abroad by Australian citizens.[10] The Philippines, Thailand, South Korea, Sri Lanka, and Hong Kong are some of the primary Asian destinations for organized sex tours. Indonesia and Taiwan are secondary destinations.

The former Soviet Union and Central and Eastern Europe have replaced Asia as the main source of women trafficked to Western Europe. Victims come from Russia, Ukraine, Belarus, Moldova, and several Central and southeastern European countries, especially Albania, Bulgaria, Romania, and Lithuania. The main destination countries are Belgium, Germany, Greece, Italy, and the Netherlands.[11] Western European countries are also destination points for victims from other parts of the world, including Africa, Latin America, and Southeast Asia. In addition, several Central and Eastern European countries are reported to be source, receiving, and transit countries.

Since the economic and political turmoil after the collapse of the Soviet Union, trafficking from the region has escalated from a minor problem before 1991 into a major international concern. Most Russian and Eastern European victims are believed to be sent to Western European countries. A substantial number are also sent to the Middle and Far East (especially Japan and Thailand). Many wind up in the United States or Canada.[12] During the conflicts in Bosnia and Kosovo, traffickers found new opportunities in the former Yugoslavia and the Balkans.[13]

The sexual exploitation of women and children in the Middle East usually involves importing women from other regions. Women and children, mostly from Asia, are trafficked as domestics, prostitutes, or brides to the Middle East. Domestic workers are not protected under labor laws in many countries of the Middle East and North Africa, which makes them especially vulnerable to abuse. Some countries do little to punish traffickers. At the same time, trafficked women in the region risk punishment for illegal prostitution. Women from the former Soviet Union are sent to Israel. According to the Israel Women's Network, at any given time, an estimated 3,000 women, traded for prostitution, are in Israel. Hundreds of women from Russia and the former Soviet Union are brought reportedly to Israel by well-organized criminal groups.[14]

Countries of Latin America and the Caribbean are reported primarily as countries for trafficking victims, although many serve as transit and destination countries. The largest number of victims is trafficked from Brazil, Colombia, the Dominican Republic, Guatemala, and Mexico. The principal destinations are North America and Europe.[15] Tens of thousands of Latin American and Caribbean women and children are believed to be trafficked for sexual exploitation each year.[16] Impoverished children are particularly vulnerable to trafficking for prostitution. The Central American countries and Mexico are also transit countries for trafficking to the United States.

The presence of sex tourists from Europe, North America, and Australia has significantly contributed to the trafficking of women and children. A growing number of sex tourists are going to Latin America, partly as a result of recent restrictions placed on sex tourism in Thailand, Sri Lanka, and other Asian countries. Favored sex tourism destinations are Brazil, Argentina, the Dominican Republic, Mexico, Honduras, Costa Rica, and Trinidad and Tobago.

Africa is a source region of women, especially for individuals trafficked to Western Europe and the Middle East. Western Africa is also believed to be a major destination region. Victims are trafficked to Nigeria, Gabon, Ghana, and South Africa.[17] Principal source countries are believed to include Nigeria, Benin, Ghana, and Morocco.

The United States is primarily a destination country. As many as 17,500 people are trafficked to the United States each year, according to recent State Department estimates.[18] Most come from Southeast Asia and the former Soviet Union. About half of those are forced into sweatshop labor and domestic servitude. The rest are forced into prostitution and the sex industry or, in the case of young children, kidnapped and sold for adoption. While many victims come willingly, they are not aware of the terms and conditions that they will face. Women trafficked to the United States most often wind up in the larger cities in New York, Florida, North Carolina, California, and Hawaii. But the problem is also migrating to smaller cities and suburbs. Russian crime groups are said to have become actively involved in trafficking and the sex industry in the United States in the 1990s.[19] The United States is also the major destination country for young children kidnapped and trafficked for adoption by childless couples unwilling to wait for a child through legitimate adoption procedures and agencies. The largest source country is Mexico. Mexican children are also kidnapped and trafficked to the United States for child prostitution.

U.S. EFFORTS TO COMBAT INTERNATIONAL TRAFFICKING

Before 2000, U.S. laws were widely believed to be inadequate to deal with trafficking in women and children or to protect and assist victims. Substantial antitrafficking legislation and programs have been implemented since 2000 with the hope of significantly improving the situation. The human trafficking problem gained attention in the United States and worldwide in the late 1990s. It was addressed as a priority by Congress, as well as the Clinton and Bush administrations. As part of former President Bill Clinton's announced International Crime Control Strategy, an interagency working group was set up to address international crime implications of trafficking. On March 11, 1998, President Clinton issued a directive establishing a U.S. Government antitrafficking strategy of prevention, protection and support for victims, and prosecution of traffickers. The strategy had strong domestic and international policy components.

The Department of State sponsored the creation of a database on U.S. and international legislation on trafficking. An Interagency Council on Women formed by the Clinton administration established a senior governmental working group on trafficking. The council sponsored a meeting of governmental and nongovernmental representatives from source countries, transit countries, destination countries, and international organizations to call attention to the trafficking issue and to develop strategies for combating the problem. The Clinton administration worked with Congress on what it considered urgently needed legislation to fight trafficking at home and abroad, building on its framework of prevention, protection, and prosecution to strengthen tools available for the fight and to help advance U.S. policy on trafficking in other countries. The administration also urged the enactment of legislation to encourage and support strong action by foreign governments and to help the work of nongovernmental organizations in this area.

Several bills were introduced in the 106th Congress on human trafficking. H.R. 3244 was introduced by Representative Christopher Smith (R–NJ) on November 8, 1999. A similar bill was sponsored in the Senate by Senator Sam Brownback (R–KS). In conference, the bills were combined with the Violence against Women Act of 2000 and repackaged as the Victims of Trafficking and Violence Protection Act of 2000, along with miscellaneous anticrime and antiterrorism provisions. President Clinton signed the bill into law on October 28, 2000 (P.L. 106–386).

The Bush administration and Congress continued the antitrafficking effort with strong bipartisan support. Attorney General John Ashcroft announced in March 2001 that the fight against trafficking would be a top priority for the administration and that U.S. law enforcement agencies, including the FBI, the Immigration and Naturalization Service, and the Justice Department's Civil Rights Division, would cooperate closely to upgrade their efforts to combat trafficking. The Justice Department also announced new guidelines for Federal prosecutors to pursue trafficking cases.[20] The State Department issued its first congressionally mandated report on worldwide trafficking in July 2001.

On January 24, 2002, the U.S. Attorney General announced the implementation of a special "T" visa, as called for in P.L.106–386, for victims of trafficking in the United States who cooperate with law enforcement officials. Under the statute, victims who cooperate with law enforcement against their traffickers and would be likely to suffer severe harm if returned to their home countries may be granted permission to stay in the United States. After 3 years in T status, the victims are eligible to apply for permanent residency and for nonimmigrant status for their spouses and children.[21] On February 13, 2002, President George W. Bush signed an executive order establishing the Interagency Task Force to Monitor and Combat Trafficking in Persons.

The task force is charged with strengthening coordination among key agencies and identifying what more needs to be done to protect potential victims, punish traffickers, and prevent future trafficking.

In 2003, Congress approved the Trafficking Victims Protection Reauthorization Act of 2003. The President signed the act into law on December 19, 2003 (P.L. 108–193). The act authorized substantial increases in funding for antitrafficking programs in fiscal years 2004 and 2005 (over $100 million for each fiscal year). P.L. 108–193 refined and expanded on the minimum standards for the elimination of trafficking that governments must meet and placed on such governments the responsibility to provide the information and data by which their compliance with the standards could be judged. The legislation created a special watch list of countries that the Secretary of State determined to require special scrutiny in the coming year.

The Trafficking Victims Protection Reauthorization Act of 2005 (P.L. 109–164) was introduced in the House of Representatives on February 17, 2005, by Representative Christopher Smith (R–NJ) and nine cosponsors to authorize appropriations for fiscal years 2006 and 2007 and to close loopholes in previous antitrafficking legislation. Among other things, the bill has provisions to increase U.S. assistance to foreign trafficking victims in the United States, including access to legal counsel and better information on programs to aid victims. It addresses the special needs of child victims, as well as the plight of Americans trafficked within the United States. The bill directs relevant U.S. Government agencies to develop antitrafficking strategies for postconflict situations and humanitarian emergencies abroad. It seeks to extend U.S. criminal jurisdiction over government personnel and contractors who are involved in acts of trafficking abroad while doing work for the government. It addresses the problem of peacekeepers and aid workers who are complicit in trafficking. The bill was passed by the House and Senate in December 2005 and signed into law by the President on January 10, 2006.

On June 5, 2006, the State Department issued its sixth annual report on human trafficking, as mandated by P.L.106–386, P.L. 108–193, and P.L. 109–164.[22] The report reviews recent trends in the fight against trafficking and rates countries according to whether they meet minimum standards with regard to their antitrafficking commitment and policies.[23] Secretary of State Condoleezza Rice introduced the latest report, stressing that the U.S. commitment to ending human trafficking is part of President Bush's National Security Strategy. She also indicated that it was a key component of U.S. "transformational diplomacy."

THE INTERNATIONAL RESPONSE

Human trafficking has gained prominent international attention in the past decade. Individual governments and international organizations have taken significant steps to address it. A number of countries have passed comprehensive legislation and launched programs to fight traffickers and save their victims, and the United States has been in the forefront of these efforts. In addition to clamping down on trafficking to and within the United States, the Federal Government and Congress have initiated programs to assist other countries in fighting trafficking. In response to congressional directive, the report also summarizes actions taken by international organizations to fight trafficking and especially to stop trafficking and sexual exploitation by peacekeepers and humanitarian aid workers. The organizations involved include the United Nations (UN), the North Atlantic Treaty Organization, and the Organization for Security and Co-operation in Europe (OSCE).

The United States and the European Union (EU) agreed on a joint initiative to combat trafficking in November 1997.[24] U.S. and EU officials met in Luxembourg to launch a jointly funded initiative against trafficking in women from Russia and Eastern Europe. It is primarily an information campaign and an education program for law enforcement, customs, and consular officials to heighten awareness of the problem. Pilot projects were launched in Poland by the EU and in Ukraine by the United States. The United States initiated bilateral cooperation programs in a number of countries.

In 2002, the Council of the European Union took a major step in the fight against human trafficking, reaching agreement on a broad new framework decision. The decision sought to strengthen police and judicial cooperation and to harmonize the laws and policies of member states in areas such as criminalization, penalties, sanctions, aggravating circumstances, jurisdiction, and extradition.

At the OSCE summit meeting in Istanbul in November 1999, leaders of the 55 OSCE member states agreed to make combating trafficking in the OSCE area (where some 200,000 people are trafficked annually) a priority issue. A follow-up meeting on trafficking was held in Vienna on June 19, 2000. The participating states agreed on steps to increase their efforts and better coordinate actions to fight the problem. The OSCE sponsored a conference in Bangkok in June 2002 to deal with the trafficking issues. Speaking at the conference, Helga Konrad, who heads the OSCE task force on human trafficking, said that the approach taken to date to fight trafficking has failed. She argued that closer collaboration between source and destination countries was vital.[25]

The international community began meeting in 1999 to draft a Protocol to Prevent, Suppress, and Punish Trafficking in Persons, especially Women and Children in conjunction with the UN Convention Against Transnational Organized Crime. The United States, along with Argentina, introduced the draft protocol in January 1999. Negotiations were concluded in 2000 on a revised draft. On November 15, 2000, the UN General Assembly adopted the Convention on Transnational Crime, including the Protocol on Trafficking. The Convention and Protocols, formally signed in Palermo, Italy, in December 2000, were designed to enable countries to work together more closely against criminals engaged in cross-border crimes. The United States signed the UN Protocol on Trafficking in December 2000 and ratified and became party to it on December 3, 2005, following Senate advice and consent on October 7, 2005. At present, 94 countries are party to the protocol. The United States is party to two other international agreements that have been adopted to address aspects of trafficking in children. The International Labor Organization Convention 182, concerning the Prohibition and Immediate Action for the Elimination of the Worst Forms of Child Labor, was ratified by the United States in December 1999.[26] The Protocol to the Convention on the Rights of the Child on Sale of Children, Child Prostitution, and Child Pornography was signed by the United States in July 2000 and ratified in December 2002. In January 2002, the protocol went into force, having been signed by 88 countries and ratified by 16.[27]

INDIVIDUAL COUNTRY PROGRESS IN 2006

The State Department's June 2006 *Trafficking in Persons* (TIP) *Report* is more comprehensive than in previous years, focusing on 158 countries. In addition to the 149 countries that are ranked, the report discusses trafficking in 9 "special case" countries where sufficient information was not available to provide a ranking. The number of countries covered has grown steadily over the past 6 years. In addition to Tiers 1 through 3, there is a fourth category of countries, the "Tier 2 Watch-list." The Department of State is required to issue an interim report on how these countries are performing by February 2007 in advance of the 2007 TIP Report. Ambassador John Miller has indicated that the Watch-list is an effective tool, with many of the countries on the list improving their performance. The report includes information about law enforcement efforts in other countries and U.S. efforts to prosecute traffickers and help victims.

P.L. 106–386 subjects to sanctions those countries listed in Tier 3 (beginning with the 2003 State Department report), including termination of nonhumanitarian, non-trade-related assistance, and loss of U.S. support for loans from international financial institutions. Sanctions may be imposed if such countries have not improved their performance by the date by which the President is required to make a determination (within 90 days from the release of the report).[28]

The report acknowledges the progress made by countries against trafficking. However, the report is critical of many governments and law enforcement agencies for placing too much emphasis on whether a person's movement across borders is coerced or voluntary in deciding who is a trafficking victim. Too often, movement by victims is voluntary, in search of better opportunities. The report emphasizes that moving to a new location is incidental and that the defining element of trafficking is the force, fraud, or coercion against the victim to provide or continue service to a "master."

Also, some governments are thought to rely too heavily on victims of trafficking coming forward and identifying themselves. The reality, according to the report, is that most victims are afraid to identify themselves to law enforcement officials on first contact. Therefore, it stresses that governments need to put in place other ways to identify trafficking victims, including through extensive interviews and counseling.

The priority placed on stemming illegal immigration in many countries has often resulted in treatment of trafficking cases as a problem of illegal immigration, thus treating victims as criminals. When police raid brothels, women are often detained and punished, subjected to human rights abuses in jail, and swiftly deported. Few steps have been taken to provide support, health care, or access to justice. Few victims dare testify against the traffickers or those who hold them, fearing retribution for themselves and their families, as most governments do not offer stays of deportation or adequate protection for witnesses.

In the TIP Report, countries are ranked in four groups. Countries not included are either not seen as having a significant trafficking problem as source, transit, or destination countries (meaning more than 100 cases per year) or there is insufficient information about their role. Tier 1 is made up of countries deemed to have a serious trafficking problem but fully complying with the minimum standards for eliminating trafficking. Tier 2 includes countries not fully complying with those standards, but that are seen as making "significant efforts to bring themselves into compliance." A Tier 2 Watch-list was added as a category in 2004 to flag countries that are on the border between Tier 2 and Tier 3. P.L. 108–193 requires that the Department of State issue an interim report on how these countries are performing by February 2007, in advance of the 2007 TIP Report.[29]

In Tier 3 are those countries not fully complying with standards and not making significant efforts to do so. These countries are subject to possible U.S. sanctions if they have not improved their performance within 90 days after being placed on Tier 3, although the President has authority to waive the sanctions.

Twenty-six countries are included in the group of best performing countries (Tier 1). Five countries were moved up to Tier 1, including Finland, Ireland, Malawi, Singapore, and Switzerland. Ireland was previously unranked; the others had been in Tier 2. In addition, the Czech Republic, Nepal, and Portugal were moved down to Tier 2 from their previous placement in Tier 1 in 2005.[30]

The largest group of countries is placed in Tier 2, implying that they have not done enough to fight trafficking but are making a serious effort. A total of 79 countries are included on this list, up from 77 in 2005. Twenty-four countries are new from 2005. Of these, three were moved down from Tier 1, three were previously unranked, and the rest moved up.[31] The Tier 2 Watch-list is made up of 32 countries. All except seven are new to the list from 2005. Fifteen were moved down from Tier 2. Seven were moved up from Tier 3. Three of the countries were previously unranked.

The list of worst performing countries includes 12 countries (down from 14 in 2005), of which 6 are new: Belize, Iran, Laos, Syria, Uzbekistan, and Zimbabwe. Moved up from Tier 3 were eight countries: Bolivia, Cambodia, Ecuador, Jamaica, Kuwait, Qatar, Togo, and the United Arab Emirates. Ecuador was moved to Tier 2; the rest were placed on the Tier 2 Watch-list.[32] A number of these countries are on the list for their failure to address forced labor among foreign migrant workers. From the 2005 Tier 3 list, Burma, Cuba, North Korea, Saudi Arabia, Sudan, and Venezuela remain on Tier 3 in the June 2006 TIP Report.

PROSPECTS

The issue of how success can be measured in the fight against human trafficking and the adequacy of legislation and policies implemented to date remains unresolved. So far, few reliable indicators have been identified. Despite the heightened attention, significant legislation, and extensive programs to combat human trafficking since 2000, there is disagreement over how much progress has been achieved. The new estimates of numbers of trafficking victims in the United States seem considerably lower than some of the previous estimates. Whether these figures reflect the success of U.S. policies and programs or more accurate data gathering is unclear. Hard evidence with regard to the results of the more vigorous international campaign against trafficking is also lacking. Worldwide estimates of the numbers of victims seemingly have not changed much, when cross-border trafficking and trafficking within countries are taken together. The estimated number of victims remains very high. By comparison, the number of traffickers prosecuted and victims helped is still very low.[33] The 2006 GAO report concluded that U.S. Government efforts to combat trafficking have been hampered by the lack of a coordinated strategy and the absence of performance measures by which to judge the impact of its antitrafficking programs abroad.

Most experts agree that extensive international cooperation is required to stop international trafficking. Differing perspectives on what constitutes trafficking could make international cooperation more difficult. Both "carrots" and "sticks" may be needed to influence the policies of other governments, including financial and technical assistance, as well as shining a light on poor performance and the threat of sanctions. According to U.S. officials, the threat of sanctions has induced some governments to do more to curb trafficking. In other cases, sanctions have not proven an effective tool. The disinterest and even complicity of some governments in trafficking remains a problem.

In the aftermath of the terrorist attacks on the United States on September 11, 2001, there was some concern that momentum might be lost in the battle to counter human trafficking, given the new and more urgent priorities for resources and personnel. The concern has diminished in light of continued governmental and congressional focus on the problem. However, there is still some question about whether the requirements for homeland security and the war on terror might limit financial, law enforcement, and judicial resources from other efforts, including the campaign against human trafficking. Some observers also wonder if the U.S. need for support in the war on terror from certain governments will make it more difficult to pressure those governments if their antitrafficking efforts are inadequate. Alternately, enhanced homeland security, border tightening, and greater visa regulation and scrutiny may have a positive effect in making human trafficking and other crimes carried out across borders more difficult and risky.

NOTES

1. This section is based on Francis T. Miko, *Trafficking in Persons: The U.S. and International Response*, RL30545 (Washington, DC: Congressional Research Service, Library of Congress, January 19, 2006).

2. United Nations (UN) Development Programme, United Nations Presents the Human Trafficking Report for Russia, March 17, 2006, available at www.undp.ru.

3. UN Office on Drugs and Crime, *Trafficking in Persons: Global Patterns*, April 2006, 50, available at www.unodc.org/pdf/traffickinginpersons_report_2006ver2. pdf.

4. Victims of Trafficking and Violence Protection Act of 2000 (P.L.106–386).

5. Cited in U.S. Department of State, *Trafficking in Persons Report*, June 2005, 13, available at www.state.gov/g/tip/rls/tiprpt/2005.

6. See UN Development Programme, *Human Trafficking in the Russian Federation: Inventory and Analysis of the Current Situation and Responses*, March 15, 2006, available at www.undp.ru.

7. U.S. Government Accountability Office (GAO), "Human Trafficking: Better Data, Strategy, and Reporting Needed to Enhance U.S. Antitrafficking Efforts Abroad" (GAO–06–825), July 2006, 3, available at www.gao.gov/new.items/ d06825.pdf.

8. Information in this section is summarized from a wide range of official and nongovernmental organization sources. Specific estimates of numbers trafficked to and from individual countries and regions are not included; their accuracy is uncertain, and the numbers presented by different sources are dated and cannot be reconciled.

9. UN Office on Drugs and Crime, 88, 89, 103.

10. See Marianna Brungs, "Abolishing Child Sex Tourism: Australia's Contribution," *Australian Journal of Human Rights* 8, no. 2 (December 2002), 101–124.

11. UN Office on Drugs and Crime, 90–95, 103–104.

12. Ibid.

13. Organization for Security and Co-operation in Europe (OSCE), OSCE Mission in Kosovo, *Background Report: Combatting Trafficking in Kosovo*, June 5, 2001, available at www.osce.org/documents/mik/2001/06/986_en.pdf.

14. See Israeli Women's Network at www.iwn.org.

15. UN Office on Drugs and Crime, 96–98, 104.

16. See also Clare M. Ribando, *Trafficking in Persons in Latin America and the Caribbean*, RL33200 (Washington, DC: Congressional Research Service, Library of Congress, December 15, 2005).

17. UN Office on Drugs and Crime, 85–87, 102.

18. U.S. Department of State, *Trafficking in Persons Report*, June 2005.

19. U.S. Department of State, Bureau of Consular Affairs, *Fraud Digest*, November/December, 1997.

20. John D. Ashcroft, "Worker Exploitation," news conference, March 27, 2001, available at www.usdoj.gov/archive/ag/speeches/2001/032701workerexploitation.htm.

21. U.S. Department of State, International Information Programs, Washington File, January 24, 2002, accessed at http://usinfo.state.gov.

22. U.S. Department of State, *Trafficking in Persons Report*, June 2006, available at www.state.gov/g/tip/rls/tiprpt/2006.

23. Governments meeting *minimum standards* are defined in the Trafficking and Violence Protection Act of 2000 and the Trafficking Victims Protection Reauthorization Act of 2003 as those that (1) prohibit and punish acts of trafficking; (2) prescribe punishment commensurate with that for grave crimes, such as forcible sexual assault, for the knowing commission of trafficking in some of its most reprehensible forms (trafficking for sexual purposes, trafficking involving rape or kidnapping, or trafficking that causes a death); (3) prescribe punishment that is sufficiently stringent to deter and that adequately reflects the offense's heinous nature; and (4) make serious and sustained efforts to eliminate trafficking. The fourth minimum standard was amended and supplemented by the Trafficking Victims Reauthorization Act and now calls for consideration of 10 criteria.

24. Fact Sheet: "US–EU Initiative to Prevent Trafficking in Women," USIS Washington File, December 5, 1997.

25. Agence France-Presse, June 20, 2002.

26. See the International Labor Organization Web site at www.ilo.org/public/english/standards/ipec/about/factsheet/facts23.htm.

27. See the UN Children's Fund Web site at www.unicef.org/crc.

28. As a result of the findings in the 2003 *Trafficking in Persons Report*, the President imposed sanctions on five countries (Burma, Cuba, Liberia, North Korea, and Sudan) due to their poor records in combating trafficking. In the case of Liberia and Sudan, the sanctions were partially waived to give the United States greater leverage in seeking to end conflicts in those countries. See "Presidential Determination with Respect to Foreign Governments' Efforts Regarding Trafficking in Persons," Memorandum for the Secretary of State, Presidential Determination No. 2003–35, September 9, 2003, available at www.whitehouse.gov/news/releases/2003/09/20030910-1.html.

29. The Tier 2 Watch-list of countries includes Algeria, Argentina, Armenia, Bahrain, Bolivia, Brazil, Cambodia, Central African Republic, China, Cyprus, Djibouti, Egypt, Equatorial Guinea, India, Indonesia, Israel, Jamaica, Kenya, Kuwait, Libya, Macau, Malaysia, Mauritania, Mexico, Oman, Peru, Qatar, Russia, South Africa, Taiwan, Togo, and the United Arab Emirates.

30. Tier 1 includes Australia, Austria, Belgium, Canada, Colombia, Denmark, Finland, France, Germany, Hong Kong, Ireland, Italy, Lithuania, Luxembourg, Malawi, Morocco, the Netherlands, New Zealand, Norway, Poland, Singapore, South Korea, Spain, Sweden, Switzerland, and the United Kingdom.

31. Tier 2 includes Afghanistan, Albania, Angola, Azerbaijan, Bangladesh, Belarus, Benin, Bosnia-Herzogovina, Bulgaria, Burkina Faso, Burundi, Cameroon, Chad, Chile, Costa Rica, Cote D'Ivoire, Croatia, Czech Republic, Democratic Republic of Congo, Dominican Republic, East Timor, Ecuador, El Salvador, Estonia, Ethiopia, Gabon, the Gambia, Georgia, Ghana, Greece, Guatemala, Guinea, Guinea-Bissau, Guyana, Honduras, Hungary, Japan, Jordan, Kazakhstan, Kyrgyz Republic, Latvia, Lebanon, Macedonia, Madagascar, Mali, Malta, Mauritius, Moldova, Mongolia, Mozambique, Nepal, Nicaragua, Niger, Nigeria, Pakistan, Panama, Paraguay, Philippines, Portugal, Romania, Rwanda, Senegal, Serbia-Montenegro, Sierra Leone, Slovak Republic, Slovenia, Sri Lanka, Suriname, Tajikistan, Tanzania, Thailand, Tunisia, Turkey, Uganda, Ukraine, Uruguay, Vietnam, Yemen, and Zambia.

32. Tier 3 includes Belize, Burma, Cuba, Iran, Laos, North Korea, Saudi Arabia, Sudan, Syria, Uzbekistan, Venezuela, and Zimbabwe.

33. U.S. Government Accountability Office, 21.

CHAPTER 4

Addressing the Nuclear Smuggling Threat

David Smigielski

In the decade following the collapse of the Soviet Union and end of the Cold War, the focus of America's nuclear anxiety began to shift. No longer primarily concerned with the threat of a massive Soviet nuclear strike, American policymakers grew increasingly troubled by the lack of security surrounding nuclear materials within the former Soviet Union. As the 1990s progressed, reports of fissile material missing from formerly top secret nuclear cities—coupled with the very public breakdown of the Russian military and reports of tens of thousands of Russian nuclear scientists going for months without pay—fed Western concerns that the formerly traceable Soviet nuclear threat had developed into something much more insidious. The primary fear of policymakers—global thermonuclear war between the superpowers—has been replaced by a fear of rogue regimes and terrorist groups becoming nuclear players via the illicit transfer of nuclear materials, technology, and expertise.

As the threat has grown, and especially in light of the September 2001 terrorist attacks on New York City and Washington DC, the United States and its allies have taken substantial steps toward addressing the threat posed by nuclear smuggling. U.S. policy, specifically the Cooperative Threat Reduction (CTR) Program, has understandably focused on what Senator Joseph Biden termed Russia's "candy store of nuclear arms."[1] Future antismuggling efforts, however, must look beyond the former Soviet Union, while at the same time taking lessons from our experiences to date.

NUCLEAR SMUGGLING IN A NUTSHELL

To gain a clearer understanding of the threat posed by nuclear smuggling, and how to counter it, one must first gain a better understanding of the types of materials that pose the greatest risk. Both state and terrorist groups have actively, but unsuccessfully, sought out a complete nuclear bomb. When unable to do so, a state would likely attempt to acquire the fissile material, industrial capability, and expertise necessary to build its own indigenous nuclear device. Nonstate or terrorist groups, on the other hand, would likely seek out nuclear materials and know-how for other reasons, such as the production of low-tech radiological weapons (that is, the so-called dirty bombs). Ultimately, the goal of the end user and the types of material available dictate the nature of the smuggling threat. There are four general categories of "merchandise" that would be most valuable on the nuclear black market: complete nuclear weapons, raw nuclear materials, nuclear components and technology, and nuclear know-how.

Complete Nuclear Weapons

To the aspiring nuclear state or would-be nuclear terrorist, the successful theft of a working nuclear weapon remains the Holy Grail of nuclear smuggling. For states that lack the necessary infrastructure and knowledge base to produce an indigenous nuclear weapon,[2] obtaining a handful of already built nuclear bombs is likely seen as a one-way ticket to increased influence, respect, and power. Although there have been no confirmed transfers of complete weapons to third parties, reports of various nations attempting to buy such devices continue to surface from time to time. During the 1980s, for example, Libyan leader Muammar Qadhafi reportedly offered the Chinese government nearly a billion dollars for a small number of nuclear weapons, an offer Beijing declined.[3]

Transnational terrorist groups such as al Qaeda also seem to recognize the benefit of purchasing a complete nuclear device via the black market, perhaps even more so than the more traditional rogue state. By their nature, nonstate actors lack even the territory upon which to develop a nuclear weapon of their own, making purchasing someone else's weapon imperative.

There is a notable history of attempts by terrorist groups to obtain nuclear weapons, and Chechnya is often cited as one of the more likely locales through which al Qaeda might obtain nuclear materials. In October 1995, the Russian extremist newspaper *Zavtra* published an article claiming that Chechen rebels had managed to obtain two tactical nuclear weapons. These reports were never confirmed, and the paper's editors later retracted the story claiming that it had been fed to them in an attempt to increase the political leverage of Chechen leaders.[4]

In August 1999, Yossef Bodansky, an American author, analyst, and head of the Congressional Task Force on Terrorism and Non-Conventional

Warfare, claimed that he had been told by Middle East and Russian sources that Osama bin Laden had "a few of the ex-Soviet 'suitcase' bombs[5] acquired through the Chechens."[6] Two months later, in October 1999, Bodansky told the Moscow daily *Komsomolskaya Pravda* that bin Laden had obtained 20 tactical nuclear warheads and was attempting to buy "nuclear suitcases" from Kazakhstan. The Kazakh government denied Bodansky's claim and stated that all Russian nuclear weapons had been removed from Kazakh territory in 1995 in accordance with the Strategic Arms Reduction Talks I treaty.[7] That same month, Bodansky claimed that bin Laden had purchased suitcase nuclear weapons using "$30 million in cash and two tons of Afghan heroin."[8] Bodansky's statements are best taken with a grain of salt; his sources have never been confirmed and his claims remain in doubt. In addition, one could argue that if al Qaeda had indeed obtained a nuclear device in 1999, then it would have been used by now.

While a loose nuclear weapon in the wrong hands may provoke the most concern and have the most serious consequences, it is also the most unlikely smuggling event. Nuclear bombs are a nuclear power's most important commodity and will likely be guarded as such (this does not, however, preclude acts of insider theft by rogue technicians). The result is a smuggling market in which the most valued merchandise is largely unattainable.

Raw Nuclear Materials

Due to the problems associated with stealing and smuggling a complete nuclear bomb, the majority of smuggling efforts to date appear to have focused on comparatively easier to obtain raw nuclear materials, such as uranium and plutonium. The creation of weapons-grade fissile material is a complex process requiring sophisticated refinement and separation procedures.[9] It is estimated that there are 1,000 metric tons of enriched uranium (that is, uranium that contains at least 20 percent U-235) and 160 tons of weapons-grade plutonium in Russia alone.[10] A would-be nuclear power may find it more practical simply to purchase weapons-grade nuclear material on the black market.

There is strong evidence to indicate that highly enriched uranium and plutonium have been the focus of concerted—although not always well-thought-out—smuggling operations. In August 1994, German authorities arrested two Spanish nationals and a Colombian for the attempted sale of 350 grams of Pu-239 that had been stolen from the Institute of Physics and Power Engineering in Obninsk, Russia. The intended recipient was never identified.[11] That fall, an Iraqi middleman attempted to purchase 27 kilograms of U-238 for an Iranian buyer. The smuggler was arrested in Moscow. In December 1997, International Atomic Energy Agency (IAEA) officials inspected the Vekua Physics and Technology Institute in the breakaway Georgian region of Abkhazia. There they found 2 kilograms of highly enriched uranium missing. The uranium was never recovered.

At first glance, these incidents are alarming—and certainly headline grab-
bing; however, it appears that the majority of attempts at smuggling nuclear
material involve "radioactive junk—materials that might pose environmental hazards but are useless in constructing fission weapons."[12] In 1992, for
example, Swedish authorities intercepted a shipment of copper contami-
nated with radioactive cobalt-60, which is dangerous as waste but likely
unusable as a weapon.

Additionally, the amount of weapons-grade material necessary to build
a nuclear device must be taken into consideration. Although the official
amounts are classified, it has been estimated that at least 56 kilograms of
U-235 are needed to build a crude nuclear device while at least 4 kilograms
of Pu-239 are required for the same purpose.[13] This information is noteworthy when one reviews the amounts of smuggled U-235 that have been
intercepted by authorities. Most have involved less than 10 kilograms of
U-235, well short of the amount needed to construct a bomb. The intercep-
tion of similar amounts of plutonium is slightly more troubling (considering
the small amount a nuclear bomb requires) until one considers that plutonium is highly toxic and exceptionally dangerous to handle outside of
laboratory conditions. It seems likely that smuggling a sufficient amount
of weapons-grade plutonium would be a fatal endeavor for the average—
frequently amateur—nuclear black marketeer.

This is not to say that nonfissile materials are harmless. While obtaining
enough of the appropriate fissile material to construct a nuclear bomb is
extremely difficult, constructing a dirty bomb—radioactive material placed
in a conventional bomb to contaminate the target—is relatively simple.
A dirty bomb, however, would not be a mass casualty weapon (beyond
those occurring as a direct result of the conventional explosion) and would
certainly not be considered a weapon of mass destruction. In his March 2002
testimony before the Senate Committee on Foreign Relations, the president
of the Federation of American Scientists, Dr. Henry Kelly, stated:

> While radiological attacks would result in some deaths, they would not result
> in the hundreds of thousands of fatalities that could be caused by a crude
> nuclear device. Attacks could contaminate large urban areas with radiation
> levels that exceed ... health and toxic material guidelines [and] would require
> prompt evacuation and create terror in large communities even if radiation
> casualties were low.[14]

It is for that reason radiological weapons have been popularly described
as weapons of mass disruption and may appeal to the terrorist group looking
to sow confusion and panic. To date, only one known use of a possible dirty
bomb has occurred: In November 1995, Chechen rebels placed an explosive
device laced with radioactive cesium-137 in a Moscow park. The device was
found and disarmed before it could be detonated.[15]

Compared to a fission bomb, the likelihood of a dirty bomb being constructed and used is much greater simply due to the availability of raw materials and the ease with which such a device could be constructed. Non-weapons-grade civilian nuclear materials are in widespread use throughout the world—so widespread, in fact, that unknowing bystanders have occasionally stumbled upon radioactive material in public (nonsecure) locations. In 1987, scavengers in Goiania, Brazil, found an abandoned radiation therapy unit and gained access to the cesium-137 powder inside. The cesium spread throughout the city, killing 4, contaminating hundreds, and forcing the razing of 85 houses.[16] More recently, a group of hunters in the former Soviet republic of Georgia became seriously ill when they found a Soviet-era battery containing highly radioactive strontium-90. Batteries such as this were used throughout the Soviet Union to power remote scientific stations. It is unknown just how many remain within Russia.[17] The fact that casualty levels in these incidents were relatively low may be of some comfort; however, these incidents illustrate the potential danger that non-weapons-grade nuclear material poses.

Nuclear Components and Technology

Building a nuclear device is a complicated technological task requiring not only fissile material but also precision components such as detonators and timers. The production of the bomb components themselves requires advanced, specialized machine tools and computer-aided design and manufacturing techniques (many of which are subject to international export restrictions). All of this makes the indigenous production of a nuclear device expensive and difficult. Many would-be nuclear powers simply lack the technological base necessary to support a domestic nuclear program. Therefore, purchasing already made weapons components or off-the-shelf manufacturing equipment becomes necessary for nations wishing to "skip a step" in the development of their nuclear arsenal.

There are numerous examples of states attempting to smuggle nuclear components. In early 1990, British authorities arrested four people attempting to smuggle nuclear warhead detonation capacitors into Iraq. Baghdad, for its part, claimed they were part of a university laser project.[18] In 1994, Pakistan attempted to smuggle preformed tubes used in gas centrifuges (necessary for enriching uranium) from Germany under the guise of ballpoint pen bodies.[19]

Nuclear Know-How

The successful manufacture of any sort of nuclear device is not simply a matter of obtaining the required components and material. For a would-be nuclear state or terrorist group, technicians with suitable knowledge in nuclear physics, fissile material, and bomb production are vital. Some nations, such as Iran, already have some degree of the expertise necessary to develop nuclear weapons. For those states and nonstate actors who do not, it is necessary to import the expertise from abroad.

After the collapse of the Soviet Union, significant concern was attached to the plight of scientists within the Russian nuclear community. Once the elite of Russian academic and technological society, nuclear scientists in the aftermath of the Soviet collapse suffered from some of the lowest salaries in Russia—by some reports earning as little as $50 a month.[20] The predominant fear in the West was that these experts would be lured to rogue states with promises of payment for their expertise.

The legitimacy of the brain-drain threat, however, is unclear. Save for a few anecdotal rumors regarding a handful of Russian scientists moving to Iran or North Korea, there does not appear to have been the mass exodus of nuclear technicians many had expected and feared. While it is difficult, if not impossible, to determine accurately why the mass brain drain from Russia has not occurred, national pride has likely been one factor in the equation. That said, the danger posed by the illicit transfer of information and knowledge continues to cause concern in the West.

COMBATING NUCLEAR SMUGGLING

The most comprehensive U.S. effort aimed at preventing nuclear smuggling, the Cooperative Threat Reduction Program, offers insight and lessons for future antismuggling programs. In the case of the former Soviet Union, U.S. policymakers recognized the smuggling threat early. Created by Congress in November 1991, the Nunn-Lugar Cooperative Threat Reduction Program grew out of concerns that the Russian government lacked the necessary resources to maintain adequate security around its nuclear arsenal and infrastructure. The initial CTR legislation (Public Law 102–228) allowed for up to $400 million in Department of Defense (DOD) funding to assist in, among other things, the

> safe and secure storage of fissile material ... preventing the proliferation of weapons of mass destruction (as well as their components) ... preventing diversion of weapons-related NIS [Newly Independent States, i.e., the former Soviet Union] scientific expertise to terrorist groups or third countries.[21]

Instead of responding to the results of nuclear smuggling after the fact, CTR aimed to counter smuggling at the source. By eliminating weapons-grade nuclear material and technology, helping to shore up existing (or, in some cases, nonexistent) Russian security measures, and providing alternate avenues of employment for Russian nuclear scientists, CTR hoped to make smuggling more difficult by removing the merchandise from the market.

Within a few years of its inception, CTR expanded to include six Federal agencies. The DOD CTR programs focused on securing fissile material, specifically from dismantled Russian nuclear warheads, and so-called quick fix solutions, such as improved fencing and detection and surveillance equipment for nuclear weapon storage facilities. DOD funds were used to construct the Mayak Fissile Material Storage Facility, a modern, high security facility in southern Russia designed to store securely the material from approximately 12,500 dismantled warheads.[22]

The Department of Energy (DOE) Material Protection, Control, and Accounting program was designed to shore up security at Russian nuclear facilities, as well as to assist in the "blend-down" of highly enriched uranium into non-weapons-grade, low-enriched uranium. In addition, DOE agreed to assist in the elimination of 34 tons of weapons-grade Russian plutonium and aid Russian efforts to convert its weapons-grade reactors to "proliferation proof" (that is, non-plutonium-producing) nuclear power reactors.

The DOE Nuclear Cities Initiative was designed to prevent the outflow of Russian nuclear scientists by converting Russia's nuclear cities into civilian industrial sites to provide employment for nuclear scientists and technicians. DOE also funded the Second Line of Defense program aimed at enhancing export control regimes in Russia and training and equipping Russian border guards to detect more easily attempts at nuclear smuggling.

Department of State efforts included providing grants to Russian weapons scientists to prevent their recruitment by foreign governments, as well as efforts to enhance border security. State Department funds purchased radiation detection vans for use in Russia and Poland, and radiation detection equipment to prevent nuclear smuggling across the Georgian border.[23]

U.S. Customs Service, Coast Guard, and Federal Bureau of Investigation involvement in CTR included the training of foreign border guards, and efforts to shore up the capabilities of foreign governments to prevent nuclear smuggling.[24]

INTERAGENCY COOPERATION: MAKING IT ALL WORK?

The CTR program serves as an example of just how contentious and fragile interagency operations can be and provides clues to potential problems in future U.S. antismuggling efforts.

In typical Washington fashion, CTR's problems were budgetary. While the initial funding for CTR came from the Department of Defense, divergent priorities among the players—DOD and the Departments of State and Energy—resulted in the dispersion of the CTR program and its funding to at least three different agencies. In an attempt to guarantee some sort of parity among CTR's main parties, an interagency working group was established within the National Security Council to determine where CTR priorities lay. As time went on, the differences in opinion between agencies grew. DOD remained focused on the elimination of Russia's offensive strategic nuclear weapons and the denuclearization of the former Soviet republics with weapons still on their soil. DOE was more concerned with safeguarding stockpiles of weapons-grade material in the former Soviet republics. Dispersing CTR funding was seen as a way to achieve parity between the agencies involved in the program.

This so-called balkanization of the CTR program ultimately backfired. A May 2002 General Accounting Office report was highly critical of the coordination and planning of U.S. antismuggling efforts, concluding that with no single agency coordinating efforts, the disparate agencies have "implemented their programs without coordinating their efforts."[25] This lack of coordination resulted in redundant programs, both between agencies and within agencies, a failure to set program priorities, and inaccurate assessments of recipient country's needs. There is evidence that CTR's balkanization forced multiple American agencies, all with differing priorities, to negotiate separate agreements with foreign agencies. On occasion, these agreements have come into conflict, adding further confusion to the CTR program.[26]

LOOKING BEYOND CTR AND THE FORMER SOVIET UNION

For all of its flaws, CTR's overall success in eliminating, albeit slowly, the amount of nuclear material in the former Soviet Union—in effect gradually shutting down Russia's nuclear candy store—make it an obvious model for future preventative programs. But there are lessons to be learned from CTR's implementation.

Lesson One: Antismuggling Efforts Must Be Unified under a Single Command. While it might be true that the scattering of nuclear security programs allowed for more effective lobbying on behalf of threat reduction as a whole (that is, six agencies lobbying for funding are better than one), the lack of a cohesive implementation policy led to interagency and international confusion. Future programs need clear leadership at the White House level, possibly to include a nuclear security czar to bring disparate agencies together, guarantee cohesive policies, and avoid redundancy.

Lesson Two: Look beyond a Single Country. While the focus of American antismuggling efforts to date has been on the former Soviet Union, there are other, equally serious potential threats in other parts of the world. In the fall of 2001, reports began to surface of al Qaeda operatives contacting Pakistani nuclear scientists, many of whom accepted offers to work in Afghanistan only if the Pakistani government approved their deal.[27] It seems unlikely that such approval would be forthcoming, considering Pakistani relations with the United States. Four years ago, Italian officials broke up a smuggling ring that had managed to obtain a highly enriched uranium fuel rod stolen from the Triga nuclear reactor in Kinshasa, Democratic Republic of Congo. A journalist who visited the site reported "rusted gates, fastened by a simple padlock, leading to the reactor." The journalist was able to get past the two guards by simply signing her name in a guest book.[28] As if to highlight the problem, in July 2002, IAEA officials reported a second fuel rod had gone missing from the same reactor in Kinshasa. The director of the reactor has admitted that security is "minimal."[29]

Lesson Three: It's Not All about Fissile Material. The threat posed by fissile material and nuclear bombs should not overshadow the threat from nonfissile nuclear material. As the incidents in Georgia and Brazil indicated, medical and scientific radioactive waste can have substantial destructive power, although not in the ways traditionally associated with nuclear weapons. A conventional bomb laced with cesium-137 or strontium-90 has the potential to contaminate a large area. By one account, such a device detonated in New York City would contaminate tens of square miles and require the demolition of numerous structures, resulting in potentially trillion dollar losses.[30] In fiscal year 2002, DOE earmarked $25 million to study the threat posed by dirty bombs as part of its Second Line of Defense Program; however, the fiscal year 2003 budget request for the same program fell to $16 million.[31] The dirty bomb threat requires greater attention and a greater emphasis by policymakers on the threat posed by civilian nuclear materials.

Nuclear smuggling poses a unique challenge to American policymakers and institutions. Addressing the threat requires a rational understanding of the problem, leadership at the political level, and the implementation of a clear, unified, and flexible set of policies. Only then will the United States be able to address adequately the nuclear smuggling threat.

NOTES

1. Joseph R. Biden, Jr., "Shutting Down the Russian Candy Store," *Chicago Tribune*, February 28, 2002.

2. In this chapter, the term *nuclear weapon* refers to a fission/fusion thermonuclear device. Radiological weapons, or the so-called dirty bombs, will be referred to as such.

3. Federation of American Scientists, "Libya Special Weapons," available at www.fas.org/nuke/guide/libya/index.html.

4. Scott Parrish, "Are Suitcase Bombs on the Loose? The Story Behind the Controversy," CNS Reports, November 1997, available at www.cns.miis.edu/pubs/reports/lebedlg.htm.

5. The suitcase bombs to which Bodansky refers have been the source of great consternation in the nonproliferation community. Since the 1960s, it has been technologically feasible to build a nuclear device much smaller than those traditionally fielded. Although there is considerable debate over the exact size of such devices, it is likely that they were much larger than a suitcase. They are, however, believed

to be relatively lightweight (100 to 200 pounds) and somewhat man-portable. In 1997, Russian President Boris Yeltsin's former national security advisor, General Alexander Lebed, claimed that a large number of miniature nuclear bombs designed for sabotage operations had gone missing. The Russian government vehemently denied that any such weapons existed, and the U.S. Government stated that it had no cause for concern. Two years later, the Russian defense minister told Pennsylvania Representative Curt Weldon that such devices did in fact exist but that they had all been secured and were in the process of being destroyed. For more on this subject, see Carey Sublette, "Osama, Suitcase Bombs, and Ex-Soviet Loose Nukes," October 2001, available at www.fas.org/nuke/hew/News/Lebedbomb.html; and Parrish.

6. Nick Simeone, "Bin Laden Bombing Anniversary," Voice of America, August 6, 1999.

7. "Youssef Bodansky: Terrorist No. 1 Has an Atomic Bomb," *Komsomolskaya Pravda*, October 5, 1999.

8. "Bin Laden Has Several Nuclear Suitcases," *The Jerusalem Report*, October 25, 1999.

9. "Weapons-grade" nuclear material is either uranium or plutonium of sufficient purity to maintain a nuclear chain reaction. To be considered weapons grade, uranium must contain at least 90 percent of the uranium-235 isotope (natural uranium is only 0.72 percent U-235). Pure U-235 can be extracted only from less pure uranium using complex and expensive ring magnets, gas centrifuges, or molecular lasers. Weapons-grade plutonium (Pu-239) can only be created in nuclear reactors in which uranium-238 is bombarded with neutrons to create the appropriate isotope. See Federation of American Scientists, "Special Weapons Primer," available at www.fas.org/nuke/intro/nuke/design.htm.

10. David Phinney, "Former U.S. Defense Chief Warns Aging Weapons 'Prime Source' for Terrorists," States News Service, April 26, 2002.

11. All smuggling incidents are taken from the Monterey Institute's Newly Independent States Nuclear Tracking Database (www.nti.org/db/nistraff/index.html) and the Russian-American Nuclear Security Council's unpublished "Chronology of Reported Smuggling Incidents Involving Nuclear Weapons and Materials from the Russian Federation and the Newly Independent States (1991–2002)."

12. Rensselaer W. Lee III, *Smuggling Armageddon: The Nuclear Blackmarket in the Former Soviet Union and Europe* (New York: St. Martin's Press, 1998), 15.

13. Federation of American Scientists, "Nuclear Weapon Design," available at www.fas.org/nuke/intro/nuke/design.htm.

14. Federation of American Scientists, "Testimony of Dr. Henry Kelly before the Senate Committee on Foreign Relations," March 6, 2002, available at www.fas.org/ssp/docs/030602-kellytestimony.htm.

15. "U.S. Government Chronology of Nuclear Smuggling Incidents, 1993–1996," March 21, 1996, accessed at www.usis-israel.org.il/publish/press/cia/archive/march/ca2_3-22.htm.

16. Charles J. Hanley, "U.S., Global Agencies Gear Up to Defend Against Insidious New Threat," Associated Press, June 30, 2002.

17. Richard Stone, "'Hot' Legacy Raises Alarm in the Caucasus," *Science*, February 1, 2002.

18. George Gedda, "Study Says Five Countries Develop Nuclear Capability Through Smuggling," Associated Press, April 17, 1990.

19. David A. Kay, "Proliferation Deception," in *Weapons Proliferation in the 1990s*, ed. Brad Roberts (Boston: The MIT Press, 1995), 325.

20. Lee, 37.

21. Jason D. Ellis, *Defense By Other Means* (Westport, CT: Praeger Publishing, 2001), 27.

22. All CTR program information taken from William Hoehn and Christopher Ficek, "U.S.-Former Soviet Union Cooperative Security Programs," *Arms Control Today*, January/February 2001, 6–7, unless stated otherwise.

23. General Accounting Office, "GAO-02-426: U.S. Efforts to Help Other Countries Combat Nuclear Smuggling Need Strengthened Coordination and Planning," May 2002, 7.

24. Ibid, 9–10.

25. Ibid., 11.

26. Ellis, 114; see also GAO, 11–17.

27. Jack Kelly, "Terrorists Courted Nuclear Scientists," *USA Today*, November 12, 2001.

28. Alex Belida, "Africa Nuclear Terror," Voice of America, June 24, 2002.

29. Alex Belida, "Nuclear Fuel Rod Reported Missing from DRC," Voice of America, July 3, 2002.

30. Federation of American Scientists, "Testimony."

31. Hoehn anf Ficek, 2.

CHAPTER 5

Transnational Crime and Small Arms Trafficking and Proliferation

Boris O. Saavedra

This chapter provides an overview of the different stages of the complex process of small arms and light weapons (SALW) proliferation today. Its main objective is to provide policymakers and analysts with a template illustrating the different pathways associated with small arms and light weapons proliferation and its relationship with transnational criminal activities, its direct effect in mortality and morbidity, health hazards, crime and punishment, human rights violations, and violation of international humanitarian law.

The chapter sketches a picture of the globalized system and its impact in small arms and light weapons production and transfers through a variety of circuits. The primary circuit includes mostly legal or licit transfer between producing firms and domestic and international clients. Nevertheless, in the globalized system, the circulation of arms within these complex systems can still represent a proliferation concern depending on the effectiveness of the legal and political framework of national and international controls.

GLOBALIZATION AND SMALL ARMS PROLIFERATION

Globalization is a multidimensional phenomenon: Information technologies, along with a variety of other technologies, are developing rapidly and spreading widely. Trade is expanding globally, as is the flow of private capital and investment. Interdependencies are growing in all aspects of our lives. These developments create real possibilities to achieve economic prosperity, spread political freedom, and promote peace. Yet they are also producing powerful forces of social fragmentation, creating critical vulnerabilities, and sowing the seeds of violence and conflict. Economic crises extend across state borders and are producing global hardships. All of these are aspects of what is commonly referred to as globalization, and all have important security implications.[1]

Many different aspects of globalization now combine to increase the dangers of a variety of transnational threats from weapons proliferation, cyber attacks, ethnic violence, global crime, drug trafficking, environmental degradation, and the spread of infectious diseases. Armed violence carried out primarily with small arms is a major contributing factor that has led to increasing poverty and human insecurity. Cheap, portable, and readily available small arms are the weapons of choice in gang violence, organized crime, civil war, or interstate conflict. Their widespread availability can threaten the welfare and stability of communities, states, and regions.

Discussion of the small arms crisis and the role played by globalization in the dispersal of weapons often begins with deliberate focus on measures to improve state regulatory functions. But similar to other sectors, the state is weakening in relation to the supply and demand of small arms. In other words, weak states are increasingly incapable of restraining sales and entry of firearm surplus, and the receiving states are less capable of controlling their effects. Countries with problems of governance due to the lack of institutions provide inadequate protection and surveillance over their inventory.

Globalization has contributed to a reduction of restrictions on the international movement of almost all goods and services, including stockpiled and newly produced small arms. The global expansion of markets and trade has taken place in parallel with a reduction in state capacity to maintain regulatory and oversight functions over their borders. In addition, there are new intermediaries who are able to conduct transactions in diverse and dynamic business environments, circumvent national regulations, and arrange for rapid financial transfer and shipment of goods anywhere in the world. Arms dealers are able to exploit existing overcapacity of arms production in producer states and large surpluses as a result of downsizing that result in deliberate stockpiling in weaker states.

Finally, resources that sustain war economies are tied to the global economy. Where some see economies weakened by armed conflict, criminal actors are ripe for the trafficking of arms, money laundering, abundant and cheap labor, and endless possibilities for exploitation.

MORTALITY AND MORBIDITY

On average, 300,000 intentional firearm deaths occur each year as a direct result of armed conflict. An additional 200,000 intentional firearm deaths occur in countries ordinarily classified as peaceful. Firearms are the most lethal instruments of suicide: 93 percent of attempts are completed successfully with firearms as compared with 30 percent using other means.[2]

The incidence of armed violence disproportionately affects the poorer countries of the Third World. Experts have typically focused on a combination of factors: social and economic exclusion, competition over economic resources, rent-seeking and grievances; the erosion or absence of democracy and the institutions of governance; and the lack of respect for international norms. On the other hand, observers have emphasized the socialization of violence among males and the culture of violence nurtured by patriarchal societies. While there has not been a proliferation of conflicts in the last decade, there has been a proportional rise in regionalized internal conflict. Light weapons have been the only weapon used in approximately 95 percent of the 49 regional conflicts started since 1990.[3] Civilian deaths are known to stay steady and even rise in post-conflict situations, largely because the boundaries between war and peace, as between war and crime, tend to be blurred and SALW play an important role.

HEALTH HAZARDS

Death and injury resulting from firearms have been classified simultaneously as a scourge, epidemic, and a preventable disease. The medical community's efforts to recast the problem as a measurable public health issue amendable to medical intervention, as well as identifying new and emergent threats, has greatly contributed to sensitizing the international community.

The implications of firearm injury at the local and individual level are profound. The costs extend to treatment, medication, physiotherapy, and counseling: loans and informal credit; the closure of businesses and repositioning of assets; and long-term, even permanent, psychosocial trauma and marginalization. The indirect effects of SALW on health, while not captured in the statistics, relate to the diminishment of the quality of life of individuals and entire communities.

CRIME AND PUNISHMENT

Controlling arms-related violence through appropriate legislation and action is part of a state's inherent obligation to ensure and protect human rights. With the declining control over stockpiles and inventories and the desire to generate much-needed foreign exchange, the preferred tools of criminals are more readily available than ever before. In response, citizens are increasingly resorting to other forms of protection. Fear of crime and violence has led to fortress-like communities that are emblematic of the widening divide between the haves and have-nots and a militarized mentality in communities.[4] Those who cannot afford protected castles and the commodification of their security are forced to organize their self-defense outside legal parameters.

The emergence of privatized security firms follows. Depending on the region, private security firms have had a grip on the provision of public safety that amounts to a monopoly for the past 50 to 200 years. The tools of violence have been transferred from the public to the private domain. Since the early 1990s, private security has come to represent a lucrative growth industry, with significant numbers of corporations and states relying on contracted or in-house services, rather than public policing. This emerging private service has been viewed as threatening to democratic and judicial institutions as they prioritize the profit-motive over the public good of communities.[5]

In some cases, particularly among developing countries, criminal elements are better equipped and armed than state military and police apparatus. The increased economic potency and international networks developed by organized crime, coupled with the new space afforded by expanding markets and rapidly moving capitals, have permitted underground or shadow economies to flourish.

HUMAN RIGHTS

The humanitarian discussion of the impact of SALW revolves around two overlapping areas: first, the violation of international humanitarian law resulting from legal, grey, or clandestine shipments to particular regimes; and second, the violation of international humanitarian law and the human rights of civilians and humanitarian personnel during armed conflict.

The first perspective—advanced by certain like-minded states, international human rights organizations, and nongovernmental organizations (NGOs) actively pursuing demilitarization—highlights the importance of supply-side controls on producer and exporting states to regimes abusing human rights. It takes the view that states that distribute to regions in conflict are, by either commission, omission, or sheer neglect, accessories to committed abuses. If the abuses rise to the level of war crimes, even perpetrators of genocide argue that the major exporting states have the moral obligation to impose restrictions on licensing arrangements and sales to abusive regimes.

The second approach—favored by enlightened United Nations (UN) donors, the International Committee of the Red Cross, and major international relief agencies—seeks to heighten international awareness and actively respond to the impact of armed violence on noncombatants. Agencies are alarmed that civilians and humanitarian and development personnel are increasingly the primary target of attack. For this and other reasons, increasing hostage-taking, banditry, and violent theft is common in the aftermath of conflict. Consequently, demands for protection have risen to the top of the humanitarian agenda.

INTERNATIONAL ORGANIZATIONS AND SMALL ARMS CONTROL

The problem of small arms trafficking, proliferation, and misuse have a long history. However, it was not until the end of the Cold War that these issues emerged on the international agenda. In the early 1990s, increased attention was focused on the ways in which the proliferation and misuse of small and light weapons contributed to the incidence of armed conflicts, violent death, and massive human rights abuses. The UN is particularly well positioned to address one of the most dangerous and important aspects of the small arms trafficking. The first UN General Assembly resolution on arms transfer was adopted in 1988. This resolution resulted in a voluntary UN Register of Conventional Arms, which was established in 1992. But only 92 governments submitted data in 1997, and it is estimated that nearly all transfers of listed systems were reported by the exporting or importing country or both.

The 2001 UN conference on illicit trade in SALW—with the participation of member states, many international and regional organizations, and about 120 NGOs—put these issues on the international agenda and widened the discussion of small arms issues beyond the arms control perspective. Nevertheless, many participants were aware of the compromises and weaknesses in the final Program of Action (POA) on SALW. While governments and NGOs have committed more resources than ever before to develop small arms policy and initiatives, and though states are working unilaterally, bilaterally, regionally, and globally on small arms illicit trafficking, action in this area remains at times ad hoc and unfocused. The POA does not satisfactorily address some of the key human rights, humanitarian, developmental, or crime prevention dimensions of the problems associated with SALW.

The weaknesses in the POA developed by the 2001 UN conference make it difficult to discern a coordinated approach. There has been little discussion as to how implementing the steps outlined in the POA will be monitored. Moreover, because the program of action is not a legally binding treaty but rather a declaration of intent by states, there are no punitive measures if states do nothing about small arms. Nevertheless, all the states have a legal obligation under Article 41 of the UN Charter to abide by arms embargoes enacted by the Security Council, which in recent years focused increased attention and resources on the issue of arms embargoes and their enforcement as reflected in the special investigations undertaken to assess the effectiveness of the embargoes imposed on Rwanda and the National Union for the Total Independence of Angola.

In the preparation for the 2001 UN conference on SALW, there was a relatively intense process of international meetings and regional initiatives during the period, which contributed to the overall negotiation process. The

Inter-American Convention against the Illicit Manufacturing and Trafficking in Firearms, Ammunition, and Explosives and Other Related Materials and associated Inter-American Drug Abuse Control Commission Model Regulations had already been agreed in 1997 and 1998, respectively. In Africa, the Economic Community of Western African States (ECOWAS) moratorium was signed in October 1998 after 2 years of discussions. The Southern African Development Community (SADC) countries developed a Southern Africa Regional Action Program on Light Arms and Illicit Arms Trafficking in Conventional Arms (1997), a Code of Conduct on Arms Exports (1998), and a Joint Action on Small Arms (1999). During the lead-up to the 2001 UN SALW conference, development of regional initiatives intensified. For instance, the Organisation for Security and Co-operation in Europe (OSCE), Organization of African Union, and the European Union (EU) developed together their program of action on SALW in December 2000, to which the Brazilian Declaration of Latin American and Caribbean States agreed on November 24, 2000.

Importantly, a parallel international process had been launched, under the auspices of the UN Economic and Social Council. This led to an agreement on a UN Convention against Transnational Organized Crime in December 2000 and, in spring 2001, to the adoption of a protocol to the conventional dealing with illicit firearms manufacturing and trafficking. The UN Firearms Protocol was the first instrument on small arms to be agreed upon at the global level. Having finally received sufficient ratifications by signatory states, the UN Firearms Protocol came into force in July 2005.

There are many regional initiatives and agreements that address aspects of the SALW problem and other substantial international agreements, particularly the UN Firearms Protocol. The development of the POA was facilitated by the regional initiatives taken by the Organization of American States (OAS), OSCE, SADC, ECOWAS, EU, Nairobi Initiative States (Eastern Africa), and others before 2001. It is firmly established that the POA sets minimum global standards; regional agreements should be consistent with it and seek to promote implementation and further development of the POA according to circumstances and opportunities.

The POA specifies certain follow-on measures. In particular, there is a Biennial Meeting of States (BMS) that convenes every 2 years to consider implementation of the program of action. The first and second BMS took place in 2003 and 2005, respectively. The mechanism adopted in each conference was informal consultations on the issues, a review of the progress on implementation, which implies a broader aim of assessing progress, and a review of the adequacy of existing commitments, and an implementation of activities. This may lead to decisions aimed at not only promoting better implementation but also strengthening the POA itself and setting priorities for the next conference that will take place in 2007.

INTERNATIONAL PROGRESS

While references in the POA to principles relating to transfer controls remain underdeveloped, a concerted effort has nevertheless been made on the part of both government and civil society organizations. There are three major international processes related to transfer controls. These three initiatives are direct but closely linked and reinforce the UN small arms process and POA commitments on transfer controls.

The United Kingdom (UK) government has led the Transfer Control Initiative (TCI), which sought to secure international agreement to common standards on SALW transfers at the UN Program of Action Review Conference in 2006. Currently, the TCI focuses on working at a regional level with governments to gather information on what transfer controls exist within countries in order to build consensus on the need to strengthen control on SALW transfers.

The second of the three parallel global initiatives is the Consultative Group Process (CGP). The CGP has involved over 30 governments from different regions, including Europe, Africa, Asia, and the Americas, as well as international experts from NGOs and UN agencies. In late 2004, the CGP published a chair's report, which drew together the progress made by the CGP in building common understanding on transfer control guidelines and on the second aspect of the CGP's work, restricting transfers to nonstate actors.

The third of the current initiatives is the effort to establish an International Arms Trade Treaty. The initiative centers upon a set of global principles governing arms transfers that were compiled with the help of a team of international lawyers and that codify existing state responsibilities under international law. This initiative has the backing of over 600 civil society organizations worldwide and is the main international objective of the Control Arms Campaign. The governments of Tanzania and the United Kingdom have led the process of building support for the treaty. Finland hosted a meeting of governmental experts in 2004, and a follow-on meeting was held in Dar es Salaam in 2005.

REGIONAL PROGRESS

The establishment of multilateral SALW transfer controls has thus far been most successful at the regional or the subregional level. Since 2003, the most encouraging regional progress on the issue of transfer principles has been in Africa. The SADC Firearm Control Protocol came into force in 2004, containing a commitment for governments to harmonize import, export, and transit control. Also, the 11 signatory states to the Nairobi Protocol in the Great Lakes and Horn of Africa signed the Best Practice

Guidelines for the Import, Export, and Transit of Small Arms and Light Weapons in 2004.

The countries of the Andean community in South America have agreed to the Andean Plan to Prevent, Combat, and Eradicate the Illicit Trade in SALW in All Its Aspects, which obliges states to exercise effective control over the production, import, export, transfer, trade, brokering, marketing, and registration of SALW.

NATIONAL PROGRESS

One hundred seven states surveyed have some legislation covering exports. Indeed, only 54 states have conducted a review of their SALW export legislation since 2001. A norm is developing for criteria-based licensing systems, although in many countries the actual criteria used are often confidential. A number of countries in eastern Africa are undertaking legislative review following the signing of the Nairobi Protocol. The different criteria standards for operating in different regions and the lack of regional agreements in some areas (for example, South Asia) further highlight the need for common international standards governing arms transfers.

STATES MISUSE OF SALW

Although state misuse of SALW was not addressed by the program of action, it is nevertheless an important and extremely relevant issue for states to consider within the context of the UN small arms process. The misuse of small arms by government security forces is a major source of human rights violations and an important factor in driving the demand for SALW on the part of civilians and other nonstate actors. Nonetheless, states have a responsibility to use SALW in accordance with the internationally agreed standards. These include the UN Code of Conduct for Law Enforcement Officials (1979), the UN Basic Principles on the Use of Force and Firearms by Law Enforcement Officials (1990), and the UN Principles on the Effective Prevention and Investigation of Extra-Legal, Arbitrary, and Summary Executions (1998). These agreements require law enforcement officials to "use force only when strictly necessary and to the extent required for the performance of their duty" and require that intentional lethal use of firearms may only be made when strictly unavoidable in order to protect life or under exceptional circumstances including war or threat of war.

There is considerable international consensus that, when making decisions on licensing transfers of SALW, states take full account of a recipient's record in upholding international standards for the use of SALW in law enforcement. In this regard, states should refuse SALW transfers if the weapons are likely to be used to violate international human rights standards.

RESTRICTING TRANSFERS

In recent years, the issue of SALW transfers to nonstate actors has been one of the most controversial and debated subjects in the international arms control arena. In 2001, a small number of states, led by the United States, refused to accept the inclusion in the POA of a ban on such transfers, despite strenuous counterarguments, particularly on the part of members of the African group. Unfortunately, the absence of a consensus on the issue has created one of the major gaps within the POA. However, the flow of SALW to rebel groups, terrorist organizations, and similar nonstate actors remains an urgent concern for the international community.

Strictly speaking, any transfer of arms to a nonstate actor should be authorized by the exporting government and the government of the territory where that nonstate actor is based. Failure to secure such an authorization could mean that the supplier government is guilty of interfering in the internal affairs of another state. The focus of the international debate has thus primarily centered upon the possible supply of arms to entities that are not authorized by their national government as legitimate recipients of SALW. Nonetheless, the specific prohibition on providing weapons to terrorists is an important development that will become especially significant if the UN adopts a definition of terrorism as has been proposed. At the most recent meeting in Rio de Janeiro, Brazil, participants from Latin America and elsewhere debated the subject at length and concluded that while a ban on unauthorized transfer of SALW to nonstate actors would represent the best form of agreement, some way should be found of bringing on states that do not support a ban into an international control regime.

MANPADS

The proliferation of the man-portable air defense system (MANPADS) has been of increasing concern to the international community, especially since the failed attack on an Israeli passenger aircraft flying out of Mombasa in November 2002 highlighted the threat posed to civilian aviation. Although MANPADS is a specific subcategory of light weapons, they are being dealt with separately from broader SALW issues in a number of international forums.

The production of MANPADS is currently limited to a small number of manufacturers, but the number of companies and countries manufacturing them has increased since the 1980s. At present, at least 15 companies and consortia produce MANPADS in more than 15 countries. The number of complete systems in existence is in the region of 100,000. Many of the approximately 105 states that stockpile units experience problems with security. At least 13 nonstate groups possess MANPADS, some of which are considered terrorist organizations. It is estimated that of the approximately 1,000 Stinger missiles transferred to the Afghan mujahideen by the Central Intelligence Agency (CIA) in the mid 1980s, between 200 and 600 were never returned to the United States. The CIA estimates that there are from 2,000 to 6,000 units at large worldwide, after determining that at least 4,000 of the weapons from Iraq's prewar arsenals cannot be accounted for.

At the Evian Summit in June 2003, the Group of Eight (G-8) countries also expressed concern about the increasing number of MANPADS in worldwide circulation. The G-8 committed to reduce proliferation and called on all countries to strengthen control of their MANPADS stockpile. The G-8 states have also agreed to implement some steps called Elements for Export Control of MANPADS and to exchange information on national measures related to the implementation of these steps.

There have also been a number of bilateral and national initiatives to control MANPADS:

- In February 2005, the Russian Defense Minister Sergey Ivanov and the U.S. Secretary of State Condoleezza Rice signed the U.S.-Russian Arrangement of Cooperation in Enhancing Control of MANPADS.
- In May 2004, the Cambodian army destroyed its entire stock of 233 MANPADS with the assistance of the U.S. Government.
- In May 2004, Nicaragua, which reportedly had some 2,000 surface-to-air weapons obtained from the Soviet Union during the 1980s, announced that it destroyed a portion of its stock (333 missiles).
- In February 2005, a North Atlantic Treaty Organization (NATO) Partnership for Peace trust fund project was established to help Ukraine destroy stockpiles of surplus ammunition and SALW, including MANPADS.

INTERNATIONAL COOPERATION AND ASSISTANCE

International assistance is an essential element to implement the POA, and commitments to provide such assistance form a key part of Section III of the program. Even before July 2001, a number of donors were providing important support for efforts to prevent and reduce SALW trafficking, proliferation, and misuse. At least 22 states have provided some form of bilateral assistance to SALW-related projects since 2001. Most of these have provided only quite modest aid in resource terms and in a limited number of areas. However, there are some with relatively substantial SALW programs, adding up to the equivalent of millions of U.S. dollars annually.

Most of these are developed countries and long-established members of the so-called donor community. But some are not. For example, Pakistan provided specific assistance to Afghanistan, relating to disarmament of ex-combatants. Countries such as South Africa and Thailand are emerging as significant contributors to their neighbors. In fact, the number of developing and transitional states that are assisting neighbors in some way is probably greater than indicated; they simply do not report it as bilateral aid. In practice, there is a greater scope for developing countries to provide assistance to others in a similar situation, at least because they have intimate knowledge of many of the challenges.

MULTILATERAL OR REGIONAL ORGANIZATION AID

A number of countries also provide resources to enable multilateral or regional organizations to develop substantial international assistance programs in this area. Among the most significant are the UN Development Program, UN Department for Disarmament Affairs, UN Regional Centers, OSCE, NATO, and the Stability Pact. The EU structures involve the regular and reliable resources of its budgets for this purpose, rather than the ad hoc support on which most other regional and international bodies depend in this context.

The review and examination of the development and implementation of international assistance programs related to SALW since 2001 has identified a number of emerging issues and themes:

- ensuring scope and focus for SALW aid programs
- supporting regional cooperation
- learning lessons
- coordinating donor issues and capabilities
- integrating SALW programs aid with other assistance programs.

ANALYSIS AND ASSESSMENT

The POA clearly remains an important framework for promoting cooperation to prevent and combat illicit trafficking and uncontrolled proliferation of SALW at all levels. However, it is similarly clear that the international community is still far from having prevented or eradicated the illicit trade in SALW in all its aspects. Indeed, overall it seems that the problem remains as serious and damaging as ever. Although there has been progress in efforts to control the availability and flows of SALW and to reduce their damaging impact, there is little evidence to suggest any overall success so far.

The primary responsibility for preventing and reducing illicit trafficking and proliferation of SALW, and for implementing the program of action, continue to lie with states. Nevertheless, the problem of SALW trafficking and proliferation are complex, cross-cutting, and difficult. They cannot effectively be tackled without developing partnership, not only within the government but also between governments, international and regional organizations, and civil society groups.

International cooperation and assistance is an essential aspect of progress toward implementing the POA. However, international assistance is not a panacea in these places where international assistance plays a key role in helping to stimulate, facilitate, and support effective use of these national (and regional) resources. Financial and technical assistance is needed to build capacity and to support implementation programs directly.

Also there are four major issues related to cooperation assistance to support POA implementation:

- Issues of local ownership and determination of priorities for support continue to be prominent. In principle, each country and region should develop its own implementation of the POA and then identify those areas where it needs assistance and establish priorities.
- Bilateral donor agencies and relevant international and regional donor organizations need to address problems with their own capacity to provide appropriate assistance for all key aspects of the POA. This is partly a matter of establishing cadres of staff with the appropriate expertise and experience with SALW-related programming.
- There is a need to take measures to mainstream SALW dimensions into more established dimensions of international assistance, such as governance, security sector reform, and poverty alleviation.
- There is a continuing problem with matching needs to available assistance and with donor coordination. The immediate priority continues to be at least to ensure effective information exchange and consultation among donors and their partners.

CONCLUSIONS

Globalization is shaping the international proliferation and diffusion of firearms while simultaneously creating opportunities for global interagency action. Advances in technology, not to mention economies of scale, have increased civilian access to weapons of high lethality and destruction. The availability of SALW is fueling real and perceived insecurity. Partially as a result of the growing awareness of the problem, the discursive response of the effects of SALW has become increasingly varied, and the contours of analysis are broadening rather than narrowing. More and more actors are calling for a multidisciplinary and integrated approach to disarmament that takes into consideration public health, criminology, as well as humanitarian and international organizations.

The UN Program of Action on Small Arms remains the framework for comprehensive international efforts to cooperate to prevent, combat, and eradicate illicit trafficking, proliferation, and misuse of SALW. Unfortunately, only a limited number of countries and regions have so far demonstrated a sufficiently serious commitment to implementing the POA commitments that they entered into in 2001.

Indeed, arms trafficking and proliferation are not the sole or the main cause of tensions and conflicts in this globalized world. Regulating and controlling SALW transfers to conflict areas is just one of the potential tools for achieving a more peaceful world.

NOTES

1. Robert O. Keohane and Joseph S. Nye, Jr., "Introduction," in *Governance in a Globalizing World*, ed. Joseph S. Nye, Jr., and John D. Donahue (Washington, DC: Brookings Institution Press, 2000).

2. Franklin E. Zimiring and Gordon Hawking, *Crime Is Not the Problem: Lethal Violence in America* (Oxford: Oxford University Press, 1997).

3. Michael Klare, "The Kalashnikov Age," *Bulletin of the Atomic Scientists* 55, no. 1 (January–February 1999), 18–22.

4. Jenny Irish, *Policing* for *Profit: The Future of South Africa's Private Security*, Graduate Institute of International Studies Monograph Series 39 (August 1999), available at www.iss.co.za/Pubs/Monographs/No39/Contents.html.

5. Graduate Institute of International Studies, "After the Smoke Clears: Assessing the Effects of Small Arms Availability, in *The Small Arms Survey: Profiling the Problem* (Oxford: Oxford University Press), 2001.

PART III

Regional Studies

CHAPTER 6

Balkan Trafficking in Historical Perspective

Esther A. Bacon

The role of early Balkan organized crime, in the form of outlaws and bandits, is traditional. In some ways, the outlaws and bandits were the catalysts for revolution against the Ottoman Empire and certainly were facilitators in the formulation of the modern Balkan states. The trafficking of weapons from one Balkan state to another[1] and contraband to finance support for rebels fueled the fall of the Ottoman Empire.

The downward spiral of the Ottoman Empire was most evident about the turn of the century when merchants began profiting without paying taxes to the state. These opportunistic merchants, mostly of Balkan Orthodox or Greek nationality, lived from border smuggling and legitimate trade. They included Greek ship captains who owned a schooner or two, Serbian pig farmers taking hogs to markets in Hungary, and Bulgarian dockside traders who imported Russian furs. People of this kind created the revolutions that completed the pattern of Ottoman decline.

The bandit tradition in the Balkans, along with the cooperation between state bandits in forming the modern states, is a model that has led to modern bandits or criminals and organized crime. The term *organized crime* was itself only invented in the 1920s, originally referring to smuggling activities such as those in which armed bandits and tribes of the Balkans had previously been involved but which were increasingly being clamped down on by state authorities (in the case of weapons) or were being newly prohibited (such as drugs) and therefore a new commodity to be trafficked in this way.[2]

Rebel movements against the Ottoman Empire largely handled the smuggling and trafficking of illicit goods in the Balkans. The main source of smuggling was arms merchants who supplied obsolete Russian army rifles that had been acquired as a consequence of the Russo-Turkish War of 1877–1878. One of the ways contraband was smuggled over the borders is still familiar today in the Balkans: hidden in bags of rice and tobacco carried by a mule train. Following the World War I, Turkey and Yugoslavia were increasing their supplies of morphine, heroin, and cocaine to Europe. By 1936, they were the main suppliers of European and U.S. drug manufacturers.[3] From this time forward, Turkey has been a main supplier of drugs into Western Europe.

THE BALKAN ROUTE IN MODERN PERSPECTIVE

Modern smuggling and trafficking through the Balkans was prominent during the era of Josip Broz Tito. Yugoslavia's intelligence agencies and its criminal underworld worked together in an alliance that served to communalize political society. Serbia's mafia was established at this time because of its control of the Balkan route[4] for smuggling of heroin.

The war in Yugoslavia reactivated the circuits of illicit trade in arms that had been established during the Iran–Iraq conflict and had since fallen into disuse, particularly after the first Gulf War.[5] After the war in Bosnia and the Western sanctions on Serbia, former Serbian President Slobodan Milosevic profited greatly because of the ability to exploit market shortages. Smuggled cigarettes, for example, accounted for an estimated 70 percent of domestic consumption. During the wars, Milosevic carried out transfers through banks in Greece, Cyprus, Austria, Bulgaria, and Switzerland to avoid international economic sanctions against Yugoslavia. These bank accounts, along with a network of front companies used by Milosevic, bought U.S., Russian, and Israeli military equipment for Serbia's wars.[6]

Over the past decades, the Balkans became a nexus of criminal activity in Europe. Its powerful criminal structures play a pivotal role in smuggling illegal immigrants into the European Union (EU); the trafficking of prostitutes and establishment of brothels in the EU; the infiltration of untaxed tobacco products into the EU; the transit of drugs bound for the EU; the sale and export of weapons which have been found in the possession of illegal organizations as far apart as northern Ireland and Angola.[7]

WHAT IS SMUGGLED AND TRAFFICKED

The Balkans are a clearinghouse for drugs, arms, cigarettes, and humans in Western Europe. Some of these "items" originate in the region; others are just transported, but all pass, in one way or another, through the Balkans. The profits from these commodities made by organized crime are laundered for the most part within the borders of the Balkans. Some of these profits are linked with terrorist groups.

It is estimated that 75 to 80 percent of drugs in Europe have been trafficked through the Balkans.[8] The Drug Enforcement Agency (DEA) estimates that 4,000 to 6,000 kilograms of heroin are smuggled from Afghanistan to Western Europe every month, largely through the Balkans. With a kilogram of heroin worth between $50,000 and $200,000 on the street, the European traffic generates a market worth $7 billion a year, making it easily the biggest regional industry in the Balkans. The drug is transported by land and sea, in trucks, minibuses, and cars, as well as in speedboats and large ships that park in international waters and transfer their illicit cargo to small vessels such as fishing boats.

According to the DEA, cigarette smuggling in the Balkans is rivaling drug trafficking. The center of traffic is reportedly situated in Kosovo, with probes linking high-ranking Montenegrin officials to the rise in that marketplace for smuggled cigarettes.[9] Cigarette smuggling in the region has continued to deprive governments and local economies of millions of euros in tax revenues. Furthermore, incomes earned from smuggling often go to finance organized crime. In 1999, according to the World Customs Organization, 4 billion smuggled cigarettes were seized in Western Europe, many coming from the Balkans. Indeed, 85 percent of the cigarettes in Serbia were smuggled in 2000. At $35,000 per load, the cost incentive for organized criminals is high.[10]

Five hundred thousand illegal immigrants travel into Europe through the Balkans a year. Of the estimated 1 million women and girls forced into prostitution worldwide each year, 200,000 of them are trafficked into the whole of Europe, through the Balkans, out of Central and Eastern Europe and the former Soviet republics. Kosovo and Bosnia Herzegovina are trafficking destinations in the region, while Moldova, Albania, and Romania, followed by Bulgaria, are the most significant originating countries in the Balkans and the neighboring countries. Each country or territory is to varying degrees a country of origin, transit, or destination.

The Italian police estimate 13,500 tons of arms passed through Italy to be sold in the Balkans, especially to the Croatian army in the 1990s when former Yugoslavia was under an arms embargo. Current estimates are difficult to track. However, arms are flowing from Kosovo Albanians to rebels in Macedonia.

ROUTES

Afghanistan

Afghanistan is an originating country for heroin that is smuggled through the Balkans for Western European markets. According to United Nations (UN) statistics, opium production increased between 1988 and 1991 by 100 percent, and between 1991 and 1999, from an estimated 2,000 tons to a record 4,600 tons. In 1999, Afghanistan produced 75 percent of the global supply of opium. By 2005, it accounted for 92 percent of the global illicit supply.[11] Most recently, due to the chaos and lawless conditions in many regions of the country, an almost record drug harvest increased 59 percent for 2006.[12] Of these totals, about 20–30 percent is transported to Europe via the Iran-Turkish route, continuing on through the Balkans to its destination. Approximately 50 percent of drugs travel via Central Asia to Russia and Eastern European states.

Afghanistan is the original source of most of the opiates reaching Turkey. Afghan opiates, and also hashish, are stockpiled at storage and staging areas in Pakistan where large quantities are assembled and then smuggled by overland vehicles to Turkey via Iran. Multiton quantities of opiates and hashish also are moved to coastal areas of Pakistan and Iran, where the drugs are then loaded on ships waiting offshore. The contraband is then smuggled to points along the Mediterranean, Aegean, or Marmara Sea coastal areas of Turkey. Opiates and hashish also are smuggled overland from Afghanistan via Turkmenistan, Azerbaijan, and Georgia to Turkey.

Turkey

Turkey is a transit and originating country for drugs, humans, and cigarettes that travel through the Balkan route. It is also a major operating base for international narcotic traffickers responsible for all aspects of trafficking and refining drugs and serves as a key link to Afghanistan. Turkey is one of the most advanced countries in the region in terms of countering illicit drug trafficking. Turkish authorities continue to seize large amounts of heroin and precursor chemicals, such as acetic anhydride, and to disrupt heroin laboratory operations at various locations around the country. Precise data on the amount of heroin and other opiates trafficked via Turkey are difficult to determine, but the DEA estimates that trafficking operatives in Turkey are involved in the smuggling of at least 4 to 6 tons of heroin per month.[13]

Turkish-based traffickers and brokers operate directly and in conjunction with narcotic suppliers, smugglers, transporters, laboratory operators, drug distributors, money collectors, and money launderers in and outside Turkey. They negotiate, arrange, finance, control, direct, and engage in the smuggling of opiates (whether in the form of opium, morphine base, or heroin) to Turkey and from Turkey to markets largely in Western Europe.

The precursor chemical acetic anhydride, which is used in the production of heroin, is illegally acquired from sources in Western Europe, the Balkans, and Russia. During the 27-month period from July 1, 1999, to September 30, 2001, over 56 metric tons of illicit acetic anhydride were seized in or destined for Turkey. Turkish-based traffickers operate illicit laboratories, refining morphine base into heroin at various locations in Turkey. Some Turkish criminals operate heroin laboratories in Iran, near the Iranian-Turkish border. The ready availability of opiates originating from Afghanistan and precursor chemicals from other countries enables major traffickers in Turkey to continue to operate illicit laboratories converting morphine base into heroin. These heroin laboratories continue to pose a problem for law enforcement authorities and to provide Turkish-based traffickers with heroin, enabling them to control much of the heroin marketed to Western Europe.

Bulgaria

Bulgaria is both an originating country for arms and humans, as well as a transit country for drugs and humans. Indeed, according to a 1995 Europol report, Bulgarian organized crime groups established themselves particularly in trafficking women for sexual exploitation, along with debit-card fraud and Euro-counterfeiting.[14]

Small quantities of opium poppies and cannabis are grown in Bulgaria. Clandestine laboratories produce amphetamines, and diverted acetic anhydride is transported from Bulgaria to Turkey.

According to the head of Bulgaria's Customs Service, a total of 2 metric tons of drugs were seized at Bulgarian border crossings between January and November 2001. Of that amount, some 1.5 metric tons was heroin. By comparison, 2,541 kilograms of narcotics were seized in 2000, of which 1,785 kilograms was heroin. Following a wave of killings among underworld figures, the Sofia police began a crackdown on drug dealers and stepped up efforts to keep street dealers away from schools.

Heroin from the Golden Crescent and Southwest Asian sources, most notably from Afghanistan, remains the main illegal drug transiting Bulgaria, though some marijuana and cocaine also transit the country. The northern Balkan route from Turkey through Bulgaria to Romania is the most frequently used overland route. Other routes go through the Former Republic of Yugoslavia (FRY), now called Serbia and Montenegro, and the Former Yugoslav Republic of Macedonia (Macedonia). In previous years, Bulgarian officials have noted the transit of increasing amounts of Brazilian cocaine. Furthermore, the trend in which precursor chemicals pass from the former Yugoslavia through Bulgaria to Turkey has increased steadily over the past decade.

Bulgaria is a source and transit country and, to a lesser extent, a destination country for women and girls trafficked for sexual exploitation. After narcotics trafficking, human trafficking is rated by some experts as the second most lucrative criminal business for Bulgarian organized crime.[15] Women originating in, or transiting through, Bulgaria are most often trafficked via Albania and end up in France, Spain, the Netherlands, and Greece. Other trafficking victims are from Georgia, Ukraine, Moldova, Romania, Russia, Lithuania, and Latvia.

Albania

Albania is a transit country for drugs, humans, and cigarettes, as well as an originating country for humans and arms. Albanian police claim that approximately 10 speedboats carrying trafficked persons depart from Vlora bay and other coastal points each night. The number of trafficked people during the summer is reportedly between 2,500 and 3,000 a month. Many are Kurds entering Albania from Greece.

Organized crime groups involved in the trafficking of women are located in Tirana, Shkodra, Korca (which is the main transit city between Macedonia and Greece), Berat, Vlora, and Fier. Trafficking of women is often closely linked with the smuggling of drugs and arms as the routes are often the same due to the fact that most transits are conducted via fast boats to Italy and Greece and from there to other EU countries, such as Belgium, France, and the Netherlands. The women are provided with false documents and then transported out of the country. Widespread corruption has led to the complicity of local authorities, both in Albania and Italy, who are either involved or turn a blind eye to the level of human trafficking between the two countries.

Albania is also one of the main transit countries for the trafficking of women and girls from Central and Eastern Europe. Victims transiting Albania come mostly from Romania and Moldova, with smaller numbers from Bulgaria and Ukraine. Young boys are trafficked from Albania to work as beggars in Italy and Greece.

The main human trafficking routes into Albania follow the arms and drug smuggling routes. These are through Romania, Serbia, and either Montenegro or Macedonia, from which women and girls are trafficked into Western Europe or Greece. Different routes to move women are used, though the main route is from the country of origin such as Moldova or Ukraine to Serbia, Montenegro, Albania, and onto Western Europe. Shkodra is usually the first main transit town in Albania for trafficking from Montenegro, and Korca is the main transit city for traffic from Macedonia. Women are generally bought and sold in these cities and then sent to the ports of Durres or Vlora, bound for Italy. Similar markets are reported to exist in Berat, Elbasan, Durres, Fier, Tirana, and Vlora.

Organized crime groups use Albania as a transit point for drug and other types of illicit goods due to its strategic location, weak police, and judicial systems, as well as lax border controls. The most common illegal drugs are heroin, cocaine, and marijuana. Heroin is typically routed through the Balkan route of Turkey-Bulgaria-Macedonia-Albania, and from there to Italy and Greece. Cocaine is smuggled by air from the United States and South America, passing through Albania on its way to Western Europe.

In 2001, Albanian police arrested 353 people for drug trafficking. All but four of them were Albanian nationals. During the same year, Albanian authorities reportedly seized 4.5 kilograms of heroin, 266 grams of cocaine,

6,915 kilograms of marijuana, 600 grams of cannabis seeds, 2.8 kilograms of red poppy seeds, and 1.3 liters of methadone. The authorities also destroyed three cannabis laboratories. According to the Albanian counternarcotics service, police targeted larger smuggling operations in 2001, resulting in several key arrests and the seizure of $1 million in U.S. cash.

Macedonia

Macedonia is a transit and destination country for drugs, arms, humans, and cigarettes. It is further an originating country for refined heroin, humans, arms, and cigarettes. Macedonia lies along one of several overland routes used to deliver Southwest Asian heroin passing through Turkey on its way to Western Europe. In recent years, this route has also been used to deliver high-grade Albanian hashish to Turkey where it is often exchanged for heroin. While limited amounts of marijuana are grown in Macedonia, the market for it is small because it cannot compete with the higher quality, lower priced Albanian product. Macedonia is not known to produce precursor chemicals.

The Sar Mountains north and west of Tetevo are controlled by rebel Albanian groups (the Liberation Army of Preševo, Medveda, and Bujanovac in Macedonia). The destabilization caused by civil unrest and nationalist uprisings leaves the borders porous and uncontrolled, facilitating smuggling routes through the Tetevo region that continue to the Kosovo border. The towns of Pec and Prizren in Western Kosovo are bases for trafficking gangs who then move shipments west over the Albanian border, into the lawless Tropoje area centering on the town of Bajram Curri, 6 miles west of the Kosovo border. On the Albanian side, the Haklaj clan is dominant; on the Kosovo side the Thaci and Haradinaj clans are allegedly central to the trade in the Drenica and Pec areas respectively.[16]

Macedonia is a transit and destination country for women and children trafficked for prostitution from the former Soviet Union and Eastern Europe (most notably Ukraine, Moldova, Romania, and Bulgaria). Some victims remain in Macedonia; others are trafficked to Albania, Kosovo, or Italy.

Serbia/Montenegro

Serbia/Montenegro is a transit country for drugs, humans, and cigarettes, and an originating country for humans and arms. FRY authorities reported 3,060 seizures in 2001, up from 2,307 in 2000. As a result of the seizures, FRY authorities confiscated 2,350 kilograms of marijuana, 60 kilograms of heroin, 10,435 ecstasy tablets, 590 grams of hashish, and 2.5 kilograms of cocaine.

Montenegro. Cigarettes purchased from offshore companies and then smuggled into the EU from Montenegro cost approximately $3.4 billion in lost taxes in a 2-year period.[17] Indeed, in the same year, 50 percent of the Montenegrin gross domestic product was attributed to cigarette smuggling.[18] The problem of the government sharing in the profits of criminal commerce is great for this developing area. The issue of the collusion of government officials in criminal profiteering is a highly problematic one for other countries wishing to render foreign development assistance.

Serbia. Milosevic's corrupt reign in FYR abetted the Belgrade mafia in establishing control of the Balkan route for heroin with the full support of the Yugoslav intelligence apparatus (including fake passports, assumed identities, cover stories, safe houses, and impunity). Proceeds from illicit trafficking were deposited in Cyprus and other offshore banking centers. Smuggling included cigarettes, arms, drugs, and humans. What remains of Milosevic's political-criminal network is enduring. There are no distinct statistics.

Kosovo. In the first 2 months of its operations, the Kosovo Force made interdiction an integral part of its mission, seizing more than 600 rifles, including 45 machineguns; 48,829 small-arms rounds; more than 1,000 antitank weapons; 2,438 antitank rounds; 658 mortar rounds; nearly 1,400 grenades and mines; and piles of support equipment such as uniforms, boots, medical supplies, and flak jackets.[19]

In September 2005, in a joint operation, UN police along with the local Kosovo Police Service arrested three UN police officers and four foreigners for human trafficking in northern Kosovo. The arrests came only days after the UN Mission in Kosovo launched a toll-free help line for victims of sex-based violence in Kosovo, including victims of human and sex trafficking. Amnesty International claims that the presence of international peacekeepers in Kosovo has fueled the sexual exploitation of women and encouraged trafficking. Amnesty International has long claimed that UN and North Atlantic Treaty Organization (NATO) troops in the region are using the trafficked women and girls for sex and that some have been involved in trafficking itself.

Indeed much of FRY is a transit/source and destination country for women and girls trafficked for sexual exploitation. Victims are from Moldova, Romania, Ukraine, and Bulgaria, and largely end up in Kosovo, Bosnia, and Albania, as well as Western Europe.

Much of the smuggling and trafficking activity in FRY is enabled by rampant corruption. In 2001, for example, over 1,200 cases of general police corruption resulted in termination of employment or fines.[20] Due to years of chaos and disorder, control has landed in the hands of local power bosses who mete out justice as they see fit. The justice system is particularly susceptible to hijacking by personal interests and lacks sufficient oversight and accountability.

Cyprus

Cyprus has a large offshore banking sector that serves as a center for money laundering of the proceeds of much illicit activity. It also serves as a broker point where dealers meet potential buyers and negotiate the purchase of future smuggled goods. Since 1975, 37 offshore banking units and more than 30,000 offshore companies have registered in Cyprus. After the collapse of the Soviet Union, Cyprus was a favorite country for Russians to launder the proceeds of arms and narcotics smuggling operations as well as to avoid taxes. Since September 11, 2001, the country has imposed tough anti-money laundering legislation to avoid being placed on the international anti-money laundering blacklist.

Greece

Greece is a transit country and a destination market for drugs, humans, and contraband cigarettes. Heroin and hashish originating in the Middle East and Southwest Asia enter the country from Turkey, while cannabis and other drugs from Bulgaria and Macedonia enter Greece through Albania. Large shipments are smuggled into Greece in shipping containers, on bonded TIR (Transit International Routier) trucks, in automobiles, on trains, and in buses. Indeed, the ingenuity of the smugglers is almost boundless with schemes ranging from the brazen use of open trailers of narcotics to false walls, ceilings, and floors in freight compartments packed with illegal cigarettes. Trucks cross through the Turkish border, transit Greece, then cross the Adriatic by ferry to Italy.

Some schemes are so convoluted that they appear to be the stuff of fiction. For example, Turkish-refined heroin has been known to be traded for Latin American cocaine that, in turn, transits Greece to end up in other parts of Europe. The original cocaine has been shipped by Greek shipping concerns from Latin America to Greece, mixed with other cargo, and then sent on to other ports in Europe. For example, in August 2000, Greek authorities arrested six drug traffickers in connection with Operation *Link*, a continuing international maritime drug smuggling investigation that led to the arrest of a number of Colombian drug couriers and to the seizure of over 4 tons of cocaine.

In a similar operation the following year, in October 2001, Greek authorities seized 201 kilograms of cocaine, arrested 5 Greek nationals, and effectively dismantled a Greek-based maritime drug-smuggling organization that was attempting to smuggle large amounts of cocaine from South America to Europe.

Greece is primarily a destination country and, to a lesser extent, a transit country due to the fact that it lies in the middle of the traditional Balkan route for trafficked women and children. Major countries of origin include Ukraine, Russia, Bulgaria, Albania, FRY, and Romania. Women from North Africa (Tunisia, Algeria, and Nigeria), Asia (Thailand and the Philippines), the Middle East, and other countries, such as Moldova, Georgia, Poland, and Kazakhstan, are also trafficked to Greece.

Hungary

Hungary is an originating, transit, and destination country for the traffic in humans. Women and girls are trafficked from Romania, Ukraine, Moldova, Poland, Yugoslavia, and China to and through Hungary to Austria, Germany, Spain, the Netherlands, Italy, France, Switzerland, and the United States. Men are also trafficked for forced labor through Hungary to EU countries. The majority of them come from Iraq, Pakistan, Bangladesh, and Afghanistan.

After Bulgaria and Romania, Hungary is the next primary transit country on the main narcotics smuggling route from Southwest Asia to Western Europe. It is a destination for synthetic drugs and marijuana from the Netherlands and heroin that passes through the Balkan route. Hungary has also been an important transit country for the smuggling of arms, stolen art works, and vehicles.

Italy

Italy is a transit country for drugs and humans from the Balkan route and is a destination country for drugs and humans. While Italy is almost legendary for its organized crime groups, foreign groups have moved to the country and established operations under the strict tutelage of Italian crime bosses. Albanian heroin traffickers, for example, work with members of the Italian mafia families as transporters and suppliers of drugs. Others include Russian, Kosovar, Serbian, and Turkish organized crime groups who have negotiated "franchise operations" or who pay "taxes" to Italian organized crime groups. The Italian mafia seems to prefer to receive arms, narcotics, or simply cash as their profit rather than engage in human trafficking themselves.

Italy is a destination and transit for trafficked men, women, and children from Albania, Eastern Europe, the former Soviet Union, South America, Africa, and Asia. Nigeria is the main source of women trafficked to Italy.[21] Women and girls are trafficked for prostitution, and some Chinese men are trafficked for forced labor in industry.

Cocaine, destined for Italian and other European consumption, originates with Colombian and (more recently) Mexican criminal groups.

In 2005, the Italian police apprehended 18,000 people on narcotics-related offenses and seized approximately 27,000 kilograms of narcotics including 1,168.4 kilograms of heroin, 3,714 kilograms of cocaine, 19.947 kilograms of hashish, 2,024 kilograms of marijuana, as well as 284,310 ecstasy tablets.[22] The major nationalities of those arrested were Moroccan, Tunisian, Albanian, Algerian, Nigerian, Spanish, Senegalese, and Colombian.

In October 2005, the Italian police mounted an international counternarcotics sting operation that involved Spain, Argentina, France, and the

Netherlands. The operation netted approximately 1.5 tons of cocaine and over 120,000 ecstasy tablets and led to the arrest of 60 people. That same month, the Italian *Carabinieri* broke up an international drug trafficking network based in southern Italy and arrested 40 members of the group.

Czech Republic

The Czech Republic is an originating country for arms and a transit country for drugs originating in Turkey. Albanian organized crime reportedly maintains warehouse operations in the country for these transit operations that make it a critical locus for these criminal operations. The Czech Republic is also a growing money laundering center. The major organized crime groups that utilize the country are Albanian, Nigerian, Vietnamese, and some criminal groups of the former Soviet Union.

Heroin from the south (mostly from Turkey, moving north via the Balkans) also transits the Czech Republic en route to Northern and Western Europe. Czech authorities attribute most of this activity to Kosovar-Albanian drug mafias. As with other drugs that transit the country, some heroin also ends up on the streets of the Czech Republic. Cocaine and marijuana reach the Czech Republic, mostly in transit to Northern and Western Europe, although some is sold to Czech residents and tourists visiting Prague. The use of ecstasy has increased in recent years, and police are concerned that PMA (an ecstasy-like "club drug") and GHB (the so-called date rape drug) have begun to appear on the Czech market. Pervatine (a Czech produced methamphetamine) is produced in the Czech Republic, primarily for local consumption. Czech counternarcotics police believe that Russian-speaking and Asian gangs now control about half of the pervatine market and that increasing amounts of the drug are now exported to neighboring countries such as Germany and Poland.

Slovakia

Slovakia is an originating and transit country for drugs. Smuggling occurs primarily from Russian and Ukraine. Russian organized crime groups are very active in the heroin trafficking business.[23] In recent years, Slovak authorities have placed increased emphasis on the Balkan route and the suspected Albanian criminal organizations that use it. Albanian traffickers cooperate with criminal organizations in neighboring countries to move the heroin to market. Albanian organized crime groups are responsible for 90 percent of all drug trafficking in Slovakia.

Slovenia

Slovenia is not a major transit or a destination country for drugs or humans. Slovenian authorities believe that its borders with Italy, Austria,

Hungary, and Croatia, as well as its short Adriatic coastline, make Slovenia a relatively easy target for Albanian, Turkish, and Italian criminal organizations smuggling heroin into Western Europe via the Balkan route. Slovenia's main cargo port, Koper, located on the North Adriatic Sea, makes it a particularly attractive transit point for South American cocaine and North African cannabis destined for Western Europe.

Slovenian authorities seized 198 ecstasy tablets in the first 11 months of 2004, compared with 2,536 ecstasy tablets in the first 9 months of 2003, 7,051 tablets in 2002, and 1,773 tablets in 2001. In 2004, 148.6 kilograms of heroin was seized compared with 77.24 kilograms in 2003, 65.6 kilograms of heroin in 2002, and 88.9 kilograms of heroin in 2001. In addition, 16.6 kilograms of marijuana and 4,893 cannabis plants were seized in 2004, compared with 144.37 kilograms of marijuana seized in 2003, 1,083.8 kilograms of marijuana in 2002, and 170.56 kilograms of marijuana in 2001. In the first 11 months of 2004, 104.8 kilograms of cocaine was seized by Slovene authorities.[24]

Slovenia is a transit country for women and girls from eastern, southeastern, and Central Europe being trafficked to Western Europe, the United States, and Canada. It is also a destination country for women and teenage girls, mostly from other former Yugoslav republics, as well as from Ukraine, Moldova, Romania, the Czech Republic, and Bulgaria.

Croatia

Croatia is a transit country for weapons and drugs (controlled by Albanian organized crime groups) that pass primarily through the port of Rijeka. The main drugs trafficked through the country include heroin, cocaine, hashish, marijuana, amphetamines, LSD, and ecstasy. With an approximately 1,000 kilometer coastline (added to this number are 4,000 kilometers on its 1,001 islands), Croatia is a smuggler's paradise for moving such contraband as narcotics and cigarettes into Western Europe. Heroin and marijuana moving through the country often land on the streets of the country to be sold to the local population. Croatian officials estimate that there are approximately 12,000 heroin addicts, consuming between 400 to 500 kilograms of cut, street-ready heroin annually.

Bosnia Herzegovina

Bosnia Herzegovina is a regional hub for narcotics transshipment. It also serves as a transit country for drugs, humans, and cigarettes. It is both a country of origin and destination for humans and cigarettes. Money laundering, often through charity groups, has been traced to al Qaeda and other terrorist organizations in the region.

Years after civil war tore apart Bosnia Herzegovina, international authorities in Sarajevo estimate there are 5,000 trafficked women in the country at
any given time and that many are used by NATO peacekeepers and foreign
police officers. Local police are also reportedly a major clientele group for the
sex trade industry, which only serves to feed the cycle of violence and lawlessness in the country by ensuring that the trade continues uninterrupted.[25]
The International Office of Migration in Sarajevo estimates that there are
between 600 and 3,000 trafficked women in Bosnia Heregovina at any given
time.[26]

In 2004, 280 criminal reports were filed for the unauthorized production,
process, and sale of drugs (a 13 percent decrease in comparison with 2003),
and 980 criminal reports for possession of drugs (a 215 percent increase in
comparison with 2003). The increase of reports for drug possession is attributed to the implementation of the Federation Criminal Code, which criminalized drug possession. Federation counternarcotics operations resulted in
the seizure of 34 kilograms of marijuana, 3.323 kilograms of heroin (a 50
percent increase over 2003 levels), and 1,214 ecstasy tablets (a 50 percent
increase over 2003 levels).[27]

There is mounting evidence of links between, and conflict among, Bosnian
criminal elements and organized crime concerns in Russia, Albania, FRY,
Croatia, Austria, Germany, and Italy. Much of the ethnic fragmentation that
was evident among the three main groups—the Christian Croats, Christian
Serbs, and Muslim Bosnians—has continued to be played out in the criminal
underworld and is, arguably, responsible for the growth of a number of
criminal empires. Bosnia Herzegovina has 432 border crossings but only 39
of them are controlled. Moreover, border police are so underpaid—the top
salary is about $300 a month—there is an almost overwhelming temptation
to accept bribes.

THE WAY AHEAD

The U.S.-initiated Southeast European Cooperative Initiative (SECI) was
launched on December 6, 1996.[28] Its objective is to enhance regional cooperation and thereby guarantee stability among the countries of Southeastern Europe through cooperative and transboundary solutions to shared
economic and environmental problems. Accordingly, under the auspices of
SECI, participating countries jointly seek to address relevant developmental
aspects of the region by improving information exchanges, planning multi-
state programs, and attracting private capital to complement bilateral and
multilateral sources of funding.

There are many factors that enable the growth of organized crime and
the circumstances that facilitate smuggling and trafficking in the Balkans,
such as weak governance, official corruption, ineffective customs and border
controls, displaced people, and extensive criminal activity. Corruption in the

Balkan countries, including the corruption of border officials, law enforcement officers, and political elites, only exacerbate the existing problems.

But there is hope. For instance, with sponsorship from the SECI, law enforcement agencies in the Balkans came together in November 2000 to establish the Regional Center for Combating Transborder Crime. This center aims to tackle the problem of organized crime and trafficking in drugs, humans, and arms in the region. There are 29 permanent liaison officers from various member countries based in Bucharest who specialize in customs, border policing, narcotics, contraband, and human trafficking. Individuals from several U.S. agencies, including the DEA, Federal Bureau of Investigation, and the Department of Homeland Security (Immigration and Customs Service) assist SECI operations. With this kind of regional and international cooperation, the long-standing smuggling and trafficking problems of the Balkans could begin to diminish.

NOTES

1. The possession of weapons by non-Muslims during the Ottoman Empire was prohibited.

2. Sappho Xenakis, "The Challenge of Organized Crime to State Sovereignty in the Balkans: An Historical Approach," (Cambridge, MA: Harvard University, July 2, 2001), available at www.ksg.harvard.edu/kokkalis/GSW3/Sappho_Xenakis.pdf.

3. S.H. Bailey, *The Anti-Drug Campaign: An Experiment in International Control* (London: Edinburgh Press, 1936), 57.

4. From Afghanistan and Iran through Turkey-Bulgaria-Yugoslavia-Hungary, or Albania to Western Europe.

5. Fondzaione Rosselli, "Organized Criminality Security in Europe," European Commission Working Paper, 1999, 10.

6. Kerin Hope, "Bank linked with Milosevic arms purchases," *The Financial Times*, June 17, 2002.

7. Misha Glenny, "Balkans challenges for the West," BBC World News, July 1, 2001, available at http://news.bbc.co.uk/hi/english/world/europe/newsid_1416000/1416145.stm.

8. Heroin, cocaine, methamphetamines, amphetamines, cannabis, ecstasy, and LSD.

9. Nicholas Forster and Sead Husic, "Probe into Montenegro's role at illegal cigarette trade," *The Financial Times*, August 9, 2001.

10. In Greece, there are possible links between cigarette smuggling and groups such as Hezbollah, making this more than just a criminal venture.

11. Testimony of Karen P. Tandy, Administrator of the U.S. Drug Enforcement Administration, before the House Armed Services Committee, U.S. House of Representatives, June 28, 2006.

12. United Nations Office on Drugs and Crime, "Afghan Opium Cultivation Soars 59% in 2006 UNDOC Survey Shows," September 6, 2006.

13. In 2001, U.S. Customs and the Coast Guard seized over 5.1 tons of heroin, 10.1 tons of hashish, and 1.7 million synthetic drug pills. There were 9,064

drug-related arrests and a significant increase in seizures of precursor chemicals, particularly acetic anhydride. Most of the hashish seizures came from the eastern part of Turkey, whereas heroin seizures were mostly from border gates in the western part.

14. Matthew Brunwasser, "A Killing Complicates Bulgaria's EU Hopes," *International Herald Tribune*, December 1, 2005, 1.

15. Berry LaVerle, Glen E. Curtis, John N. Gibbs, Rex A. Hudson, Tara Karakan, Nina Kollars, and Ramón Miró, "Nations Hospitable to Organized Crime and Terrorism," Library of Congress, Federal Research Division, October 2003, 39.

16. Neil Barnett, "The Criminal Threat to Stability in the Balkans" *Jane's Intelligence Review*, April 1, 2002.

17. Forster and Husic.

18. Ibid.

19. Alissa J. Rubin, "U.S. Patrols Smuggling Routes to Macedonia: Balkans: American peacekeepers in Kosovo intercept weapons on way to rebels" *Los Angeles Times*, August 20, 2001, 1.

20. For complete crime statistics for the Former Republic of Yugoslavia, see Richard Monk, *Study on Policing in the Federal Republic of Yugoslavia* (Belgrade: Organisation for Security and Co-operation in Europe, July 2001), available at www.osce.org/documents/spmu/2001/07/17633_en.pdf.

21. Esohe Aghatise, "Trafficking for Prostitution in Italy," in *Violence Against Women* 10, no. 10, October 2004, 1127.

22. "Major Hit Against Albanian Ethnic Organized Crime Group Involved in Drug Trafficking," EUROPOL Press Release, The Hague, October 29, 2005.

23. International Narcotics Control Strategy Report, Bureau for International Narcotics and Law Enforcement Affairs, U.S. Department of State, 2005.

24. Ibid.

25. LaVerle et al., 79.

26. Countries of origin of women assisted by the International Police Task Force in Bosnia Herzegovina in 2000 are: Moldova, 48 percent; Romania, 33 percent; Ukraine, 16 percent; and Other, 3 percent.

27. International Narcotics Control Strategy Report, Bureau for International Narcotics and Law Enforcement Affairs, U.S. Department of State, 2005.

28. Albania, Bosnia Herzegovina, Bulgaria, Croatia, Macedonia, Greece, Hungary, Moldova, Romania, Slovenia, and Turkey.

CHAPTER 7

Drug Smuggling in Central Eurasia

Svante E. Cornell

Since the end of the Cold War and the subsequent rise of nontraditional and often transnational security threats, the need to widen the concept of security and to distinguish between "hard" and "soft" security threats has been increasingly accepted by academics and policymakers alike. This evolution of security threats has been especially evident in developing and post-Communist bloc areas. Among transnational threats, the trade in illicit drugs arguably carries the largest social, political, and economic consequences following terrorism. Aside from the obvious social consequences of increased addiction problems and ensuing epidemics, the growing strength of transnational organized crime in Central Eurasia has had significant implications for the stability, security, and development of these societies. The most alarming consequences have been through the twin relationships between organized crime and insurgency, as well as between organized crime and politics. In fact, both politics and insurgency in this region have become increasingly criminalized lately, with important implications.

At its extreme, drug production and trafficking are leading sources of financing for terrorist and insurgent organizations. The drug trade also exacerbates corruption in already weak states, impairing their economic and political functioning. Finally, though not least threatening to security, the associated costs of drug addiction, drug-related crime, and disease, the drug trade also threatens the fabric of societies.[1]

Nowhere is the damning effect of the drug trade on these multiple aspects of security more visible than in the Central Eurasian region.[2] With rapidly increasing production of opium in war-torn Afghanistan and increasing trafficking of heroin northward through Central Eurasia to markets in Russia and Europe, the adverse impact of the drug trade on the wider Central

Eurasian region is now increasingly apparent. In fact, the security of the region can no longer be separated from the adverse impact that the drug trade and its rising influence has had. Despite the perils associated with this phenomenon, systematic research into the phenomenon has been relatively scant.[3] Given the importance of the region to U.S. national security interests, the adverse effect of the regional drug trade is bound to have a negative impact on U.S. interests in Central Eurasia.

This chapter surveys the development of narcotics smuggling in Central Eurasia. Building on an overview of smuggling patterns, the chapter focuses on two crucial issues that make the drug trade a threat to security in the region: the link between narcotics and terrorist/insurgent groups and the link between narcotics and state officials.

CENTRAL ASIAN CONDITIONS

At independence, the successor states of the former Soviet Union were particularly vulnerable to illicit smuggling activities for a number of reasons. Most had either never existed before as independent states or briefly attempted independence between the collapse of the Russian empire in 1917 and reintegration into the Soviet Union in 1920–1922. Few had a homogeneous population, with the norm being multiethnic populations with kinship links across borders, including both the erstwhile Soviet administrative borders and with populations outside the Soviet Union. Hence, borders have limited legitimacy for the population, and basic state institutions such as border controls were either absent or grossly dysfunctional and had to be built up from scratch. Moreover, the economic collapse that nearly all former Soviet states suffered made corruption a way of life in government bureaucracies and a necessity to survive. These factors acted as tremendous lubricants of illicit smuggling activities across the former Soviet space. These include a multifaceted combination of consumer goods, human beings, arms, materials for weapons of mass destruction, and narcotics. Since the mid-1990s, Central Asia has emerged as a leading smuggling conduit, especially in the context of the trade in illicit narcotics. In addition to the typical problems of post-Soviet societies, Central Asia suffered the added complication of being landlocked, a fact that put additional strain on its economy.

Central Asia is characterized by the weakness of the states in the region and their deep economic and social difficulties, which are intimately interrelated. Before 1991, no independent state, kingdom, or emirate had existed with the same name or similar borders as the five post-Soviet Central Asian states that suddenly gained independence in 1991. These territorial units were created by the Soviet central government in the 1920s, and the delineation was plagued by arbitrary decisions, much like colonial border delimitations in Africa and elsewhere. Topography, ethnic settlement patterns, and natural resources in many cases have little relation to these borders. Especially in the Fergana Valley, which straddles southern Kyrgyzstan, northern Tajikistan, and eastern Uzbekistan, borders are an obstacle to transportation and economic relations between and within countries in an area that historically constituted a single economic space. More poignantly, the border delimitation created economically unviable states whose component parts are geographically isolated from one another. Numerous enclaves and small territorial units belonging to one state but encircled by another exist, but more crucially, topography forms a formidable impediment to the physical unity of states, especially in Kyrgyzstan and Tajikistan. Since independence, this has grown to be a significant impediment to trade and economic relations, especially with the securing of borders following the Islamic insurgency of the late 1990s.[4]

The absence of historical statehood and the existence of practical boundary problems contributed to existential fears among Central Asian ruling elites. The weak legitimacy of states, internally and externally, was exacerbated by the absence of vital state institutions at independence. These factors contributed to making state-building and consolidation of sovereignty a primary priority for ruling elites in all countries. In turn, they eschewed deeper regional cooperation, which was understood as a weakening of sovereignty.[5] The states of Central Asia were mainly raw material producers in the Soviet command economy and were assigned the role of cotton producers, while traditional agriculture was downgraded. Their industrial products were expensive, of low quality, and not in demand internationally, while the cost-efficiency of their primary products was uncompetitive. Moreover, their integration into the world economy was complicated by their landlockedness, as Afghanistan's unrest prevented the restoration of traditional trade routes to South Asia and sustained economic dependence on Russia.

Afghanistan has by contrast existed as a distinct entity for two centuries, but its slow process of state-building was completely undone by the Soviet invasion of 1979 and the ensuing civil war that lasted for a generation with various configurations of power.[6] The war led to the collapse of Afghanistan's infrastructure and economy and to its international isolation, especially during the 1996–2001 Taliban government. The historical heart of Central Asia, Afghanistan's centrality to the political and economic future of the entire Central Asian region became increasingly clear by the late 1990s. It was at one and the same time not only the main security threat to the Central Asian region through its exportation of Islamic radicalism but also the hope for Central Asia's economic reintegration into the world economy, as transportation links through Afghanistan to Pakistan and onward were understood to be crucial to the region's future.

With galloping production of opium in war-torn Afghanistan and increasing trafficking of heroin northward through Central Asia to markets in Russia and Europe, the adverse impact of the drug trade on the wider Central Asian region is now increasingly apparent and deeply affects the security of the region. Despite the perils associated with this phenomenon, systematic research into the phenomenon has been relatively scant.[7]

DRUG TRAFFICKING ROUTES

Drug trafficking in the Central Asian and Caucasian context is normally equated with heroin, which is increasingly the overshadowing drug in the region. It should be noted, though, that the smuggling of other licit and illicit commodities as well as human beings is gradually increasing in the region. That said, this chapter focuses on the narcotics trade because of its specific relevance to security. Opium production has skyrocketed in Afghanistan since the mid-1990s, coupled with increasing processing of opium to heroin inside Afghanistan's territory, whereas earlier it was refined along the smuggling routes. As a result, the amount of heroin transiting Central Eurasia is increasing in absolute terms as well as relative to other drugs. Nevertheless, it must be noted that cannabis products grow naturally in the regions and are cultivated on large territories within Central Asia and the Caucasus (as is ephedra), and it is also noteworthy to point out that synthetic drugs are gradually increasing in importance across Asia and the post-Soviet space.

While the consumption of cannabis is rampant across the region, its social and financial implications are limited compared to the impact of heroin. Central Asia and the Caucasus are not important producers of opium, nor is opium refined into heroin to a significant extent as it currently stands. Kyrgyzstan was a leading producer of licit opium in the Soviet era but has discontinued production. In the late 1990s, a considerable proportion of seizures of drugs were in the form of raw opium, indicating a possibility that refining was taking place along the Kyrgyz smuggling chain. Since the early 2000s, however, the increasing processing of opium into heroin inside Afghanistan has been reflected in Central Asia as seizures of opium have decreased, while seizures of heroin have increased.

Before analyzing trade routes, it is important to note the methodological difficulties associated with obtaining exact information on trafficking. To overcome these inherent difficulties, United Nations (UN) figures mainly utilize seizure data to estimate trafficking flows, yet the highly varied efforts of transit countries to fight trafficking make this methodology fundamentally flawed. Turkmenistan's refusal to report any data on seizures of the past few years illustrates this. In general, seizure data cannot be considered informative in isolation without contrasting it with an analysis of the corruption of state authorities and the efficiency of law enforcement. UN figures on production and consumption of drugs, then, are reliable enough to provide a foundation from which analytical conclusions about the regional narcotics trade can be based. Compiled with data on corruption trends, this chapter goes one step further to provide a valuable methodological edge in understanding drug trafficking flows.

PRODUCTION TRENDS IN AFGHANISTAN

The year 2004 marked a major development in Afghanistan's opium production. While the years 2002 and 2003 could be summarized by the restoration of opium production to the levels of the late 1990s, in 2004 a major increase in production took place, estimated by the UN Office on Drugs and Crime (UNODC) at 64 percent in terms of cultivated area to 131,000 hectares. Because of unusually unfavorable climatic conditions, however, the yield of the opium crop (particularly in the southern areas) was low, resulting in an increase in opium production of only 20 percent to 4,200 tons. The 2004 harvest by far surpassed the bumper crop of 1999 in terms of cultivated land, though not surpassing it in terms of production.

The 1999 crop led to the creation of huge stockpiles, as existing trafficking routes to consumer markets were not in a position to absorb this large increase in production. Whether this is also the case today is unknown, although demand is likely higher than in 1999: the stable consumption of the Russian market is one example, as are indications of increasing export to China.

In the 1990s, Afghan opium was mainly produced in the Nangarhar and Helmand areas and adjacent territories, with relatively small production taking place in the northern province of Badakhshan. Production was focused in the south and west of the country, which also reflected the main direction of smuggling. Recent changes in patterns of opium production in Afghanistan thus act as an initial confirmation of the switch of trafficking routes to the north. Production in the south has gradually receded and shifted toward the inner and northern parts of the country. The largest increases in production are taking place in the northern parts of Afghanistan, although the traditional producing provinces of Nangarhar and Helmand experienced a rebound in 2004. Importantly, by 2004, all provinces of Afghanistan produced opium.

Concomitantly, the amount of opium, and therefore heroin, available in Central Eurasia's neighborhood has increased considerably. In Badakhshsan and adjacent provinces, approximately 72 tons of heroin equivalent was produced in 2004, with an additional 53 tons in the northern and 34 tons in the northwestern provinces. About a third of Afghan heroin, or up to 160 tons, was produced in the northern half of the country, and given the current security dynamics in the country, it is likely that the majority of these shipments were trafficked through Central Asia as the northern route would technically offer greater ease of movement and relatively quick distribution along the initial rungs of the smuggling chain.

CONSUMPTION TRENDS

Afghanistan's opiates are consumed in an increasing number of countries and regions. Previously, opium production in the Golden Crescent served mainly the Iranian opium market. As Iran clamped down on opium following the 1979 Islamic revolution, a significant proportion of production moved to Pakistan and subsequently into Afghanistan. This shift was preceded by Turkey's success in eradicating opium production by the 1960s. With this geographical shift, drug consumption markets also changed. Afghan and Pakistani opiates were smuggled westward in ever-increasing proportions, reaching the ever-growing Western European consumption markets through Iran and Turkey. For a short time, even a large proportion of heroin consumed in the United States originated in this region. This was nevertheless replaced mainly by Mexican and Colombian opiates. Western Europe remains a major destination for Afghan opiates, with 1.5 million addicts consuming approximately 40 to 60 tons a year.[8] This is the most lucrative market, with heroin prices up to $100,000 per kilogram. In terms of quantity, however, the consumption in Iran, Russia, and Pakistan is equally important.

Afghanistan in 2004 produced approximately 420 tons of heroin equivalent, and Myanmar produced approximately 40 tons (compared to 80 tons in 2003 and 110 tons in 2000). Myanmar's production is mainly feeding China, Australasia, and, in minor quantities, the United States and Europe, though the halving of production in 2004 is likely to generate important shifts especially as Chinese consumption is concerned. The overwhelming majority of Europe's heroin is of Afghan origin. Over 80 percent of China's has been of Burmese origin and approximately 20 percent from Afghanistan. Europe, the former Soviet Union, Iran, Pakistan, and 20 percent of China jointly consume the lion's part of Afghanistan's exports, but even high estimates of consumption in these countries would not exceed a need for 250 to 320 tons of heroin. In addition, small quantities of Afghan heroin are consumed in South Asia and the Middle East.

This rudimentary analysis of the consumption of heroin in areas supplied by Afghanistan fits well with estimates of Afghanistan's actual opium production. Hence, there is significant reason to believe that large stockpiles are kept inside Afghanistan. Afghanistan simply produces more opiates than its known consumer markets can absorb.

TRAFFICKING TRENDS

Trafficking patterns in Central Asia and the Caucasus differ. In Central Asia, a major heroin trafficking route in and by itself, heroin trafficking is the prevailing form of organized crime and overshadows other forms of smuggling in terms of monetary value—though, by volume alone, smuggling of illicit goods is rampant in the region. In the South Caucasus, the heroin trade constitutes one of several other significant activities, such as human trafficking and nuclear and arms smuggling. The South Caucasus is sandwiched between two major trafficking routes, and sections of both traverse the area. The amount of heroin transiting the South Caucasus is therefore more difficult to estimate, given the lack of large seizures, as well as conflicting and complex trafficking patterns.

The heroin consumed in the former Soviet Union is known to be almost exclusively of Afghan origin and smuggled to and through Central Asia (and, to a limited extent, from Iran to the Caucasus). This suggests that at least 80 to 100 tons of heroin is smuggled through the region. Pakistan and Iran are clearly not supplied through Central Asia, implying 90 to 120 tons of Afghanistan's heroin is smuggled south. In sum, it appears logical to assume that at the very least one third of Afghanistan's opiates are smuggled north and slightly over a third south and west. The only real question surrounds the routes through which heroin transits in order to end up in Europe. The significant seizure rates in Turkey, reports from the Balkan route, and the involvement of ethnic Albanian communities in some Western European countries all suggest that a substantial smuggling of heroin still takes place through the Balkan route. Conversely, there are smatterings of reports of heroin from Central Asia and Russia reaching the European Union (EU), but the expected avalanche has not taken place; Russia and other newly independent states all the way to the Baltics seem to absorb most of the heroin smuggled through Central Asia. Only a limited portion of the heroin transiting Central Asia reaches the EU, and no major publicized seizures in Europe have been identified as transiting Central Asia. That said, a truck apprehended with 50 kilograms of heroin on the Russian-Finnish border in the summer of 2005 indicates that this route is being used for smuggling to and possibly through Scandinavia.

THE BALKAN ROUTE VERSUS THE NORTHERN ROUTE

Although expectations of an onslaught of heroin to Europe through Russia did not materialize in the 1990s, the reverse view (that heroin remains trafficked almost entirely through the Balkan route) is not correct, either. Swedish police, for example, have managed to trace back—through operational cases—heroin shipments to Ukraine and from there on to Turkmenistan. A Western police officer visiting Tajikistan, given the honor by Russian border guards of incinerating a shipment that he estimated to be no less than half a ton of pure white heroin, noted this shipment was packed in common European (including Swedish, French, and Finnish) coffee packages. Subsequent investigations showed excess empty coffee packages had been sold from a factory in Denmark to a company in Lahore, Pakistan. Isolated incidents of heroin seizures in Scandinavia, especially Finland, have identified a connection to Russia. But in general, very seldom are forensic tests of seized heroin undertaken, which implies that the specific origin of the drug is not ascertained, thereby making assertions about the trafficking patterns unclear. At present, although most heroin trafficked to Europe follows the Balkan route, there are strong indications suggesting that the Northern route through Central Asia is becoming prominent.

An attempt to improve these conclusions through an analysis of seizure rates generates only limited results. Seizures in Central Asia are thought to represent as little as 5 percent or less of total smuggling. Turkmenistan, which reportedly seized 2 tons of heroin in 1997, has subsequently refused to report seizures since 2000. The near total lack of reliable information from Turkmenistan is a major problem in arriving at reliable figures. Tajikistan, on the other hand, reports seizing an average of 4 tons of heroin a year. Yet even in spite of the lack of information from Turkmenistan, seizure rates indicate that Central Asia's importance as a transit region is gradually increasing.

Since 2001, Central Asian seizure rates of pure heroin have been larger than those in Iran. Nevertheless, these figures do not account for the significant seizures of morphine in Iran. While these figures do not mean that Central Asia has eclipsed Iran and Pakistan as the primary transit corridor for Afghanistan's heroin, they do suggest that Central Asia's proportion in drug trafficking out of Afghanistan is rapidly rising. This is all the more the case given the formidable financial resources and manpower invested by the Iranian government on its border with Afghanistan and Pakistan, compared with the relatively limited resources of Central Asian states.

Extrapolation from production, seizure, and consumption patterns (that is, analysis of widely available information) leads to the conclusions that heroin consumed in Europe is primarily smuggled through the Balkan route but a gradually increasing proportion reaches Europe through Central Asia, the Caucasus, Russia, and Ukraine, perhaps up to a quarter of the total.

SPECIFICS OF THE NORTHERN ROUTES

Breaking this estimate down into more exact information on the individual countries of the region is more complicated. In fact, Central Asia's five states are a leading example of the unreliability of analysis built on officially documented seizure rates. Based solely on these official figures, it would appear that only Tajikistan is heavily used by traffickers. Indeed, seizure rates in Tajikistan display the establishment of a continuous and alarming rate of drug trafficking in the country.

Whereas the weakness and relative openness of Tajikistan after its civil war have brought attention and publicity to that country's problems with drug trafficking, very little hard evidence is available on what is the other most likely major artery of the Central Asian drug trade: Turkmenistan.

While seizures of narcotics skyrocketed in all other countries of Central Asia in 1995–2001, the numbers in Turkmenistan actually dropped from 2 tons in 1997 to 180 kilograms in 2000.[9] This has raised significant suspicion among analysts watching the regional drug trade. Even the United Nations diplomatically noted that "it seems surprising that drug traffickers were not making use of these links."[10] The UN backed this conclusion by citing the fact that Turkmenistan was the only Central Asian country that bordered both Afghanistan and Iran and that enjoyed political relations with both the Taliban and the Northern Alliance—and it also had established commercial relations with the Taliban-controlled regions of Afghanistan. This UNODC analysis assumes that seizure figures provide an indication of the actual amount of drugs being smuggled through a country. In the case of Turkmenistan, one of the most closed societies in Eurasia comparable to North Korea, seizures are not likely to give much indication of what is really going on in the country. In fact, accusations of high-level penetration of the Turkmen state by drug trafficking networks abound.

This implies that an analysis of drug trafficking routes in Central Asia is impossible without taking qualitative factors into account. These include the relationship to the patterns of production in Afghanistan; drug use and Human Immunodeficiency Virus (HIV) epidemics in the region; assessments of actors in organized crime in the countries; information from available investigated trafficking cases; appraisals of the counternarcotics capacities of the regional states; and accounting for the level of criminal infiltration into state authorities and the endemic corruption in each country.

PRODUCTION AND CONSUMPTION

As already indicated, one important indication of evolving trafficking patterns is geographical (that is, provincial) changes in Afghan opium production. The general move to northern provinces has already been noted. Afghanistan's opium production has traditionally taken place in the vicinity of neighboring countries through which the drugs are then trafficked (for example, production within the Nangarhar has traditionally been trafficked through Pakistan's North-West Frontier Province, and Helmand production normally transits through Pakistani Baluchistan or directly into Iranian Sistan-Baluchistan). Likewise, production in Badakhshan is assumed to be trafficked almost exclusively through Tajikistan, although some shipments may now be trafficked through the Wakhan corridor to China. However, in the past 2 years, the diversification of supply inside Afghanistan has made it difficult to extrapolate directly (and solely) from production areas. One important factor is the very rapid increase, albeit from low levels of production, in Afghanistan's northwestern provinces. This increase of production near Turkmenistan's border could signify a move of production closer to export markets, minimizing the risk of seizures inside Afghanistan. Production

TABLE 7.1
Estimates of Drug Users in Central Asia

Country	Registered Users, 2003	UNODC Estimate, 2002	Prevalence Rate (%)
Kazakhstan	50,000	165,000–185,000	1.1
Kyrgyzstan	5,600	80,000–100,000	1.8
Tajikistan	8,800	45,000–55,000	0.85
Turkmenistan	N/A	N/A	N/A
Uzbekistan	21,300	65,000–90,000	0.3

figures alone nevertheless continue to lend credence to the domination of Tajikistan as a primary artery for Afghan opiates.

A second indication of trafficking routes is the emerging patterns in drug addiction. As the historic experience of Pakistan and Iran reveal, domestic drug use often acts as a natural reflection of a country as a transit state. This nevertheless depends on the type of trafficking taking place. Highly organized trafficking in large shipments, especially if taking place in collusion with officialdom, has less risk of leading to large spread of drug use among the local population.

On the other hand, small-scale disorganized smuggling making use of local couriers, often paid in kind rather than in cash, usually leads to a large and rapid spread of drug use in transit areas. Finally, economic factors are of importance, too: higher living standards imply a larger potential benefit from selling drugs locally. In Central Asia, the weak state authorities make statistics on drug use and HIV unreliable. Turkmenistan claims not to have an HIV problem, though anecdotal evidence indicates widespread drug addiction (including the injection of drugs) in the country. Other states of the region do cooperate with international organizations on these issues, but the stigma surrounding drug use and HIV has led to remaining problems in estimating the true size of the epidemic. A UNODC Rapid Assessment survey in 2000–2002 was the first estimate of drug use that went beyond depending on officially registered users (see Table 7.1).

The information in Table 7.1 is clearly a rough estimate. As Kairat Osmonaliev notes, it likely overstates drug abuse in Kyrgyzstan and possibly also in Kazakhstan, while understating it in Tajikistan and Uzbekistan.[11] Figures nevertheless show alarming increases in drug users and HIV cases in all republics. Given the absence of data from Turkmenistan, the only real conclusion that can be drawn from the consumption statistics is that Uzbekistan appears to be only a secondary trafficking route and that the most likely origin of most heroin smuggled to Kyrgyzstan and Kazakhstan is Tajikistan. As only limited guidance is available from known data on consumption, a short overview of the regional countries is in order.

Tajikistan

Proximity to production areas, ethnic ties with Afghanistan, and seizure rates all testify to the leading role Tajikistan plays as a drug trafficking route. The relative openness of the country due to the weakness of state institutions and authorities, and its dependence on international support, are major factors in allowing external access to a wealth of information on the country.

Tajikistan is also the country in the region with the most significant international drug control presence. It conceived a Drug Control Agency (DCA) in 1999, for which it gained UNODC funding (provided mainly by the United States). The agency now employs 360 personnel and has the status of a law enforcement agency. Moreover, the Russian 201st motorized rifle division, tasked to guard large sections of the Afghan-Tajik border, is a main player in countering the drug trade in the region. Although these institutions have made inroads in stemming the drug trade, both institutions are riddled with internal problems. The Drug Control Agency has been widely lauded in the West as an honest and corruption-free institution. Nevertheless, the appointment of General Ghafor Mirzoyev as head of the DCA in January 2004 led to significant concern. A warlord during the civil war, it is strongly believed that his great personal wealth was accumulated from involvement in the drug trade in the mid-1990s. Mirzoyev's appointment led to a collapse of morale in the DCA and seizures dwindled. His subsequent dismissal and arrest in August 2004 may have alleviated the problem, but his appointment stands as a dangerous precedent that questions the Tajik leadership's true commitment to drug control. At the very least, it shows that internationally funded drug control is a tool in the domestic politics of the country. Secondly, the Russian military may be instrumental in seizing large quantities of heroin, but the Russian military's involvement in the drug trade is widely recognized and has of late been publicly acknowledged.[12]

In desperately poor Tajikistan, great wealth is ostentatiously displayed in the construction of palaces belonging to government ministers and other members of the ruling elite in the capital as well as the provinces. These physical reminders of the corruption and criminalization of the country's elite are compounded by a wealth of information implicating leading figures in the heroin industry. As for the Russian military and the Tajik political elite, the question is whether involvement in the drug trade is evidence of corruption or systematic collusion. Indeed, Tajikistan is permeated by the heroin trade, a fact that is made all the more blatant given the lack of other sources of income in the country.

Turkmenistan

In the late 1990s, Turkmenistan was a leading country in the seizure of drugs of Afghan origin. Heroin seizures peaked at nearly 2 metric tons in

1997, by far the largest amount seized in Central Asia at the time. Similarly, 4.6 tons of opium were seized in 1999.[13] Hence, until 2000, large shipments of illicit drugs and precursors were evidently seized in Turkmenistan. In 1996–1998, 77 percent of heroin seized in Central Asia was apprehended in Turkmenistan. During 1995–2000, more than 198 tons of precursor chemicals were seized in the country, mostly acetic anhydride, used in the manufacture of heroin.[14] However, Turkmenistan has not been providing any data on drug seizures since 2000. This suggests that smuggling networks were built up in the country and that a substantial quantity of Afghan heroin did transit Turkmenistan, even though little or no production took place in the provinces in the vicinity of Turkmenistan's border at the time. Whether this heroin was mainly of northeast Afghan origin or from Helmand is unknown.

Since Turkmenistan stopped reporting drug seizures in 2000, however, there is no evidence that the smuggling of drugs through the country has abated. Quite the contrary, evidence from police cases in Western Europe has uncovered links to Turkmenistan in cases of heroin smuggling via Ukraine, as stated by the Swedish police's criminal intelligence division. Anecdotal evidence of grave addiction problems in the country also indicates that smuggling continues to be a growing problem. In December 2003, Chief Prosecutor Kurbanbibi Atajanova was arrested, after 15 kilograms of heroin were seized from her husband in a border region. She was nevertheless present at a government meeting shortly afterward, indicating that she was not released from her duties, let alone charged. While this indicates the presence of heroin in the country, it is also a rare example of direct information on government corruption. Allegations by exiled former government officers pointing to high-level collusion with the drug trade abound, as discussed below.[15] Incidentally, Turkmen President Saparmurad Niyazov has publicly stated that smoking opium is good for health.[16]

A recent International Crisis Group report cites numerous eyewitnesses reporting government involvement in the drug trade from the lowest to the highest levels.[17] No reliable estimates are available: widely cited "unofficial" sources estimate that up to 120 tons of heroin are trafficked through the country each year, though this figure is highly unlikely, since that would constitute close to a third of Afghanistan's production and more than the estimated entire amount transiting Central Asia. In fact, all estimates available seem to be based on scarce evidence and guesses rather than sound methodology. Unlike Tajikistan, Turkmenistan does not have a Drug Control Agency, and it has allowed a minimal international presence that has any relevance to drug control. Its long and porous border with Afghanistan is considered by UNODC as uncontrolled on both sides.[18] Hence, Turkmenistan is in all likelihood an important chain in the Eurasian heroin industry. Estimates of the quantity of drugs passing through Turkmenistan are nevertheless unavailable. The most logical estimate is that Turkmenistan is second only to Tajikistan in terms of the amount of drugs trafficked through the country directly from Afghanistan.

Kyrgyzstan

Though not directly bordering Afghanistan, Kyrgyzstan is one of the countries most heavily affected by the Afghan drug trade. A weak and impoverished state, Kyrgyzstan has proven vulnerable to the penetration of its territory by drug traffickers. Almost all drugs enter Kyrgyzstan from the southern areas of Osh, Jalal-abad, and Batken. In the late 1990s, the major trafficking artery was along the highway from Khorog in Tajikistan's Gorno-Badakhshan province to Osh, which developed into a major center of the regional drug trade. From 1999 onward, the routes shifted to the southwestern Batken region, where drug trafficking routes from Tajikistan coincided with the regions affected by the militant incursions of the Islamic Movement of Uzbekistan (IMU) in 1999 and 2000. Osh is crucial to illicit trafficking of narcotics due to its geographic location, close to the Uzbek border and at the head of the only road connecting the northern and southern parts of Kyrgyzstan. Hence, both trafficking routes linking Tajikistan to Uzbekistan's Ferghana Valley and routes onward to northern Kyrgyzstan, Kazakhstan as well as to Uzbekistan pass through Osh. As a result, powerful local criminal groups have emerged in the region. Kyrgyz officials note that governmental control over the southern areas of the country is significantly weaker than in the north. Even when aware of drug shipments transiting toward the northern part of the country, law enforcement normally waits for the shipments to arrive in the north before intercepting them, fearing reprisals by drug traffickers. As Osmonaliev notes:

> In May 2004 officers of the Southern counter-narcotics department of the Kyrgyz Ministry of Interior detained a citizen of Tajikistan with 3 kg of heroin. Later, these officers were attacked by an unknown group from Tajikistan, who demanded the release of the drug courier. Armed with three machine-guns and a Makarov pistol, they shot twice in the air and took their compatriot, presumably an accomplice, away.[19]

This episode illustrates how weak state control over the territory in southern Kyrgyzstan is, a predicament that seriously complicates the country's counternarcotics efforts. Based on the Tajik model, a Drug Control Agency with a staff of over 250 has been created with support from the UNODC. In spite of this, drug seizures in Kyrgyzstan remain low and haphazard.

Uzbekistan

Uzbekistan has avoided the fate of Tajikistan and presumably Turkmenistan of being considered a major direct transit corridor for Afghanistan's opiates. Largely due to the short 137-kilometer border (90 miles) that it shares with Afghanistan and the relative strength of the Uzbek state, the border is not known to be penetrated by trafficking groups in any significant way. Instead, drugs seem to enter the country mainly through Tajikistan and Kyrgyzstan. One trafficking route hence crosses into Uzbekistan, carrying drugs northward into Kazakhstan.

While punishments are severe, corruption in the ranks of the Uzbek law enforcement structures is endemic, as in other countries of the region. Indeed, the interior ministry appears highly autonomous from the presidential office, enabling drug trafficking networks to infiltrate the law enforcement structures in spite of what seems a government commitment to fight drugs. The fact that Uzbekistan hosts both the regional office of UNODC as well as the U.S. Drug Enforcement Agency's office in the region does not necessarily mean the country is devoid of problems in its own ranks.

Kazakhstan

Due to its large landmass and the fact that Kazakhstan is the only Central Asian country bordering Russia (the main immediate destination of most Afghan drugs transiting the region), much of the heroin transiting the countries bordering Afghanistan appears to transit Kazakhstan before being smuggled onward. As a result of this, as well as Kazakhstan's economically advantageous situation in regional terms, the country has become a heroin market in its own right. This explains the higher recorded prevalence of drug use in the country compared to the rest of the region.

Drugs have been noted to enter Kazakhstan through myriad routes, including from Tajikistan across Kyrgyzstan; via Uzbekistan's long border with Kazakhstan; and via Turkmenistan or Uzbekistan toward the western part of the country and the port of Aktau on the Caspian Sea. Kazakhstan's membership in a customs union with Russia, Ukraine, and Belarus facilitates this traffic. Once cargo enters any of the customs union countries, customs officials consider it as domestic cargo, and it is therefore not subject to inspection as long as it remains sealed. Kazakhstan is also a producer of precursors; this particularly occurs in the city of Shymkent in Southern Kazakhstan.

SECURITY IMPLICATIONS

The economic and political impact of the drug trade in these states has also been significant, especially in the weakest states of the region, Tajikistan and Kyrgyzstan. In the absence of a strong licit economy—and in the case of Tajikistan, a war-ravaged one—the large turnover and profit margins of drug trafficking have a serious impact on state and society. This has created a severe corruption problem across the region at all levels, especially among low-paid government officials in law enforcement. High-level government officials have also been known to be involved in the trafficking of drugs, raising the question whether systematic criminal infiltration into state authorities is taking place. Meanwhile, the Islamic insurgencies that the region has experienced have been tied intimately to the drug trade.

Though the Islamic Movement of Uzbekistan's (IMU) armed incursions of 1999 and 2000 were ostensibly waged in the name of the creation of a Caliphate with a base in the Ferghana Valley, a strong body of evidence suggests that they are in fact best explained by more mundane motivations, especially the drug trade. The geographical areas targeted, the timing of the attacks, and the tactics used all point in this direction. The IMU was in fact a leading actor in the drug trade in its own right. The group was singularly well placed to control the drug trade from Afghanistan to Central Asia. It had well-established links with the Taliban government and al Qaeda,[20] while maintaining close contacts with old comrades-in-arms in the former Tajik opposition, who were now in government. The Tajik government in turn had close links with the ethnic Tajik-led Northern Alliance under Ahmad Shah Masoud. Opposing political forces were hence controlling the main production areas in Afghanistan and the main transit corridor in Central Asia. Only the IMU had a network of contacts on all sides, which enabled it to move across Afghanistan and Tajikistan unlike any other known organization.

In 1999 as in 2000, the IMU's attacks occurred in the summer season, roughly a month after the latest opium harvest in Afghanistan, allowing for the processing of opium into heroin before smuggling it out of the country. The launching of simultaneous but small-scale incursions by comparatively small groups of fighters into Kyrgyzstan as well as Uzbekistan makes little military sense, unless understood as a diversionary measure intended to create instability, confuse law enforcement and military structures, and allow for the use of mountain passes for trafficking. The IMU had made a practice of staging August incursions, but this did not take place in 2001. While other factors may have been at work, it is an interesting coincidence that 2001 was the year in which the Taliban ban on opium had gone into effect: there was simply no harvest in Taliban-held Afghanistan that the IMU could smuggle out to Central Asia. There were nevertheless large stockpiles of opiates left in the country following the large harvests in 1999 and 2000, which the IMU may or may not have had access to.[21]

An increasing consensus has indeed developed that the IMU was strongly involved in drug trafficking from Afghanistan toward Osh in Kyrgyzstan, where the opiates were likely handed to trafficking networks that could ship them further north and west. Drug control experts concurred with the estimate that the IMU controlled up to two-thirds of opiates entering Kyrgyzstan.[22] Ralf Mutschke of the Criminal Intelligence Directorate of Interpol labeled the IMU "a hybrid organization in which criminal interests often take priority over 'political' goals," adding that "IMU leaders have a vested interest in ongoing unrest and instability in their area in order to secure the routes they use for the transportation of drugs."[23] During and after the 1999 incursion, law enforcement officials noted a threefold increase in trafficking attempts. Kyrgyz government officials noted that the volume of drugs trafficked into Kyrgyzstan increased significantly after the 1999 incursion.[24] The IMU never lived up to the reputation of a monolithic, hierarchically structured organization. Most studies of the movement seem to indicate the coexistence within the IMU of a more guerrilla-oriented and criminal faction and a more religious one. As such, a set of different motivations likely were behind the IMU's actions. As Frederick Starr has termed it, the IMU is best understood as an "amalgam of personal vendetta, Islamism, drugs, geopolitics, and terrorism."[25]

CONCLUSIONS

In countries such as Afghanistan, Tajikistan, and now Kyrgyzstan, voluminous accusations of high-level participation in the drug trade by high government officials raise the question whether these states are infiltrated by criminal interests to an extent that merits the use of the term *narco-state*. In this context, the vague concept of corruption is unsatisfactory to understand the processes occurring in South and Central Asia. The World Bank uses the term *state capture* to describe attempts by organized forces, whether legal or illegal, to buy, control, or otherwise influence administrative decisions, legislative acts, court verdicts, or state policy in general. State capture involves turning the institutions of the state to serve narrow interests rather than the interests of the population at large. This is conducted by businesses, regional interest groups, and the like in many developing and postcommunist states.

The World Bank definition does not differentiate between the types of interests that seek to influence state institutions. However, when organized crime infiltrates the state in order to influence or affect its decision-making mechanisms, the process is qualitatively different than ordinary state capture, in fact amounting to a criminalization of the state. Organized crime has infiltrated state authorities in Central Eurasia with an increasing degree of success, not only because of its absolute and relative financial strength in the region but also because organized criminal networks have a greater interest than most actors in capturing the state, since the state poses the main impediment to the development of organized crime. Consequently, the pervasive state weakness in Central Eurasia has enabled the gradual criminalization of state authority in the region.

At present, the question is whether drug trafficking in Central Asia is turning into a business conducted by states or individuals in official positions in states—and whether government complicity is in fact a main reason for the booming organized crime in the region. In this sense, there is substantial reason to argue that the crime-terror nexus in the region has been paralleled by a crime-state nexus. This development has very significant interests for the United States; it undermines the prospects of building stable, prosperous states in Central Asia with a participatory political system. Processes taking place in Kyrgyzstan and Tajikistan are empowering criminal forces with connections to terrorist organizations such as the IMU. In other words, there is a risk of a "black hole" scenario developing where individuals in important state positions are connected not only to organized crime but also to militant religious extremism and terrorism. This could be illustrated by a triangle uniting the crime-terror nexus and the crime-state nexus with a state-terror nexus. While this has not yet taken place, the increasingly influential role of figures with connections to organized crime in Kyrgyz politics and the continued strength and influence of Tajik warlords with connections to the IMU is a distinct cause for worry. The situation is exacerbated by the difficulty in predicting the motivations behind the actions of this type of political figures. Much suggests they are driven mainly by power and money and not religious extremism, but the murkiness of the web of interactions between state, crime, and terror in Central Asia is a cause of concern for the interests of the United States.

NOTES

1. Tamara Makarenko, "Terrorism and Transnational Organised Crime: The Emerging Nexus," *Transnational Violence and Seams of Lawlessness in the Asia-Pacific: Linkages to Global Terrorism* (Honolulu: Asia Pacific Center for Strategic Studies, 2004); Kimberley L. Thachuk, "Transnational Threats: Falling Through the Cracks?" *Low Intensity Conflict & Law Enforcement* 10, no. 1 (2001); Sabrina Adamoli et al., *Organized Crime Around the World* (Helsinki: HEUNI, 1998); Barbara Harris-White, *Globalization and Insecurity: Political, Economic and Physical Challenges* (New York: Palgrave, 2002); Ian Griffith, "From Cold War Geopolitics to Post-Cold War Geonarcotics," *International Journal* 30, no. 2 (1993–1994); Richard Matthew and George Shambaugh, "Sex, Drugs, and Heavy Metal: Transnational Threats and National Vulnerabilities," *Security Dialogue*, vol. 29 (1998), 163–175.

2. Defined as including the former Soviet republics of the South Caucasus (Armenia, Azerbaijan, Georgia), Central Asia (Kazakhstan, Kyrgyzstan, Tajikistan, Turkmenistan, and Uzbekistan), as well as Afghanistan and the Western Chinese Xinjiang-Uyghur Autonomous Province.

3. The literature on the drug trade in Central Asia consists mainly of United Nations Office on Drugs and Crime reports and a handful of articles and working papers. These include Martha Brill Olcott and Natalia Udalova, *Drug Trafficking on the Great Silk Road*, Working Paper 11 (Washington, DC: Carnegie Endowment for International Peace, March 2000); and Alexander Seger, *Drugs and Development in the Central Asian Republics* (Bonn: Deutsche Gesellschaft fur Technische Zusammenarbeit, 1996).

4. Svante E. Cornell and Regine A. Spector, "Central Asia: More than Islamic Extremists," *The Washington Quarterly* 25, no. 1 (Winter 2002).

5. S. Frederick Starr, "Central Asia in the Global Economy," Supplement to *Foreign Policy*, September 2004.

6. Larry P. Goodson, *Afghanistan's Endless War* (Seattle: University of Washington Press, 2001); Ralph H. Magnus and Eden Naby, *Afghanistan: Mullah, Marx and Mujahid* (Boulder: Westview, 1998).

7. Olcott and Udalova; Seger.

8. Assuming an average usage of 30 to 40 grams per user per year. This is double the use in the United States, where heroin is very expensive. In Britain, where the price is lower, a figure of 40 grams has been recorded. Purity levels, the amount of time addicts serve in treatment or jail, price differentials, and use of other drugs make estimates very difficult. Evidence from the region indicates that the usage per addict is fairly high; therefore, the use of the 30- to 40-gram bracket.

9. United Nations Office on Drugs and Crime, *The Opium Economy in Afghanistan: An International Problem* (New York: United Nations, 2003), 160.

10. Ibid.

11. Kairat Osmonaliev, *Developing Counter-Narcotics Policy in the Central Asian States: A Legal and Political Assessment* (Uppsala: Silk Road Studies Program, January 2005), 5, available at www.silkroadstudies.org/Silkroadpapers/Osmonaliev. pdf.

12. Asal Azamova, "The Military is in Control of Drug Trafficking in Tajikistan," *Moscow News*, May 30, 2001. This is the first acknowledgment of Russian officials of the long-suspected involvement of its troops in Tajikistan in the drug trade. See also "Civil Order Still a Distant Prospect in Tajikistan," *Jamestown Monitor* 7, no. 137 (July 18, 2001); Jean-Christophe Peuch, "Central Asia: Charges Link Russian Military to Drug Trade," Radio Free Europe/Radio Liberty, June 8, 2001.

13. Regional Office of Central Asia, *Drug and Crime Situation in Central Asia: Compendium Analysis* (New York: United Nations Office on Drugs and Crime, 2003).

14. United Nations Office on Drugs and Crime, "Illicit Drugs Situation in the Region Neighboring Afghanistan and the Response of ODCCP," October 2002, 13, available at www.unodc.org/pdf/afg/afg_drug-situation_2002-10-01_1.pdf. Some Central Asian countries have their own large chemical industries, which make it possible to divert chemicals required for heroin manufacture. During 1995–1998, 77.6 tons of precursor chemicals were seized in Uzbekistan.

15. Rustem Safronov, "Turkmenistan's Niyazov Implicated in Drug Smuggling," *Eurasianet*, March 29, 2002; Alec Appelbaum, "Turkmen Dissident Accuses Niyazov of Crimes," *Eurasianet*, April 26, 2002; "Russia Turns its Back on Turkmenbashi," Gazeta.ru, May 27, 2003.

16. International Crisis Group, *Cracks in the Marble: Turkmenistan's Failing Dictatorship*, January 2003, 27–28, available at www.crisisgroup.org/home/index.cfm?l =1&id=1445; "Turkmen Addiction Rising," *IWPR Reporting Central Asia*, no. 64 (August 10, 2001).

17. International Crisis Group; Safronov.

18. Vladimir Fenopetov, statement at Silk Road Studies Program seminar, Uppsala, October 2004.

19. Oibek Khamidov, "Drug Courier Was Taken Abroad," *Vecherny Bishkek*, May 19, 2004.

20. See, for example, Michael Fredholm, *Uzbekistan and the Threat from Islamic Extremism*, Conflict Studies Research Centre, Report no. K39 (Sandhurst: United Kingdom Royal Military Academy, March 2003), 9–10.

21. Associated Press, May 25, 2001.

22. Author interview with international drug control officials, Washington, DC, May 2001; Tamara Makarenko, "Crime and Terrorism in Central Asia," *Jane's Intelligence Review*, July 2000.

23. Ralf Mutschke, "The Threat Posed by the Convergence of Organized Crime, Drugs Trafficking and Terrorism," Testimony before the Subcommittee on Crime of the Judiciary Committee, U.S. House of Representatives, December 13, 2000. Also testimony to the same hearing of Donnie R. Marshall, director of the Drug Enforcement Administration.

24. Bolot Januzakov, quoted in Glenn E. Curtis, *Involvement of Russian Organized Crime Syndicates, Criminal Elements in the Russian Military, and Regional Terrorist Groupings in Narcotics Trafficking in Central Asia, the Caucasus, and Chechnya* (Washington, DC: Library of Congress, Federal Research Division, October 2002), 14.

25. Bloomberg News, March 12, 2002.

CHAPTER 8

Smuggling and Trafficking in Africa

Audra K. Grant

INTRODUCTION

The end of the Cold War saw the beginning of ethnic and local conflicts in Africa that had been previously subsumed under larger U.S.-Soviet rivalries. The political vacuum produced by the cessation of Cold War proxy wars created an environment for political and economic competition among well-armed factions. This environment has escalated into some of the world's most devastating conflagrations. The struggles that have dominated Africa since the 1990s have weakened already fragile states, thereby exacerbating internal instability and providing fertile ground for illicit trade activities. Trafficking in Africa is a complex phenomenon shaped by overlapping and interrelated dimensions, as illicit trade in commodities, weapons, narcotics, and humans and other items cross numerous countries within and beyond the region, causing civil strife, the use of military force and other forms of violence, and ultimately human suffering.

Trafficking in Africa is also characterized by the related creation and maintenance of strategic transnational alliances. These alliances involve an amalgam of state and substate actors that include criminal groups, militias, firms, and government officials. Contacts and cooperation among these actors is facilitated and enhanced through increased international trade, personal mobility, and access to porous borders. While some of these alliances take place in close geographic proximity, other arrangements exist that are not limited by location. African substate actors involved in illicit trading, for example, have established ties with substate entities on other continents as far as Asia and Latin America, a phenomenon that reflects the extent to which substate actors are able to exploit weak international legal regulation and poor state enforcement.[1]

It is against this backdrop that illicit trade networks in Africa have proliferated, emerging as a significant challenge to the integrity of the state, and
thus to the national security for the African region as well as to the security
of the international community. Trafficking, however, also raises concerns
for human security, as it contributes to the persistence of the intra- and interstate conflicts in a way that stymies economic growth, development, and
the provision of public safety. Equally important in this regard is the link
between trafficking and the spread of diseases such as Human Immunodeficiency Virus/Acquired Immune Deficiency Syndrome (HIV/AIDS).

This chapter, then, assesses patterns of the illicit trade in Africa with the
aim of highlighting major items of trafficking, the impact of trafficking on the
political and economic environment of countries, as well as the implications
for national and human security. First, however, the discussion begins with a
brief overview of the factors that cause and perpetuate illegal trade activities
in Africa.

OVERVIEW: TRAFFICKING IN AFRICA

Weak States and Diminishing Central Authority

Trafficking in Africa, as in other regions of the world, is attributed to a
weakening of the state. Ineffective governance, limited resources, and the absence of rule of law severely undermine state authority and control, creating
power vacuums ready to be exploited. Indeed, the decline in central authority is one of the major root causes of trafficking. Political structures are
no longer able to provide the public goods of security and stability for the
populace and, thus, can no longer protect citizens' interests. Corruption is
also extremely debilitating as it has contributed to trafficking in Africa and
has eroded the legitimate foundations of traditional state institutions. Corrupted state structures and actors become both complicit and casualties of
illicit activities, and it is in this environment that illicit substate actors and
trade activities proliferate, gaining political and economic power. Fragile
law enforcement and monitoring infrastructure are challenged by the substantial task of suppressing illicit trafficking through more rigorous border
control and enforcement of international regulations. Some assert that these
substate actors represent a new form of authoritarianism against the backdrop of the decline of the traditional authoritarian state. Substate actors, as
authoritarian states, use similar tools of coercion and illegitimate violence
to further their aims.[2]

Instability, War, and Complex Conflicts

Strongly related to weak central authority of African states is the existence of prolonged conflict, civil strife, and militarism, which have mounted

serious challenges to security in Africa. The end of Cold War competition in the geostrategic theater of Africa unleashed ethnic and local rivalries among factions that were armed. Presently, West and Central Africa are among the world's most unstable areas. A number of Africa's wars are appropriately described as "complex conflicts," marked by internal civil wars that defy conventional notions of "contained violence." Angola, Sierra Leone, and the Democratic Republic of Congo (DRC), for example, experienced civil wars fueled by considerable external regional dynamics. At least five states have been involved in the conflict in the DRC, including Uganda, Rwanda, Zimbabwe, and Angola. The war is cited as the widest in African history and also one of the most complicated and troubling conflagrations in the world, whose effects still reverberate.[3] Meanwhile, in Sierra Leone, the conflict is influenced by Liberian and Nigerian intervention and also involved Guinea. Observers have referred to this conflict in West Africa as even more complicated than the war in the Great Lakes region and is perhaps the most resilient and destructive of contemporary conflicts.

Adding to this potent mix, however, are the activities of substate private actors—criminal networks—that are engaged in illegal trading activities that include funding warring factions.[4] The economic devastation wrought by civil wars causes ordinary citizens to also become involved in illicit trading in the absence of legitimate economic activities.

The greater the number of actors involved in wars, the more complex the conflict and the more difficult the chances are for stemming the violence. The existence of opportunities for economic gain from illicit trade activity only contributes to a cycle of the provision of mutual incentives that is difficult to break. Ultimately, however, instability even in a more general form creates illicit markets for available goods, especially gems, other valuable natural resources, drugs, and arms.

Economic Instability and Diminished Opportunity

The economic vacuum and stagnation created by weak states permit a thriving environment for illicit trade networks, as local actors seek to exploit whatever opportunities will provide maximum economic gain or as they attempt to sustain a minimal level of subsistence in the absence of other alternatives. Underdevelopment, economic stagnation, and disruption of economic activities due to conflict all limit the availability of economic opportunities, creating uncertainty and instability. Many of the African countries that are most affected by trafficking rank at the bottom of the United Nations (UN) Development Programme Human Development Index and have the lowest per capita gross national income levels in the world, according to the World Bank.[5] Illicit trade networks quickly occupy the space under such conditions, as dearth of economic opportunities push actors toward corruption and illegal trading. For some civilians, trafficking of commodities is the only means of survival.

Population Flows

Large movements of people across borders in the way of refugee flows and immigrant workers are related to illicit trafficking in Africa. Each of the above factors causes sizeable movements of people across borders in varying levels. Population flows throughout Africa are characterized by labor migrants who leave countries seeking work in other states, and by refugees who leave a country seeking the protection of another, often because they are in fear for their lives due to conflict, war, or political oppression. While some individuals are legal migrants and enter countries with the permission of state bureaucracies, many are illegal and evade the detection of authorities in countries, which often lack the capacity to monitor borders effectively. War, natural disasters, and loss of economic opportunities are also sources for large movements of people.

Criminals and rebels often travel with such mass migration flows, bringing their activities with them. Displaced persons, however, in search of income in order to survive are also vulnerable to traffickers seeking personnel or persons to exploit in illicit markets themselves. Large population flows also weaken state capacity, which affects governing capacity, thus contributing to the intricate web of instability and trafficking.

Natural Disasters

Natural disasters that disrupt agricultural productivity and other forms of economic production facilitate massive human migration flows, forcing populations to seek economic alternatives and shelter in other states. Natural disasters also stretch state resources and their capacity to address the aftermath of disasters and to create economic opportunities for populations. As alluded to above, displaced populations face increased economic and political insecurity that increases the likelihood of their exposure to illicit trade activities, either as participants or victims.

The Challenge of Regulation and Cooperation

Supply and demand processes in other countries—developed and less developed—for illegal goods challenge international law enforcement efforts to stem global trafficking. One complication is related to the transnational dynamics associated with complex networks and the multidimensional nature of the sources of illicit trafficking, which make substantive monitoring difficult. In addition, regulatory mechanisms at the regional and international levels are also difficult to enforce, as countries often lack the infrastructure and resources to manage illicit trading activities. Importantly, international regulatory schemes must overcome the primacy of state sovereignty and the pursuit of narrower interests of actors.

PATTERNS OF TRAFFICKING IN AFRICA

The transnational nature of trafficking in Africa and the factors that provide a permissive environment for trafficking are a point of departure for a discussion of trafficking trends in Africa. Illicit trade in narcotics, weapons, natural resources, humans, and endangered species are core transnational issues that have created security challenges for the African continent.

Narcotics

Narcotics trafficking is an industry that is extraordinarily lucrative. The 2002 UN Bi-Annual World Drug Report estimates indicate that the retail value of illicit drug trade is around $321 billion. Narcotics trafficking has distinct stages of production and distribution at both the wholesale and retail levels, which provide various levels of opportunity for profit.[6] It is also an industry in which there is little competition and availability of substitute products. The economic benefits and power for the organization controlling the trade are enhanced because the poor farmers who grow the commodity receive few dividends. Drug trafficking funds are also a source of government corruption and have allowed for the establishment of terrorist organization bases. Ultimately, organizations have enhanced economic power, which can be used to corrupt military elites and members of law enforcement.

In global terms, narcotics trafficking in Africa is not the region's largest transnational problem, but cultivation, processing, trafficking, and drug abuse are all on the rise and are a hindrance to development efforts.[7] Marijuana, cocaine, heroin, and synthetic drugs are the most commonly trafficked narcotics, with the majority of drugs passing through Africa destined for Europe and North America. Significantly, the African countries through which drugs pass are also countries of consumption.[8]

The end of the Cold War opened Africa as a trade route to drug cartels from abroad. By 1996, Africa became vital for international drug trafficking as part of a pipeline that spreads as far east as Southeast Asia and as far west as the Americas. So vast and complex are activities that Latin Americans are now using African countries as trade routes. Angola, Namibia, and South Africa, for example, are believed to be the main cocaine trafficking routes for Brazilian cartels. The most notorious of all may be Nigeria. Most of the heroin seized in the United States during 1998 was linked to Nigerian smuggling groups or individuals working for Nigerians. A number of factors, such as widespread corruption, weak state structures, poor law enforcement, poverty, and social malaise, make Nigeria and other states attractive as trade routes.

Marijuana, however, is the most consumed drug in the world and is therefore the most frequently trafficked. South Africa was ranked one of the world's top four suppliers of marijuana.[9] UN statistics indicate that South Africa' share of world marijuana seizures increased from 10 to 32 percent between 1999 and 2000; by contrast, the share of the Americas dropped from 80 to 61 percent. Approximately 712 tons were seized in South Africa in 2000, an amount that translates into $23 million for producers and $1.5 billion for traffickers after it reaches U.S. and European markets.[10]

South Africa is considered a key transshipment hub for international drug trafficking activities, as significant percentages of cocaine pass through the country. The end of South African apartheid ended years of political and economic isolation, thus paving the way for the country's integration into the global economy. However, the very features that aid South Africa's participation in the global economy (that is, the county's sophisticated banking, transport, and communications infrastructure, as well as numerous points of entry for goods) are the same factors that have made the country a center for global drug trade. It is estimated that well over 200 international and local gangs are active in the country—many of which are controlled by Nigerians—each with its own network of suppliers and distributors.[11] Porous borders and insufficient control mechanisms in South Africa make for the easy proliferation and operation of drug networks.[12]

Lesotho, Swaziland, Namibia, and Mozambique also have been cited as major centers for narcotics trafficking by organized crime networks, which have made impressive inroads into these countries over the last several years. In fact, Mozambique is the second largest drug trafficking hub, and Zambia has also become a country that is frequently used as a drug trade route.

The growth of narcotics networks has led to a proliferation of money laundering, which is required to hide drug proceeds. According to the United Nations, southern African countries in particular are targeted for their inadequate level of preparation in dealing with drug cartels.

A significant feature of drug trafficking in Africa is warlordism. Warlordism in some respects goes hand in hand with drug trafficking in Africa, which became linked to drug trafficking during the late 1980s in the aftermath of the Cold War. Not only did the end of superpower proxy wars in sub-Saharan Africa open the continent to the trade route for preexisting drug organizations, but it also left an ideological vacuum in Africa, causing Africans to look to tribal and clan identities. This combined with the advent of the HIV/AIDS epidemic encouraged a reliance on traditional leaders rather than the state as the more legitimate source of authority and power.

The opportunity presented by Asian groups to participate in the drug trade was exploited by African drug warlords as a means of regaining and sustaining local and regional power, as well as a means for creating militias.

The status of the drug warlord strengthened as the authority of the state weakened. Using tools of corruption, coercion, and intimidation, drug warlords permitted an environment that led to the expansion of drug cartel activity. As their activities broadened, the economic, political, and military capabilities of the states weakened.[13]

The costs of the illicit drug trade in Africa are economic, political, and social. Economically, the illicit drug trade creates illegal economic structures that compete with legitimate, mainstream entities. The structures and incentives encouraged by drug trafficking make conventional means of economic activity less attractive. Their existence is made possible by the corruption of state officials, thereby expanding not just the economic, but *political* power of the narco-enterprises. Indeed, the more capable organizations are at corrupting officials, the more legitimate their activities become. The political cost is the disintegration of state institutions and their authority. Drug organizations have grown adept at avoiding detection and have improved their ability to operate efficiently. The increase in transnational networks also contributed to the proliferation of drug trafficking activities.

The social cost of being a drug transport point cannot be underestimated. Most countries that are transport hubs eventually become consumer countries as in South Africa and Zimbabwe. The number of drug users in countries such as Liberia and Sierra Leone, likewise, has increased and the UN Development Programme argues that increased drug use among war combatants may also contribute to the prolonging of local conflict in these two countries.

There are only a few countries that have national policies for drug control. They include Burkina Faso, Namibia, and Nigeria. Bureaucracies and structures have been established in these countries, but such efforts at effective drug control have been met with mixed success at best. Moreover, many of the major countries where drug warlords are prominent have not signed major international drug conventions of 1961, 1971, and 1988, which are meant to regulate and monitor the international drug trade.[14] Those countries include the Congo, Comoros, Central African Republic, Djibouti, Equatorial New Guinea, Eritrea, Mozambique, and Namibia.[15] South Africa, oddly, is a member of the global agreements.

Weapons

Weapons trafficking also poses a threat to stability and security in Africa, particularly in the Western portion of the region, with small- and light-arms proliferation emerging as especially problematic.[16] According to the United Nations, *small arms* and *light weapons* are defined as revolvers, self-loading pistols, rifles, carbines, landmines, submachineguns, assault rifles, and light machineguns. Small arms are typically designed for individual use. Light weapons, by contrast, are intended for use by two or more individuals. They include heavy machineguns, handheld underbarrel and mounted grenade launchers, portable antiaircraft guns, portable air tank guns, portable launchers of air tank missiles and rocket systems, and mortars.

It is estimated that there are 500 million arms on the world's weapons market, and half of that total are traded illicitly.[17] Of that number, about 7 million have made their way into the West African trafficking market and are currently in circulation.

The vast proliferation of illegal light arms can be traced to a shift in the nature of the arms trade following the Cold War. Before the collapse of the Soviet Union, arms were meant for intrastate rather than interstate struggles, and the United States and Soviet Union supplied various sorts of arms to internal warring factions. The end of the Cold War left not only an ideological vacuum but also well-armed substate actors. While some are motivated by political and territorial aims, others are motivated by economic gain and find the sale of arms to conflicting groups lucrative. So lucrative is the market that the illicit trade is associated with uncontrolled accumulation and proliferation of small arms and light weapons. Indeed, these items are widely available, durable, fairly cheap, easily transportable, and have few maintenance requirements. These features make arms attractive to smugglers, traffickers, and also terrorists.[18]

The early phase of arms trading is not entirely illegal, however. Both legitimate and illicit dealers are involved in trafficking. Entrepreneurs, government agencies, private security firms, arms dealers, brokers, and even banks that finance arms arrangements form a complex network of the illicit arms trade.[19] Arms suppliers, both public and private, have operated out of organizations in East and West Europe, Libya, North Korea, and South Africa.[20] Yet the ability to monitor weapons transactions in the legal market is complicated by the lack of transparency of transactions, accurate recordkeeping, and reliable tracing mechanisms. These things, if available, would assist governments and international organizations to distinguish between legitimate suppliers of arms and illegal traffickers. As the issue of arms trafficking has sparked substantial concerns about poor border and security controls in Africa, emphasis has been placed on the development of more effective monitoring of embargos and other arms control measures. Also important is the need to monitor borders to prevent undetected smuggling across territory.

The proliferation of arms through illicit trade prolongs conflict, mainly through their recirculation from one country in conflict to another. For example, weapons used in a conflict in Liberia may be trafficked for use in a conflict in Sierra Leone. The widespread availability of weapons also contributes to persistent conventional crime. Ultimately, this does little to advance development, postconflict reconstruction, peace, and finally security.

TABLE 8.1
Value of Diamonds per Carat in Select African Countries

	Average Cost per Carat (USD)	Number of Carats	Value in Millions (USD)
Angola	300	433,000	150
Sierra Leone	350	350,000	70
DROC	180	194,000	35

Natural Resources

Diamonds are used to fund the military activities of state and substate actors through both the mining and sale of diamonds. While other commodities are centripetal to inter- and intrastate disputes in Africa,[21] all of the conflicts that involve the trafficking of diamonds have been accompanied by large-scale human rights violations, massive internal population displacements, and the destabilization of sovereign governments. The widespread negative social, economic, and political costs of the illicit diamond trade have earned the commodity the label "conflict diamonds" due to the deadly nature of some of the major African conflagrations involving diamonds.[22]

Roughly 4 percent of the world's $6.8 billion revenue in diamond trade was generated from illicitly traded diamonds during 1999, with some figures estimating illicit revenues accounting for as much as 20 percent. Revenues from the African diamond trade have been used to fund weapons acquisitions, armies and militias, and have contributed to the devastating prolonging of conflicts and hostilities to such an extent that the trade has destabilized other governments, thereby internationalizing the conflicts. Not only do these conflicts result in disruption of economic activity and political instability, but also many of these conflicts rely on the recruitment of child-soldiers to fill the ranks of armies and militias.[23] Conflicts in Sierra Leone and Angola during the 1990s, for example, are believed to have been sustained through the acquisition and sale of diamonds for arms among groups involved.

Table 8.1 illustrates both the volume and value of the illicit diamond trade for countries involved in the DROC dispute.[24]

While these conflicts have for the most part ended, the effects of illicit diamond trading have had enormous economic repercussions in terms of disruption of economy, corruption, and ongoing political tensions.[25] The industry is still shaped by smuggling, human rights violations, and violent crime.[26] The illicit diamond trade has also been costly: Angola is believed to have lost $375 million annually due to illicit trade throughout the 1990s. Billions, moreover, were imported to Belgium from Liberia, which smuggled diamonds from Sierra Leone, making Liberia a major supplier in the illicit diamond market. Diamonds, in turn, were used to sustain internal conflicts in that country. Since Sierra Leone declared peace in 2002, illicit trafficking, in theory, has abated. However, there remains the potential for future conflict in West Africa. In the DROC, there are still volatile disagreements over the control of diamonds and other resources amid an ongoing peace process. With many vital interests at stake in this lucrative endeavor, disputes abound among state and substate actors over mining and production rights.[27]

In the Central African Republic (CAR), diamond trafficking has been linked to ongoing political conflict there (following a rebel attack during 2002, for example). Though peace negotiations there appear to have de-escalated the conflict, business among parties that participated in the diamond industry in CAR continues in the areas of mining, producing, and maintaining trade and transport networks and entities. This infrastructure, and some of the actors involved, contributed to the persistence of the conflict to begin with. The Movement for the Liberation of Congo is one such group that was involved in the DROC conflict and continues to be linked to the diamond industry.[28]

Suspicions about the development of new links in the illicit diamond trade surfaced following the terrorist attacks in New York and Washington. Significantly, reports from international investigators suggested that international terrorists, specifically al Qaeda, earned millions of dollars from the illicit sale of diamonds mined by rebels in Sierra Leone. While there is doubt regarding the quantity and quality of evidence, apprehended individuals linked to al Qaeda indicate that the organization's activities in Africa included diamond trafficking. Some analysts place al Qaeda's earnings around $15 million.[29]

The continuation of the illicit diamond trade underscores the importance of international regulation. Indeed, Africa's diamond conflicts prompted multilateral attempts to improve management of the international diamond trade. Efforts culminated in the Kimberley Process, a series of meetings convened among governments, nongovernmental organizations, and industry to establish a system of regulation. A formal system called the Kimberley Process Certification Scheme came into effect January 1, 2003. With more than 43 member states, the scheme called for all member states to establish new diamond laws and regulations that improved the transparency of diamond trading. Although the Kimberley Process has been attributed to increasing legitimate diamond exports from Sierra Leone, Angola, and the DRC, diamonds of high quality are still believed to be smuggled from these countries and find their way onto the world market.[30]

Still, the "lootability" of diamonds,[31] the fungibility of the diamond trade, and the vast reach of the global diamond market are significant challenges to policing diamond trafficking. Compounding efforts is the nature of the private legitimate diamond industry, which is insular and self-regulating. Illegal diamonds enter the legitimate market through illicit practices and subversive substate actors. Furthermore, the diamond trade is difficult to control because it is an integral part of a larger illicit market that involves arms trafficking, smuggling, and money laundering.[32]

Humans

Human trafficking is one of the unfortunate and sobering consequences of Africa's conflicts and points to one of the extremes of systematic human suffering. Human trafficking is very difficult to measure; the phenomenon has many dimensions and layers. Article 3 of the UN Protocol to Prevent, Suppress, and Punish Trafficking in Persons, especially Women and Children, in describing trafficking in persons, includes a ranges of activities and outcomes, such as recruitment, transportation, harboring, transfer, and receipt, as well as exploitation, labor, slavery, servitude, and the removal of organs.[33] Human trafficking shares many of the same causes as that of arms and drugs and is equally illicit. Weak host and origin states, substantial revenue, and the use of violence are all features that human trafficking share with other illegitimate forms of economic activity. Yet human trafficking requires maintenance of relations of exploitation in order to assure continued economic gain. This may take the form of indentured servitude, debt dependency, or outright slavery. The fate of trafficked persons is imperiled as their subjugators objectify those under their control, forcing them to work without payment, subjecting them to repeated sale, and even murder to remove evidence of illegal activity.[34]

Those most vulnerable to trafficking are women and children, particularly girls. It is fundamental to point out that boys and men are trafficked as well, as they are frequently forced to serve as combatants in military conflicts. Yet it is the social position of females and lack of rights afforded to them that make this group particularly susceptible to traffickers. The absence of political, social, and economic opportunities hinders women's efforts to secure legitimate work and forces them to seek employment elsewhere. War, civil strife, and natural disasters only increase vulnerability.

During the 1980s and 1990s, West Africa saw a significant increase in the trafficking of women. The main destination was Western Europe. This trend was followed by an increase in the trafficking of West African minors, both male and female. Many youth belonged to marginalized ethnic groups or economic classes or were from families disintegrated by war and strife. Children trafficked are integrated into a number of industries, such as the sex trade, domestic service, armed conflict, and the service industry. Still they are also involved in the more dangerous aspects of work in various manufacturing industries, such as mining, agriculture, and construction, and even begging.

According to the United Nations, trafficking in West Africa is due to a number of complex variables. First, social and normative factors make acceptable the "placement" of women and children in work. There are also traditional practices of migration, lack of education, and marriage that facilitate trafficking activities. Second, economic factors, including the search for better economic opportunities due to rural-to-urban disparities, facilitate trafficking. Third, the lack of juridical infrastructure, general lack of rule of law, and porous borders provide a permissive environment for traffickers, allowing them to evade legal responsibility and escape being subject to punitive measures.[35]

Trade routes for trafficking persons in West Africa can be traced according to dominant migratory flows. There are major migratory flows from Benin, Burkina Faso, Ghana, Mali, Nigeria, and Togo to the Congo, Côte d'Ivoire, Equatorial Guinea, and Gabon. In Togo, major flows are from Benin, Ghana, and Nigeria, with trafficking in children reflected these patterns. Children are used as traders, servants, beggars, and prostitutes. Children from Mali are trafficked to Côte d'Ivoire to work in mining and agriculture.

Reflecting patterns that have been discussed in other areas of trafficking, Southern Africa appears to be an emerging major point of destination for trafficked persons as well. Children are widely recruited for work in the sex industry by brothel owners and local gangs. Significantly, parents are often complicit in their trafficking, even though it appears to be unwittingly in many circumstances. Poverty, the disintegration of the family, and a high demand for sex with children for sociocultural reasons have led to an increase in the demand for trafficked children.

Women and children in South Africa have been trafficked from Mozambique, and refugees have been trafficked from Angola to South Africa. There are also reports that suggest trafficking occurs from Lesotho and Malawi to South Africa.

Human trafficking in Sudan has gained perhaps the most international attention. The U.S. Department of State lists Sudan among "Tier 3" countries, which are states "whose governments do not fully comply with the minimum standards" set by American law and are not making efforts to do so. In Sudan, most of those trafficked or abducted are women and children for the purposes of sexual exploitation and forced labor. Sudanese boys are sent to the Middle East where they are used as camel jockeys.

Much of Sudan's trafficking takes place in the southern and western part of the country. These areas are where central authority is weakest due to ongoing ethnic conflicts. A portion of trafficking is intertribal, reflecting the local nature of the Sudan's struggles. It is especially widespread in Dafur and Western Korodan, both of which have been long mired in fighting. Militias supported by the Sudanese government are allegedly responsible for a portion of trafficking activity. Women have been raped and trafficked for further exploitation, and children have been taken to tend to livestock.[36]

Sudan has made an effort to establish a code of law to prevent trafficking, but the enforcement of these mechanisms could be substantially improved here and in other Africa countries. Concerns have also been raised about the method of documenting trafficked persons.

Addressing trafficking calls for action on three fronts. First, prevention and deterrence are necessary to stop trafficking from occurring. This may involve alleviating the economic and destabilizing political circumstances that promote fertile ground for trafficking in persons and that make persons economically, socially, or politically vulnerable. The second is that of law enforcement and prosecution of traffickers, which are critical for deterring trafficking activities. Third, protection of trafficked persons is critical after they have been rescued. Personal safety is important if they are to avoid being prey to traffickers. Rehabilitation and reintegration into society is also important.[37] Implementation of these sorts of strategies is severely challenged by weak social institutions, a wide variety of judicial structures and laws, and poor infrastructure for dealing with trafficked persons.

Endangered Species

According to major environmental monitoring groups, virtually all of the ivory traded on the world market is from illegal and unsustainable sources.[38] Most of the unregulated domestic markets are located in Asia and Africa. International trade in ivory has been banned since 1989, following rapid depletion of the elephant population during the late 1970s and 1980s, most notably in Africa.[39] However, illegal trade in ivory has continued to increase.

Approximately 12,000 elephants are needed to supply ivory carvers each year. Despite the nearly 20-year ban, the volume of ivory traded is on the rise, a dynamic mostly attributed to an increase in demand for ivory products in China, Japan, Thailand, Myanmar, and Vietnam where ivory products are used in furnishings and crafts. These items, in turn, are frequently sold to individuals from the United States, Europe, and Asia.[40] On the supply-side, demand is also driven by poverty among African populations, many of which earn only a few hundred dollars per year.

Major countries cited as being major suppliers, manufacturers, or destination point for large amounts of illegal ivory are Cameroon, the DRC, Djibouti, Ethiopia, Nigeria, and Uganda. Angola, Burundi, Côte d'Ivoire, and Sudan also have considerable illicit ivory markets closely watched by international organizations.[41]

Somewhat optimistically, observers from the Convention on International Trade in Endangered Species (CITES) point out that poaching does not appear to be on a par with levels seen prior to the 1989 ban.[42] So great was the scale of trafficking that it has threatened African economies, requiring governments to spend vast resources to thwart poaching activities. Additionally, countries adopting more aggressive strategies saw the loss of much human life in "ivory wars."[43] However, the impact of ivory trade goes beyond ecological effects, as the illicit ivory trade is only one facet of the larger labyrinth of trafficking in Africa. Those involved in poaching are often local small farmers trying to raise income, or middlemen who are involved in the trade for the purposes of smuggling. The sale of illegal ivory, as with diamond trafficking, is sometimes used by belligerents to purchase guns whose end use is intended to supply warring factions and crime gangs.[44]

During 2004, most of the 166 signatory countries of the CITES addressed a series of new initiatives meant to strengthen law enforcement links between African countries, the international police agency, Interpol, customs officials, and airlines that might handle ivory shipments.[45] While countries such as Kenya have made significant inroads in managing poaching, the illicit trading in endangered species continues, despite CITES regulations.[46]

IMPLICATIONS FOR SECURITY

On the one hand, trafficking in Africa is a product of fracturing states structures. On the other, the persistence of trafficking activities perpetuates weak authority and at worst contributes to its further erosion. Ongoing instability and economic fragility facilitate breakdown of rule of law and threaten the viability of the nation-state in Africa. Political and economic vacuums are filled by substate actors willing to exploit the political and financial opportunities available through illicit trading—opportunities unavailable through legitimate channels. In some cases, state actors themselves are complicit in illegal trading. The sobering lessons of the regional conflicts that have plagued Africa in recent years illustrate the entangled web of country-level intervention in the conflicts of neighboring states and the role of trafficking in sustaining wars and their role in creating social and economic malaise and instability.

The alleged and disputed role of international terrorists in trafficking additionally calls attention to the potential ramifications for international security. The possibility of al Qaeda involvement in diamond trafficking to fund the organization's weapons acquisitions suggests that illicit trading is a means of sustaining the group's violent activities against other countries. Additionally, the same porous borders and poor monitoring that have been used by traffickers may also be exploited by al Qaeda, which has used Africa as a safe haven.

No less important are the ramifications of trafficking in Africa for human security at the individual and communal levels. Civil strife, social decay, and disruption of traditional economic activities in urban and rural sectors have had severely negative impacts on the personal security of individuals and communities. The lack of adequate public welfare infrastructure diminishes a state's ability to mitigate the effects of trafficking. In cases where mass population displacements occur, entire community structures and families are fragmented, as families barely live above subsistence levels. Individuals under these circumstances are also made vulnerable to the exploits of traffickers, a dynamic borne out in human trafficking, which exposes persons to poor living environments and gross violations of human rights.

Other forms of trafficking, such as that of illicit drugs, also pose a problem for human security. As the international community restricts illicit trade, traffickers are using more violent means to conduct activities. Thus, with drug trafficking come increases in conventional crime and also increases in drug consumption levels, each of which challenge the capacity of states' ability to deal with these problems, as governments do not have the resources to combat the issue.

Amid these public safety and human security concerns is the specter of HIV/AIDS, which has ravaged a number of African countries, where between 20 to 30 percent of the population in some states have the virus. Prostitution, drug use, rape, and poverty—all direct or indirect aspects of trafficking—contribute to the spread of the virus, which has stripped many African countries of critical human resource capacity, contributed to economic stagnation, crime (specifically violence against women and girls), as well as the disintegration of families and communities.

CONCLUSION

Curbing illicit trading in Africa is a formidable task for African states requiring economic, political, and bureaucratic capacity. The vast transnational nature of trafficking in Africa emphasizes the need for multilateral cooperation at the regional and international level. Monitoring accessible borders, enforcing appropriate judicial measures, ensuring regulatory frameworks in countries of both origin and destination, and alleviating the systemic economic and political sources of trafficking are necessary if activities are to abate.

The implications for national, regional, international, and human security are critical. A failure to stem trafficking activities diminishes the power and authority of states to the detriment of stability and the well-being of populations. Since the issues at stake are transnational, they influence other countries in ways that are difficult for other countries to gauge and to control. As a consequence, the impact of trafficking touches other countries that lie far beyond the locus of trafficking activities. In this sense, the ramifications for security have bearing for other countries and their populations, making the international cooperation even more urgent.

NOTES

1. Louis I. Shelley, "Transnational Organized Crime: The New Authoritarianism," in *Illicit Global Economy and State Power*, ed. Richard Friman and Peter Andreas (Lanham, MD: Bowman and Littlefield Press, 1999).

2. Ibid.

3. Timothy M. Shaw, "Human Insecurity and Problematic Peacekeeping," in *Twisting Arms and Flexing Muscles: Humanitarian Intervention and Peacebuilding in Perspective*, ed. Natalie Mychajlyszyn and Timothy M. Shaw (Burlington, VT: Ashgate Publishing, 2005).

4. Karen Ballentine and Jake Sherman, ed., *The Political Economy of Armed Conflict: Beyond Greed and Grievance* (Boulder, CO: Lynne Rienner, 1999), and Paul B. Rich, ed., *Warlords in International Relations* (London: MacMillan Press, Ltd., 1999).

5. See United Nations, *Human Development Report 2004*, and World Bank, *Development Report* (Oxford: Oxford University Press, 2003). In World Bank figures, low-income countries have annual per capita gross national income of $735 or less. The Atlas Method is applied to reduce the impact of exchange rate fluctuations in the cross-country comparisons of gross national incomes.

6. Glen Segell, "Warlordism and Drug Trafficking: From Southeast Asia to Sub-Saharan Africa," in *Warlords in International Relations*, ed. Paul B. Rich (London: MacMillan Press, Ltd., 1999).

7. Ronald Neal, "Merchants of Death Target Africa," *Africa Recovery*, vol. 12 (August 1, 1998).

8. A figure from the late 1990s maintains that trafficking revenues in Africa amounted to $500 billion, at that time surpassing world oil revenues and second to the annual earnings of the arms trade. See Alison Jameison, ed., *Terrorism and Drug Trafficking in the 1990s* (Dartmouth, NH: Aldershot, 1994), 72.

9. UN Drug Control Agency, *World Drug Report 2002*. It is difficult to perfectly measure the illicit drug trade. For many African countries, precise measurements of trafficking are not available. Consequently, seizures, arrests, and research reports are frequently used statistics.

10. Roughly 312 and 272 tons were seized in Malawi and Nigeria, respectively. UN Drug Control Agency, *World Drug Report 2002*.

11. Glen Segell and Greg Mills, *War and Peace in Southern Africa: Crime, Drugs, Armies and Trade* (Cambridge, MA: The World Peace Foundation, 1996).

12. For example, Zimbabwe only has 7 border crossing points, while South Africa has 52. Zimbabwe, moreover, has 36 international airports, many of which do not have air traffic control, policing, or immigration monitoring. See Segell and Mills.

13. Segell, 46.

14. Those conventions include the 1961 Single Convention on Narcotic Drugs; the 1971 Convention on Psychotropic Substances; and the 1988 UN Convention against Illicit Traffic in Narcotic Drugs and Psychotropic Substances.

15. Segell and Department of Foreign Affairs, Republic of South Africa, available at www.dfa.gov.za/.

16. *Small arms* and *light weapons* are further defined as weapons that can be physically carried by an individual without the need for other tools.

17. While it is impossible to list accurate figures, in one estimate, small arms alone amount to $2 to $3 billion annually. See Michael T. Klare, "Curbing the Illicit Trade in Small Arms: A Practical Approach," *U.S. Foreign Policy Agenda* 6, no. 2 (June 2001). Adekeye Adebajo and Ishmail Rashid, *West Africa's Security Challenges: Building Peace in A Troubled Region* (Boulder, CO: Lynne Rienner, 2004).

18. Adebajo and Rashid.

19. In Africa's Great Lakes region, financing arms has been arranged by banks in Asia, Europe, the Middle East, the British Virgin Islands, Hong Kong, the Seychelles, and Singapore.

20. Adebajo and Rashid.

21. Oil and timber are also natural resources that have links in the chain of trafficking of commodities, though neither of these has sparked as much controversy as diamonds.

22. There is a distinction between "conflict diamonds" and illicit diamonds, of which conflict diamonds are a part. For the purposes of this chapter, the author uses the term *illicit diamonds* to refer to both, as the emphasis of the discussion is on the overall impact of all diamonds traded illegally.

23. It is estimated that at various points, the conflict in Sierra Leone has involved as many as 5,000 child-soldiers in direct combat roles and another 5,000 in support roles. Similarly, in Angola and the DRC, roughly 7,000 to 10,000 children in those countries, respectively, are believed to have been involved as combatants. See Nichols Cook and Jessica Morrow, *Diamond-Related African Conflicts: A Fact Sheet* (Washington, DC: Library of Congress, 2003).

24. These figures have likely declined since 1999, given political changes in these countries. See Christian Dietrich, *Diamonds in the Central African Republic: Trading, Valuing and Laundering* (Ottawa: Partnership for Africa Canada, 2002); and Ian Smillie, *The Kimberely Process: The Case for Proper Monitoring* (Ottawa: Partnership for Africa Canada, 2002).

25. Angola's 27-year conflict ended in 2002, and Sierra Leone declared peace in 2002.

26. Miners are subjected to poor labor conditions, extortion, imprisonment, and even murder. Some victims have also been members of security firms—who are also perpetrators of offenses—that have been held in detention for more than a year. See "New Report Alleges Blood Still Stains Diamonds," March 10, 2005, available at www.global policy.org.

27. Nichols Cook, *Diamonds and Conflict: Background, Policy, and Legislation* (Washington, DC: Library of Congress, 2003).

28. Ibid.

29. Associated Press, "Al-Qaeda bought diamonds before 9/11," August 7, 2004.

30. Diamond Development Initiative, "Diamond Development Initiative Begins," August 15, 2005, available at www.globalpolicy.org; and Smillie.

31. *Lootability* refers to the ease with which materials can be taken by groups or individuals who are unskilled.

32. Cook.

33. Specifically, the UN Protocol to Prevent, Suppress, and Punish Trafficking in Persons, especially Women and Children, defines *trafficking* as the recruitment, transportation, transfer, harboring, or receipt of persons by means of threat, use of force or some other form of coercion, abduction, fraud deception, or abuse of power of a position or of the giving and receiving of payments or benefits to achieve the consent of a person having control over another person for the purpose of exploitation. *Exploitation* includes, at a minimum, the exploitation through the prostitution of others or forced labor or services, slavery, or practices similar to slavery, servitude, or the removal of organs. U.S. Department of State, *Trafficking in Human Persons*

Report, 2005; and Thanh-Dam Truong and Maria Belen Angeles, *Searching for the Best Practices to Counter Human Trafficking in Africa: A Focus on Women and Children* (New York: UN Educational, Scientific, and Cultural Organization, March 2005).

34. Experts acknowledge that for people who "place" family members, namely children, in the hands of traffickers, they do not immediately associate this with selling or trading their familiar. Many place their children because they did not earn enough to cover household needs. See Truong and Angeles.

35. Ibid.

36. U.S. Department of State, *Trafficking in Human Persons Report*, 2005.

37. Truong and Angeles.

38. The World Wildlife Federation and World Conservation Union are two major international monitoring organizations, which run the network called the Trade Records Analysis of Flora and Fauna in Commerce (TRAFFIC).

39. The ban was imposed by CITES. During the 1970s and 1980s, the price of ivory skyrocketed from $60 per kilogram to a staggering $300, which touched off a wave of elephant poaching for the purposes of securing ivory. During this time, the African elephant population dropped from 1.3 million to just 600,000.

40. Between January 2000 and July 2002, at least 1,063 African (and 39 Asian) elephants were reported to have been poached for their ivory, while 54,828 ivory pieces, 3,099 tusks and over 6 tons of raw ivory were seized. See Elephant Trade Fact Sheet, available at www.hsus.org.

41. See TRAFFIC bulletin, available at www.cites.org/common/cop/12/docs/eng/E12-34-1.pdf.

42. Trade in African elephants was included under Appendix 1, which halted trade in elephants and all of their parts, including ivory.

43. Elephant Trade Fact Sheet.

44. The rise in trade also raises concerns about the militarization of the ivory. During the proxy wars of the 1970s and 1980s, irregular armies used ivory to purchase heavy weaponry.

45. Daniel Lovering, "Wildlife delegates endorse plan to end Africa's illicit ivory sales," Associated Press, October 11, 2004.

46. However, numbers are nowhere near as high as figures reported during the 1980s and 1990s.

CHAPTER 9

Chinese Crime Organizations as Transnational Enterprises

Anny Wong

INTRODUCTION

Chinese crime organizations are not only a menace to societies, such as Hong Kong, Taiwan, China, and Macua, but their illicit activities also reach almost every corner of the world and have serious security ramifications: from the corrosive effect of organized crime on the rule of law and governance to spreading human immunodeficiency virus/acquired immunodeficiency syndrome (HIV/AIDS) because of intravenous drug use and prostitution. Furthermore, the mechanisms and networks maintained by Chinese crime organizations might be replicated or hired by terrorist groups to support their violent deeds. Hence, the focus of this chapter on Chinese crime organizations goes beyond the borders of Hong Kong, Taiwan, China, and Macau. It begins with a broad discussion of Chinese crime organizations, what they are, where they operate, and their smuggling activities. The second part of this chapter discusses the impact of their smuggling activities on security.

CHINESE CRIME ORGANIZATIONS

Today, Chinese crime organizations have branches and cells in many countries. They might be better viewed as criminal businesses. They live outside the law and frequently corrupt those who pass and execute laws. Growing ties between Chinese government officials and Chinese crime organizations are particularly worrisome. Corrupt Chinese officials not only make it easier for crime organizations to smuggle persons and narcotics, but they also provide a safe haven for wanted criminals and allow Chinese crime organizations (and their "customers") to acquire weapons and other dangerous materials from Chinese sources that could land in the hands of terrorists.

Chinese crime organizations[1] have grown from their beginnings as underground political revolutionaries, local crime syndicates, and ethnic-based mutual support societies into transnational enterprises. Chinese crime organizations are present in almost every place where a significant ethnic Chinese community is present, preying on them and using them to camouflage their illegal activities. They are rich in financial resources, adaptive to their environment, and skillful in exploiting opportunities and building strategic relationships to support criminal activities.

The most powerful Chinese crime organizations are based in Hong Kong and Taiwan. The largest of them were formed by Nationalists who fled China after World War II and then were defeated by the Chinese Communists in 1949. This includes the 14K in Hong Kong and the United Bamboo Gang (the largest crime organization in Taiwan). Other crime syndicates were formed by former Red Guard members who fled to Hong Kong in the 1960s (the Big Circle Boys) and groups formed by local populations in the territory, such as Sun Yee On.[2]

The economic opening of China in 1978 has made it a hotbed of activities for Chinese crime organizations. For example, China is the world's largest producer of methamphetamine. Population pressures and uneven economic development continue to drive its people to seek fortunes overseas with the services of *snakeheads* (a term used to describe human smugglers). Counterfeit goods are hidden among the millions of containers shipped out of China each year to ports around the world. Increasing capacity in information technology has also made China a major center for credit card fraud and software piracy. An environment where corruption is rife, labor is cheap, and borders are porous makes an ideal setting for the Chinese crime syndicates. For An-lo Chan, head of the United Bamboo Gang, China is a safe haven from Taiwan's law enforcement authorities. Moreover, he has found new business partners among China's Communist Party and government elites.

Chinese crime organizations are opportunistic and expand their business and influence wherever possible from towns in the Thai-Burmese borders to manage their narcotics trade to the cities in North America and Europe to distribute narcotics and run their human smuggling operations. Chinese crime organizations based in Hong Kong have also expanded their operations overseas—with many crime bosses emigrating to North America, Australia, and Europe—in the run up toward the return of Hong Kong to China in 1997.

In addition to the Chinese crime syndicates that are based in Hong Kong, Taiwan, China, and Macau, ethnic Chinese crime organizations, which are much smaller in scale but no less enterprising and violent, have sprung up in the United States and Canada where they compete and cooperate with Chinese crime organizations from Hong Kong, Taiwan, and China. One of the most powerful is the Fuk Ching, which specializes in smuggling Chinese persons into the New York City area, and the Wah Ching Gang in California. Chinese crime organizations are known to hire smaller Cambodian, Laotian, Korean, and Vietnamese street gangs in the United States and Canada as muscle. In Europe, Chinese crime syndicates are known to have significant presence in Budapest, Manchester, Paris, Vienna, Amsterdam, and Rotterdam.[3]

From their traditional "businesses" in extortion, racketeering, gambling, and narcotics smuggling, Chinese crime organizations have spread themselves into new lines of commerce, from high-tech fraud to human trafficking. Their expansion in the last 15 years, in particular, has paralleled increasing trading and human ties between China, Hong Kong, Taiwan, and the rest of the world. The fluid and cellular structure of Chinese organized crime groups makes them difficult for law enforcement to dismantle because capturing one leader does not paralyze these organizations when its parts operate relatively autonomously. The distinctive ethnic and linguistic characteristics of Chinese crime organizations pose further barriers to infiltration by law enforcement authorities. Finally, Chinese crime organizations camouflage themselves among larger ethnic Chinese populations and prey upon them as part of their illicit enterprise.

SMUGGLING ACTIVITIES

Although the discussion in this chapter focuses on the smuggling activities of organized Chinese crime groups, they are also involved in other illicit activities, such as drug manufacturing, extortion and racketeering, money laundering, credit card fraud, fake document production, and illegal gambling. Smuggling activities conducted by Chinese crime organizations cannot easily be separated from these other illegal activities because they are frequently supported by the same human network, and one often provides the means or cover for another to operate successfully.

Human Trafficking[4]

Despite being a powerhouse economy in the past decade, many parts of China still suffer severe poverty and desire a better life, so many continue to seek their fortunes overseas. Some seek the services of snakeheads to enter the United States and other developed economies, paying huge sums to be smuggled. Others, particularly women, are lured by criminals with promises of jobs. Most of these women typically end up in forced prostitution.[5] Chinese criminals—from common felons to bosses of crime organizations who seek to escape jail and possible execution—also use Chinese crime organizations to smuggle them into Europe, the United States, and elsewhere in order to find safe havens. Those arrested usually plea for asylum on humanitarian grounds to fight extradition to China, Hong Kong, and Taiwan.[6]

Human trafficking is a highly profitable business for Chinese crime organizations. For example, the price for smuggling one person into New York City was about $30,000 in the late 1990s; it rose to $60,000 by 2003 as immigration controls tightened after the September 11 terrorist attacks.[7] As for persons who are unwilling victims, such as young women who are tricked or abducted by traffickers, they become commodities that are sold and resold to operators in the flesh trade. Today, human trafficking for sexual exploitation is the fastest growing form of organized crime.

Hong Kong, Taiwan, China, and Macau are all source, transit, and destination points for international human trafficking.[8] Women and young girls from North Korea and Vietnam are commonly trafficked into China as wives. Women and children are smuggled into China from Malaysia, Burma, North Korea, Nepal, Russia, Vietnam, and Mongolia where they serve a sex industry along major transportation routes. Chinese women are trafficked to Australia, Burma, Canada, Cambodia, Malaysia, Japan, Hong Kong, Taiwan, the Philippines, Europe, and the United States for prostitution.[9]

Malaysia, Indonesia, the Philippines, and Thailand are transit points in Chinese human trafficking. Chinese crime organizations take advantage of lax visa rules in these countries and the worldwide transportation links supporting their tourism industry to move illegal migrants in and out to final destinations in Japan, Australia, North America, and Europe. Some illegal migrants end their journey in these Southeast Asian countries where they are forced to work in nightclubs and brothels operated by Chinese crime organizations and their local partners.[10] In North America, cities along the U.S.-Canada and U.S.-Mexico borders are gateways into the United States. Vancouver, Los Angeles, and other Pacific ports are used as entry points for narcotics, arms, and persons from Asia.

Chinese crime organizations recruit, move, and place Chinese illegal migrants across the world. They utilize their international networks and resources to make these clandestine journeys possible. For some Chinese crime organizations, their involvement is direct (for example, the Fuk Ching group that specializes in smuggling persons from Fujian province into New York City's massive Chinatown). For others, their involvement is more indirect (selling fake travel documents to snakeheads or providing hiding places for illegal migrants en route). One senior U.S. immigration official opined that at any time 30,000 Chinese migrants are stashed away in safe houses around the world, waiting for entry to the United States.[11] U.S. authorities estimated that up to 100,000 illegal Chinese migrants are smuggled into the country each year.[12]

Narcotics Trafficking

Chinese crime organizations have a long history of involvement in narcotics trafficking, particularly heroin and, more recently, methamphetamine.

Narcotics trafficking starts with the source countries where opium poppy for heroin is grown and synthetic drugs are manufactured. Opium poppy cultivation centers in the Golden Triangle (border regions where Burma, Laos, and Thailand intersect) where economic opportunities are few for local residents and governments have only tenuous control over these territories.[13] Chinese crime organizations control heroin production by funding its cultivation and controlling refining. They are also directly involved in smuggling it to Hong Kong, Australia, and other distribution centers and markets.

Each year, 80 percent of the 70 to 80 tons of heroin produced annually in the Golden Triangle is smuggled into China over land along the Sino-Burmese border. The 14K is reported to control heroin trafficking in the Benelux countries. Groups that smuggle heroin into the United States often operate on both sides of the U.S.-Canada border and control distribution. Chinese crime organizations are also deeply involved in the production and distribution of synthetic drugs. The 14K is said to control its production in Mong Nawng, a Burmese town near the Chinese border and works with the antigovernment Wa State Army to smuggle it into China, Thailand, Australia, and elsewhere.[14] Exploiting easy access to raw materials and corrupt officials, Chinese crime organizations have made China the world's leading producer of methamphetamine. In addition, they are selling raw materials acquired in China to production sites overseas. For example, Chinese police confiscated chemicals for manufacturing "ice" and ecstasy, which were destined for Russia, Belgium and the Netherlands, at the Heilongjian border port.[15]

Within China, narcotics trafficking and drug use have increased significantly in recent years. In 2003, Chinese police completed 94,000 drug-related cases, arrested 63,700 people, and seized 9.53 tons of heroin. Much of the drugs from the Golden Triangle enter China through Yunnan province. Narcotics traffickers exploit porous, weak border controls, corrupt officials, as well as improvements in China's transportation and communication infrastructure, to move their illicit goods.

Traffickers continuously diversify routes. They use the well-developed road system developed by Communist insurgents in Thailand, crossing mountain ranges from Chiang Mai to Lampang. Routes developed by old Chinese Nationalist forces that date back to the World War II and the Chinese civil war era are also highways for narcotics trafficking. The commercial opening of southern China and northeast India since the mid-1980s also opened new routes for narcotics trafficking. In the 1990s, ice production in Burma has revitalized the use of the Thai route. Cambodia is also increasingly used as a staging point for trafficking ice via Trat and Chanthaburi into Thailand. Vietnam, too, has become a transit point for narcotics traffickers moving to and from China, and narcotics are smuggled to Europe, North America and Australia using seaports in Hoi Anh, Danang, Vinh, and Haiphong.[16] Finally, Chinese crime organizations also use Chinese illegal migrants as mules to carry narcotics into the United States and elsewhere.[17]

Software Piracy and Smuggling

Software piracy—the illegal copy and sale of software programs, movies, music, and video games—is a big business for Chinese organized crime syndicates. Being the resourceful multinational businesses they are, Chinese crime organizations usually set up software piracy operations where a higher level of capacity in information technology is accessible and where law enforcement is weak. Some of these counterfeit operations use the best software and hardware available in the market that can easily produce thousands of copies in a matter of hours. Major counterfeit operation centers are found in Thailand, Hong Kong, China, the Philippines, and Malaysia.[18]

Another reason for locating their software piracy in these locations is access to international shipping to distribute the illegal merchandise across the globe. Hong Kong is the world's top container port, followed by Singapore (2), Kaoshiung in Taiwan (4), Shanghai (6), Shenzhen in Guangdong (11), and Port Klang in Malaysia (12).[19] Of the hundreds of thousands of containers going in and out of these ports daily, only a tiny fraction is inspected. This makes it easy to smuggle out contraband goods and even persons. Using high-tech detection devices to screen containers for persons inside them, Hong Kong authorities found 17 stowaways from Fujian province at the Kwai Chung container port in July 2003.[20] Others met a tragic end: 15 Chinese men were found dead on board the freighter Cape May in Seattle in January 2000 and another 58 had suffocated in a locked container cargo in the British port city of Dover in June 2000.[21]

Arms Smuggling

Chinese crime organizations, as any smart commercial enterprise, enter into businesses where there are profits with an acceptable level of risk. Although Chinese crime organizations have been known to move firearms and other weapons for their own use in robberies and gang warfare, more recent reports indicate that they are now involved in transnational arms smuggling for ethnic insurgents and terror groups.

Years of civil strife have left Cambodia a large stockpile of firearms, some of which Chinese crime organizations acquired and sold to rebel and terror groups. One buyer was the Liberation Tigers of Eelam in Sri Lanka. Weapons were moved through Thailand, sometimes using drug routes between Cambodia and Thailand. Other buyers are ethnic minority insurgents in Burma and southern Philippines.[22] Chinese crime organizations are also known to have sold Chinese-manufactured arms to insurgents in Burma and the southern Philippines, as well as local crime syndicates across the world.[23]

A particularly alarming report recounts the 14K smuggling arms to the Abu Sayyaf terror group in Mindanao in the southern Philippines. Abu Sayyaf has kidnapped Western tourists in exchange for money in the name of their Muslim insurgent movement. Moreover, the 14K was reported to have laundered the ransom money for the Abu Sayyaf and collected a percentage as fee for its service.[24]

Like all successful business organizations, Chinese crime organizations are quick to exploit profit opportunities. Existing assets (for example, old narcotics smuggling routes and ties with corrupt officials) are used to support their new illicit enterprises. The economic opening of China has created unprecedented opportunities for Chinese crime organizations to find new markets for narcotics, locations for counterfeiting operations, and a seemingly inexhaustible supply of persons for trafficking.

SECURITY RAMIFICATIONS

The fact that transnational organized crime represents a major threat to security is underscored by the United Nations and recognized by the U.S. and other governments.[25] *Security* here is defined as freedom from threats to the state, to individual freedom from intimidation, exploitation, and violation of basic human rights. The smuggling activities of Chinese organized crime groups clearly pose numerous threats to security.

Governance and Rule of Law

The illicit activities of Chinese crime organizations clearly break laws, whether it is trafficking either persons, narcotics, and goods or software piracy and manufacturing of fake documents. More importantly, good governance and the rule of law are compromised when government officials, police, and judges are bribed or coerced into working with criminals. Erosion of good governance and rule of law engenders public distrust in government, law enforcement, and the judiciary.

In China, smuggling of persons and goods is rampant and made possible with the collusion of officials at all levels of government. Low-level officials, for example, provide the stamps and papers necessary to move the smuggled persons or goods, or they turn a blind eye to illegal crossings and operations within their jurisdiction. High-level officials are frequently coinvestors in these illegal activities, using public funds to finance smuggling operations for example. They also abuse their authority to provide protection to criminals.[26]

Official corruption and abuse are the major source of discontent among the Chinese population. However, Beijing's response is the infrequent high-profile anticorruption campaigns that prosecute (and execute) a few high-level officials rather than introducing real reforms to curb excesses by officials of all ranks across the country. Recent high-profile prosecutions of officials tied to Chinese organized crime include the arrest of Suixin Mu, mayor of Shenyang, and his deputy Xiangdong Ma. Another was Major General Shengde Ji, head of China's military intelligence, who was sentenced to 15 years in prison for his involvement in a smuggling racket worth billions of dollars, which was operated by criminal syndicates in Taiwan and Hong Kong. Yet An-lo Chang, head of Taiwan's Bamboo Union Gang, walks free in China, although he is wanted in Taiwan for links to the murder of a legislator and construction fraud.

Public Health and Safety

Another serious security ramification is the corrosive effect of criminal activities on public health and safety. Drug addiction is a real concern for governments everywhere. Even China has openly admitted to a serious domestic drug problem, particularly in the southwestern region where narcotics traffickers are most rampant. Intravenous drug use, specifically the sharing of needles, has contributed to a rapid increase in HIV infection. Human trafficking for the sex trade also aggravates the HIV/AIDS problem. A large number of minority women in Yunnan province in China and other hill tribes in Burma, Cambodia, and Thailand are forced into prostitution. Completion of the Kunming–Bangkok highway in 2006 and plans to connect the road networks of Malaysia and Singapore will likely exacerbate cross border crime in the region.[27]

Young girls are especially in demand for prostitution because of the perception that they are not infected by HIV/AIDS or are more resistant to the virus. In reality, these women and girls are exposed to HIV and other diseases and become agents in their transmission. Men carry diseases back to their spouses, infecting them and creating dire consequences for their families. Orphans of AIDS now scatter across Thailand and many other places. The victimized women and girls are released from bondage when they can no longer turn a profit. They return to their villages physically and psychologically traumatized. Most would not speak out for fear of discrimination and help is usually not available. These tragic outcomes severely undercut the ability of the affected communities to sustain themselves socially, culturally, and economically.

Tuberculosis, avian flu, and other diseases can similarly be spread by the human trafficking activities of Chinese crime syndicates. Being illegal migrants, infected persons would unlikely seek medical attention. Highly contagious diseases can incubate and spread across a much larger population before they are detected, making it all the more difficult for public health officials to address the problem. This is a potential public health nightmare that might someday confront authorities in the United States and other places where Chinese human trafficking is pervasive.

National Security

As described earlier, Chinese crime organizations are known to work with local warlords, rebels, and other crime syndicates to control the narcotics trade in Southeast Asia, which feeds heroin and other drugs to markets across the world. Local warlords and rebels use proceeds from opium poppy cultivation, synthetic drug manufacturing, and gemstone mining in the hills of Southeast Asia to finance their cause. Chinese crime organizations are business partners with these warlords and rebels, as well as agents in selling these commodities to the outside world. Chinese crime organizations also help them to launder the proceeds, acquire commodities, such as weapons and medicine, to carry on warfare, which threatens local populations, political stability, and border security.

Another threat posed by the operations of Chinese crime organizations—or any successful crime syndicate—is their ability to maintain mechanisms and networks to support their illicit activities. These mechanisms and networks have proven successful time and again in moving vast quantities of contraband and hundreds and thousands of persons across immigration checkpoints and borders. Terrorists might find it attractive to use the services of crime syndicates, which are virtually one-stop shops, to help them sell contraband to finance their activities, acquire fake travel documents, move people, weapons, and other materiel within and across international borders. Sales of arms by the 14K to the Abu Sayyaf and its laundering of ransom money with fee for service is one example that underlines this concern.

Finally, ties between Chinese government officials and Chinese crime syndicates are a serious concern. China is an important producer of arms, chemicals, and other materiel with weapon potential. Chinese crime organizations and their Chinese government associates could become suppliers of weapons not only to criminals but also to insurgents and terrorists.

CONCLUSIONS

Chinese crime organizations have evolved today into multinational enterprises, and they conduct transnational criminal activities. They use their influence to corrupt officials, infiltrate business, and control politicians. Their actions undercut efforts to build good governance and rule of law in many places. They harm the lives of individuals and communities, promoting drug addiction and spreading diseases such as HIV/AIDS. Their expansion in recent years has benefited from the economic opening of China, which has allowed them new opportunities for cross-border smuggling into and out of China and highly profitable business deals in collusion with corrupt officials in the Chinese government and military.

Combating Chinese crime organizations will require international cooperation among law enforcement and commitment from political leaders who

will provide the necessary resources and political will to pursue these criminals. The sharing of intelligence among law enforcement authorities to trace
and stop illicit activities is a critical first step. Concerted efforts to close
trafficking routes, halt money laundering operations, and conduct arrests
will be part of the solution. Also important is training for law enforcement
officers and providing them with resources to conduct their work. Another
area in need of attention is finding ways to deal with international criminal cases when extradition treaties are absent between countries and legal
systems differ in the handling of transnational crimes.

Yet the more difficult challenge of breaking these highly flexible, innovative, and adaptive organizations persists. Hong Kong, under the British
rule, demonstrated some success in curbing Chinese organized crime. Public education campaigns, anticorruption drives, increasing transparency of
the financial system, and reform of the police were instituted to strengthen
governance and the rule of law.

The Chinese takeover of Hong Kong in 1997 has not brought about a
stronger effort to eliminate Chinese organized crime. In fact, quite the opposite has happened: Chinese crime organizations are implicitly allowed to
exist, so long as they pledge their allegiance to China. Collusive ties between
Chinese government officials and Chinese crime organizations are allowing
these crime syndicates to grow bigger, stronger, and more dangerous than
they have ever been.

NOTES

1. *Chinese crime organizations* are also referred to as *Chinese crime syndicates* in
this chapter. These two terms have a broader coverage than *Chinese triad*, which was
coined by the British authorities in Hong Kong to refer to Chinese secret societies
that were initially organized to overthrow the non-Chinese Manchu Qing dynasty
in the seventeenth century. After the Qing Empire fell in 1911, triad members,
accustomed to living underground, turned their political revolutionary groups into
criminal organizations. *Tongs* are different from the triads. Tongs were born in the
United States with the first wave of Chinese immigrants as mutual support societies.
Although many tongs became involved in criminal activities or are influenced by
established triads and crime organizations, they are not always crime organizations.

2. Jennifer Bolz, "Chinese Organized Crime and Illegal Alien Trafficking: Humans
as a Commodity," accessed at http://uninfo.state.gov/eap.

3. Glenn E. Curtis et al., "Transnational Activities of Chinese Crime Organizations," The Library of Congress, Federal Research Division, April 2003, 15 available
at www.loc.gov/rr/frd/pdf-files/ChineseOrgCrime.pdf.

4. The terms *human trafficking* and *human smuggling* are used interchangeably
in this chapter. Although human trafficking refers to illegal movement of persons
kidnapped or tricked into servitude and human smuggling describes those who ask
to be transported at their own volition, this distinction is less important than the act
of illegal movement of persons.

5. Howard W. French, "Chinese villages export their daughters," *International Herald Tribune* Online, January 4, 2005.

6. One example is Changxing Lai, one of China's most wanted criminals, who ran a $10 billion smuggling ring with corrupt Chinese officials. He remained in a Vancouver jail while the Canadian authorities debated whether to return him to China for trial. Canada has no death penalty and refrains from sending fugitives back to their home countries for trial if they could face execution. Changxing's petition for political refugee status was rejected by the Canadian courts. In a previous instance, Canada returned a Chinese criminal to China after China promised not to execute him. Upon arrival in China, however, he was sent to trial and quickly executed. See Maggie Farley, "Alleged boss of China Smuggling Ring presents Canada with a Conundrum Law," *Los Angeles Times*, December 6, 2000; and "Smuggling mastermind denied asylum," *China Daily* (English edition online), February 4, 2004.

7. Ko-lin Chin, "The Social Organization of Chinese Human Smuggling," in *Global Human Smuggling: Comparative Perspectives*, ed. David Kyle and Rey Koslowski (Baltimore, MD: Johns Hopkins Press, 2001); and Sheldon Zhang and Ko-lin Chin, *Characteristics of Chinese Human Smugglers* (Washington, DC: U.S. Department of Justice, August 2004), available at www.ncjrs.gov/pdffiles1/nij/204989. pdf.

8. Internal trafficking is also a serious problem. The ratio between men and women is 111 to 100 and worsening. Women are kidnapped and sold to men as wives. Since 2000, Yunnan police have arrested more than 6,000 suspects accused of kidnapping 3,958 women and 839 children in over 2,600 abduction cases. Infant girls are also increasingly targeted. In Guangdong province, it was reported that a village jointly purchased women and prostituted them from their homes. See Ching-Ching Ni, "China Confronts Its Daunting Gender Gap," *Los Angeles Times*, January 22, 2005; and Sophia Woodman and Stephanie Ho, "Trafficking of Women in China," Voice of America, September 27, 1995.

9. Cambodia is a major transit point for illegal Fujian Chinese on their way to Europe and North America. As of 1996, a person donating $400,000 to the Cambodian government or making $500,000 in investments would automatically receive Cambodian citizenship. It is comparatively easier for persons to enter the United States, using a Cambodian passport rather than a Chinese one. Chinese crime syndicates bribe Cambodian officials—with much smaller sums—to acquire Cambodian citizenship papers. Cambodia also provides a safe haven for both the illegal migrants and their handlers from the Chinese police. See Curtis et al., 37–47.

10. Curtis et al., 37–47.

11. Chin.

12. Bolz.

13. Cambodia, too, has become a major center in the heroin trade.

14. Curtis et al., 37–47.

15. *Ice* is the street name for a form of crystalline, smokeable methamphetamine. *Ecstasy* is a synthetic psychoactive drug chemically similar to the stimulant methamphetamine. In 2003, Chinese police seized 72.8 tons of raw materials for narcotics manufacturing. In Guangdong province, police seized 5 tons of ice, which accounted for 86.7 percent of the country's total. And underground ice factories expanded from the coastal Guangdong and Fujian provinces to inland areas. "Worsening Drug Trafficking Poses New Challenge to China," Xinhua News

Agency, February 13, 2004, available at www.china.org.cn/english/2004/Feb/87233. htm.

16. Pierre-Arnaud Chouvy, "New drug trafficking routes in Southeast Asia," *Jane's Intelligence Review*, July 1, 2002, available at www.pa-chouvy.org/JIR2.htm.

17. Chin.

18. Curtis et al., 37–47.

19. "World Top 15 Container Ports, 2000 (in TEUs)," accessed at www.ci-online.co.uk.

20. Paris Lord, "Containing Terror Threats," *The Standard* (Hong Kong), February 25, 2004, accessed at www.thestandard.com.hk.

21. David Kyle and Zai Liang, "Migrant merchants: Human smuggling from Ecuador and China," Working Paper No. 43, October 2001, UCSD Center for Comparative Immigration Studies. P. 18; and J.F.O. McAllister, "Snaking Toward Death," *Time* (Europe), July 3, 2000, accessed at www.time.com/time/europe.

22. Bertil Linter, "The Phuket Connection," *The Week* (India), April 30, 2000.

23. Curtis et al., 37-47.

24. Ibid.

25. See, for example, United Nations (UN) High-Level Panel on Threats, Challenges and Change, *A More Secure World: Our Shared Responsibility* (New York: UN, 2004); John Torres, "Pushing the Border Out on Alien Smuggling: New Tools and Intelligence Initiatives," hearing before the Subcommittee on Immigration, Border Security, and Claims of the Committee on the Judiciary, U.S. House of Representatives, 108th Congress, 2nd sess., May 18, 2004, available at http://commdocs.house.gov/committees/judiciary/hju93716.000/hju93716_0.HTM; and European Commission, Justice and Home Affairs, "A common EU approach to the fight against organized transnational crime," available at http://europa.eu.int/comm/justice_home/fsj/crime/fsj_crime_intro_en.htm.

26. Xiaobu Lu, *Cadres and Corruption: The Organizational Involution of the Chinese Communist Party* (Stanford, CA: Stanford University Press, 2000); and Louise I. Shelley, "The Nexus of Organized International Criminals and Terrorism," accessed at http://usinfo.state.gov.

27. "Calls to curb cross-border human trafficking," *China Daily* (Hong Kong), December 16, 2003, accessed at www.chinadaily.com.cn.

CHAPTER 10

Japanese Trafficking and Smuggling

Rollie Lal

The Japanese *yakuza* comprise some of the largest organized crime networks in the world and hold extraordinarily large amounts of wealth.[1] The *yakuza*, organized primarily into three main crime groups, have a total membership estimated at 80,000 or more. Although the Japanese syndicates, similar to other organized crime groups, are involved in large-scale criminal activity, they exhibit the unique advantage of relative acceptance within Japanese culture. This facet of their relationship with Japanese society has provided the *yakuza* with distinct advantages in both developing profit-making enterprises and evading law enforcement.

The *yakuza* were formed in the seventeenth century and, over the centuries, have become an entrenched part of Japanese society. The *yakuza* had gained a foothold in major urban centers by the nineteenth century and developed strong ties with both political and economic officials to expand their business interests. These groups gradually allied with the ultranationalists, assisting the Japanese militarists during the early twentieth century. These alliances were built upon long-standing shared ideological positions between themselves and the Japanese political right wing. The *yakuza* historically considered themselves the protectors of Japanese traditional culture, national honor, and the common man. After World War II, they were able to profit from both their political ties with the right and the rapid growth of their trafficking interests.

The three most powerful *yakuza* syndicates include the *Yamaguchi-gumi*, *Sumiyoshi-kai*, and *Inagawa-kai*, though many smaller crime groups also operate in Japan. Their income is derived from a variety of illegal activities, including drug trafficking, gambling, extortion, human trafficking, and legal businesses. Trafficking and smuggling drugs and people are critical areas of business for the criminal organizations.

DRUG TRAFFICKING

Drug trafficking alone is estimated to provide at least 35 percent of the income of Japanese organized crime.[2] The exceedingly fast pace of life in Japan is considered a reason for the country being the prime destination for stimulants, particularly amphetamines. Students, drivers, and many others working long hours in the office, while running low on sleep, rely upon speed to keep them awake and functional. A survey taken in 1998 indicated that at that time 2.2 million Japanese had used stimulant drugs.[3] This extremely lucrative trade in speed, commonly known as *shabu* in Japan, is controlled by the *yakuza*.

The *yakuza* procure amphetamines produced mainly in China and the Philippines, although North Korea maintains a major role and interest in the trade. Producing and marketing the drug are a vast number of countries and criminal groups spread across Asia. Consumption of the drug has become rampant in many countries, and production is growing to meet the demand. The popularity of ecstasy and other forms of amphetamines has boomed in Japan, South Korea, Hong Kong, China, Taiwan, Thailand, Indonesia, the Philippines, and Australia in recent years. As a result, syndicates in various countries have joined the game to share the profits.

China has become one of the largest producers of amphetamines, and Myanmar has developed into a major source as well, providing an estimated 800 million methamphetamine tablets per year, primarily to Thailand.[4] Syndicates have had to develop contacts with criminal elements in China and India to procure the raw materials for the trade. China and India are legally the largest world producers of a base component of methamphetamines known as ephedrine. While ephedrine production itself is regulated for legitimate pharmaceutical trade in these countries, a small amount is leaked and used for sale by drug traffickers. Some of this ephedrine is trafficked to Myanmar laboratories for production.[5]

The drugs are smuggled into Japan via sea vessels and air from myriad locations around the world. A major transit route involves the seas connecting Japan and the Korean Peninsula. Traffickers often import the drugs via fishing vessels through the waters surrounding North Korea, taking assistance and cover from officials. In a typical transaction, *yakuza* arranged for drug trafficking to take place under the cover of a Japanese trading firm. The trading firm president supervised the loading of the drug shipment near Wonsan Port in North Korea. After, the fishing vessel returned with the drugs to Japan, where it was intercepted. Apparently, the president of the trading company had supplied passes to the individuals involved in transporting, which allowed them to get by the North Korean patrol boats without trouble. The investigation revealed that the trading firm sent 40 million *yen* to North Korea as partial payment for the shipment. In other instances, North Koreans shipped the drugs directly to Japan.[6] The case highlights the involvement of corrupt officials on the North Korean side, or even possible open complicity of the authorities.

The drugs are smuggled into Japan by way of other more traditional routes, primarily disguised as tourist and business traffic coming through airports. Canadian citizens have been intercepted attempting to bring in large amounts of amphetamines through Narita Airport. In July 2004, a man and a woman were seized at the airport carrying 26 kilograms of amphetamines worth approximately 1.56 billion *yen* on the street. They had arrived on an Air Canada flight from Toronto and were planning to pass the drugs on to their contacts at a Tokyo hotel.[7] In a similar case, police intercepted a Taiwanese man, Chang Wan-Chung, attempting to board a plane at Taiwan's Chiang Kai-shek Airport with drugs. The man was carrying 2.165 kilograms of amphetamines in his luggage and was headed for Japan. Taiwanese police said that domestic drug rings, such as the one Wan-Chung was believed to work for, had become major drug exporters.[8] In addition, the Taiwanese drug syndicates had developed cooperative ties with criminal groups in Southeast Asia and Japan to move drugs efficiently to market. Malaysian women have also been caught entering Japan with amphetamines, though their intermediaries are believed to be Middle Eastern gangs rather than the *yakuza*.[9]

PROSTITUTION

Trafficking in women is also a massive business for the *yakuza*. The business of importing women for prostitution into Japan and organizing sex tours for Japanese men throughout Asia is extremely profitable and encounters less law enforcement opposition than the drug and weapons businesses. To a large extent, this is a reflection of long-standing ideas in Japanese society that prostitution is not a real problem. In Japan, the existence of hostess bars and prostitution involving illegal immigrants is given a wink and nod by government officials. The lax attitude of law enforcement has meant that women transported illegally into Japan as prostitutes have little recourse. As a result, in 2004, Japan was listed in the U.S. Department of State Trafficking in Persons Report as a country on the Tier Two Watch List. This categorizes Japan along with countries notorious for human trafficking, such as Thailand, Vietnam, and the Philippines. According to the report, "Japan lacks a comprehensive law against trafficking, and until recently there was no official, clearly defined policy to coordinate anti-trafficking efforts."[10] The report criticizes the extent of punishment available for crimes relating to human trafficking and prostitution. In sharp contrast to crimes involving drugs, perpetrators of human trafficking violations are given a slap on the wrist. The U.S. State Department also notes that the issue can be addressed by Japan if officials there can be brought to regard the problem seriously. The report states, "Considering the resources available, Japan could do much more to protect its thousands of victims of sexual slavery."[11]

Part of the glib attitude of Japanese officials and Japanese media reflects the fact that human trafficking has a long history in Japan. During World War II, for instance, the Japanese government, in collaboration with *yakuza* syndicates, arranged for thousands of Korean and other women from Asia to be made available as sex slaves or "comfort women" for the Imperial Army.[12] However, even today, the issue of comfort women is not discussed openly in public, and many Japanese refuse to believe that a crime against women occurred. In particular, many in the Japanese right wing argue that comfort women were in fact volunteers and, in any case, *necessary* to help the Imperial Army. This type of refusal to address historical issues of prostitution affects the popular perspective on current issues of human trafficking in Japan.[13]

As Japan's economy entered a boom in the 1970s, tourism to other Asian countries expanded rapidly. Growing affluence in Japan along with the strong *yen* allowed droves of Japanese to visit the rest of Asia and buy a lifestyle that was less readily available at home. Widespread poverty across the rest of Asia meant that thousands of women could be bought for very little. During this time, sex tours became increasingly popular, to the extent that Japanese tourism agencies began marketing countries for the availability of their women to the tourists. *Yakuza* entrepreneurs began profiting from this business and investing in sex tourism. Japanese sex tours in particular targeted Taiwan and Korea early on and then spread to the Philippines and Thailand.

In the early 1980s, protests against what was increasingly viewed in Asia as a new type of Japanese imperialism arose, and Japanese authorities tried to curb the flagrant sex tour industry. The Japanese economic recession also decreased the level of frivolous corporate spending available for this type of entertainment. Today, the Japanese tours continue, albeit more quietly.

Instead, the *yakuza* in the past few decades have begun new entrepreneurial activity focused upon trafficking women from Asia to Japan to meet the demand and to take advantage of a high profit margin. According to one study, an average session with a foreign prostitute in Japan in the late 1990s was $200. With an average of 100,000 prostitutes, the business would have brought in at least approximately $7.3 billion in a year, a large haul by any standard.[14]

The *yakuza* often work in coordination with the Chinese and Russian gangs, supplying women for prostitution in Japan. Japan is a major destination country for women and girls from China, Taiwan, Vietnam, Central Asia, Russia, South Korea, Cambodia, and the Philippines.[15] Japanese groups also recruit a substantial number of their sex workers from Thailand—a major source, transit, and destination country for trafficking. Thai women and girls are generally trafficked to the United States, Europe, Australia, Hong Kong, Taiwan, and Japan. Other women are trafficked into Thailand from neighboring countries, Russia, and Central Asia. Organized crime groups operating in Thailand provide a hub for much regional trafficking, providing needed facilities such as housing, banking, and protection.[16]

WEAPONS TRAFFICKING

For centuries, Japan has maintained extremely strict laws regarding the use and possession of handguns. Civilians are not legally allowed to carry a handgun and very few people own one. The only type of firearm that a Japanese citizen can legally possess is a shotgun for hunting, and for this the individual must undergo a lengthy licensing procedure.[17] As a result, *yakuza* groups attempting to arm themselves against their criminal rivals historically were at a disadvantage with regard to firepower. For decades, the price of a handgun was as much as 10 times its value in America. *Yakuza* were forced to pay a premium in price and inconvenience for acquiring their arsenal. Over time, a brisk trade in the importation of small arms developed, with the majority of the weapons coming from the United States, China, and the Philippines. Lax gun laws in the United States in particular have made it a prime shopping locale for *yakuza* in search of firepower.

In recent years, the syndicates have innovated to bring gunmakers into Japan to manufacture their weaponry locally and at a reduced cost. Filipino authorities have stated that gun manufacturers from the Philippines have been brought to Japan disguised as tourists or workers in order to produce guns there.[18] A high-ranking member of *Yamaguchi-gumi*, Akire Nemoto, was apprehended in Manila in a 2004 sting operation for firearm smuggling and drug running. Nemoto, also known as "overseas arsenal," had been involved in a transaction to sell weapons and drugs to the Taiwanese Bamboo Union gang and other gangs. Nemoto met with Taiwanese gangs in Manila to arrange the trade. Authorities believed that fishing boats were used to transfer drugs and weapons via the Philippines en route to Taiwan. The operation also revealed that the Taiwanese gangs had already placed more than $100,000 in orders for guns from *yakuza* bosses.[19]

In addition to conducting a trade in small weapons for use in arming their own gangs, North Korean defectors have testified to the U.S. Congress that the *yakuza* works with North Korea to import parts into North Korea for their missile and nuclear program.[20] American officials state that North Korea receives a significant portion of its funding and foreign currency for its arms program through drug sales. North Korean embassy officials have been intercepted in more than 20 countries for drug-related offences, a sign that official complicity in the trade goes beyond a wink and nod.[21]

The *yakuza* deals in the smuggling of other more obscure items in addition to the traditional areas of drugs, sex, and weapons. Luxury cars are smuggled out of Japan and into Thailand and other countries. Exotic animals are smuggled to and from countries, and luxury goods are smuggled into Japan to expedite money laundering.

CONCLUSION

Japan's banking crisis has revealed the extensive involvement of Japanese organized crime in creating nonperforming loans and in hindering the resolution of the problem. The crisis also uncovered the extent of organized crime's business influence in Japan. During the Japanese financial bubble of the 1980s, billions of dollars were loaned to corporations and individuals with *yakuza* involvement. Collusion between bankers, bureaucrats, politicians, and organized crime led to the disbursement of loans to unqualified recipients holding highly overvalued collateral. In the ensuing crisis, nonperforming loans extended to *yakuza*-affiliated organizations could not be recovered, deepening the problems faced by banks and the government in bailing out a decimated banking industry. The situation has forced a reassessment of the *yakuza* and its activities, including an investigation into their business dealings and the areas of their involvement in Japan's financial problems.

NOTES

1. *Yakuza* are members of traditional organized crime groups in Japan.
2. This figure is from data dating to 1989. See David E. Kaplan and Alec Dubro, *Yakuza: Japan's Criminal Underworld* (Berkeley, CA: University of California Press, 2003), 131.
3. Ibid., 244.
4. "Stimulant Abuse Rising in Asia, Opium Growth Falls: U.N. Report," Kyodo News Service, March 3, 2004; K.T. Sangameswaran, "'Ecstasy' Drugs a Nightmare, Says Expert," *The Hindu*, May 25, 2003.
5. Sangameswaran.
6. "Police Identify Leaders of Drug-Smuggling Ring," *The Daily Yomiuri* (Tokyo), March 16, 2000.
7. "2 Held for Allegedly Smuggling Large Amount of Stimulants," Kyodo News Service, July 7, 2004.
8. Lilian Wu, "Man Nabbed for Trying to Smuggle Amphetamines," Central News Agency–Taiwan, August 27, 2004.
9. "Young Malaysian Women Used as Drug Couriers," Deutsche Presse–Agentur, October 22, 2004.
10. U.S. Department of State, *Trafficking in Persons Report*, June 14, 2004, accessed at http://www.state.gov/g/tip/rls/tiprpt/2004/.
11. Ibid.

12. George Hicks, *The Comfort Women: Japan's Brutal Regime of Enforced Prostitution in the Second World War* (New York: W.W. Norton, 1994).

13. Jonathan Aiken, Atika Shubert, and Stan Grant, "Human Trafficking in Japan," CNN International Transcript, August 19, 2004.

14. Kaplan and Dubro, 239.

15. United Nations Office on Drugs and Crime, "Human Trafficking—Regional Profile 2003–3–11," available at www.unodc.un.or.th/material/document/RegionalProfile.pdf.

16. Ibid.

17. Ministry of Foreign Affairs of Japan, "National Report on the Implementation of Programme of Action (PoA) to Prevent, Combat and Eradicate the Illicit Trade in Small Arms and Light Weapons in All Its Aspects," accessed at www.mofa.go.jp/policy/un/disarmament/weapon/report0306.html.

18. Kanis Dursin, "Southeast Asia: Worried Governments Target Trade in Small Arms," Inter Press Service, May 10, 2000.

19. Deborah Kuo, "Taiwan, Philippine Police Crack Yakuza Arms Trafficking Ring," Central News Agency–Taiwan, June 4, 2004.

20. James Brooke, "Japan Lets Ferry Return to North Korea," *The International Herald Tribune*, August 28, 2003.

21. Tom Kelly, "Drug Trade Funds N. Korea Arms Programme–Pentagon," Press Association, May 21, 2003.

CHAPTER 11

South Asian Organized Crime and Linkages to Terrorist Networks

Rollie Lal

Until recently, terrorism and organized crime have been considered separate problems that should be dealt with differently. Conventional wisdom states that terrorists care little for profit, while it is the criminal's only desire. Yet consider this scenario: The powerful boss of a criminal syndicate with a vast logistical network planned to bolster his support in the Muslim community by avenging aggression against Muslims. He decided to launch terrorist attacks on the stock exchange and various other well-populated landmarks, utilizing ports and individuals whom he trusts for now bringing in tons of plastic explosives and weaponry. He recruited street criminals and trained them in terrorist camps outside the country in preparation for the attack. When the day came, simultaneous attacks were launched throughout a major city, causing destruction and chaos. Those bombings that took place in Mumbai in 1993 foreshadowed the massive terrorist attacks that occurred in the next decade.

Should these events, and other more recent instances in South Asia, cause us to rethink the conventional wisdom that terrorists and criminals ought to be assessed in quite different categories? The bombings suggest that criminal networks and terrorist groups may be deeply intertwined in ways that go well beyond tactical—and fleeting—alliances of convenience.

While organized crime has been involved in supporting international terrorist activity, including the attacks of September 11, the Madrid bombings, and the activities of militant groups in Afghanistan, global attention has focused on locating terrorist groups—that is, groups whose purpose is ideological rather than profit oriented. Moreover, the links between the two groups indicate that the issue of organized crime may need to be addressed in order to destroy the logistical network supporting terrorist groups. The case of South Asia is particularly relevant, as the region encompasses a variety of criminal and terrorist organizations that have been known to collaborate in operations internationally.

The connections between the two networks exist on a variety of levels, from purely tactical to strategic, including logistical support in weapons procurement, shared routes, training, and ideological overlap. Moreover, the possibility exists that the current cooperation between crime and terrorist groups could lead to the procurement of nuclear weapons and other weapons of mass destruction (WMD) by terrorists.

The Mumbai bombings indicated that criminal groups do not abide by state boundaries and can benefit from decentralized operations. Organized crime syndicates, such as terrorist groups, are transnational in character, and as governments increasingly focus on intercepting the criminals, the groups seek refuge primarily in Pakistan, the United Arab Emirates (UAE), and various other countries where their presence may be either tolerated or go unnoticed. The South Asian organized crime groups have also been connected with various other countries, including Canada, Thailand, Malaysia, Singapore, Kenya, and Portugal. Highly dispersed, criminal and terrorist groups have become operationally versatile and are able to supply and attack a multitude of locations in a short time frame.

At the more tactical level, terrorist groups rely upon organized crime networks to provide them with the necessary weaponry and munitions to undertake massive terrorist attacks or insurgencies. In addition, the routes that have been carefully constructed by criminal networks can be extremely useful for transporting goods on behalf of terrorist groups. For their part, criminal gangs can turn to terrorist groups to provide needed training in the use of guns and explosives and provide safe passage through militant territory for a price. Crime and terror groups are transnational and benefit from the overlap of their international routes. Criminal syndicates in South Asia are also closely connected to terrorist groups via the drug trade; both criminals and terrorists engage in drug trafficking to support their income.

Terrorist groups and criminal networks overlap in their attitude toward government authorities, and that overlap is critical. Both are engaged in illicit activities, so both networks depend upon their ability to corrupt officials and hide their activities from the government. To be effective, both networks prefer to operate in areas with weak law enforcement.[1] Crime and terror groups are transnational and can benefit from the overlap of their international routes.

Similar to terrorist groups, criminal organizations can become ideological over time. Conventional wisdom concerning criminal organizations holds that the criminals are only interested in monetary gain and thus use religious or ideological pronouncements only to cover criminal activities. Yet the South Asia cases suggest that criminal organizations have come to acquire ideological or religious predispositions that motivate their actions, not merely cover them. In South Asia, moreover, organized crime syndicates have increasingly become involved in supporting terrorist activities.

The implications of the cooperative relationship between criminals and terrorists for the spread of WMD are even more alarming. The revelations of recent nuclear transfers from Pakistan to other states raise concern that the inability of the United States and its allies to interrupt cooperation between organized crime and terrorist groups could lead to dangerous nuclear transfers in the future. Nuclear transfers to North Korea, Libya, and Iran could not have occurred without the assistance of illegal networks.[2] The ease with which the transfers were accomplished is exceptionally chilling. A.Q. Khan used false papers and front companies in several countries to transfer nuclear technology to other countries and used government cargo planes to assist in deliveries to North Korea.[3] Khan's middleman, B.S.A. Tahir, arranged for a Malaysian company to manufacture nuclear components for shipping to Libya and for Libyan technicians to be trained in the use of machines that were part of the nuclear program.[4] Tahir also assisted Khan in the transfer of centrifuge units from Pakistan to Iran.[5] Other individuals were involved in the nuclear trafficking network, including Peter Griffin, a British citizen who owned a front company in Dubai; Urs Tinner, a Swiss man who supervised work on centrifuge components; and others.[6] The scale of A.Q. Khan's illegal nuclear network and sales to various states indicates that similar sales of nuclear technology to terrorist organizations could be undertaken.

Even if states agree to international nonproliferation protocols, the existence of criminal networks engaged in nuclear trade could allow proliferation to continue. Without knowledge of where these networks operate and who is involved, interdiction becomes extremely difficult. Furthermore, authorities may not be able to identify the destination groups or countries for these illicit transfers of nuclear materials. An understanding of the case of South Asia is particularly critical at this time, as it provides insights into this dangerous trend of organized crime assisting radical Islamic groups in launching terrorist attacks and transporting nuclear material internationally.

ORGANIZED CRIME IN SOUTH ASIA

Research on organized crime based in South Asia can illuminate the connections between organized crime and terrorism, connections that may extend beyond the region, tomorrow if not today. Organized crime in this region covers a wide range of activities, including drug trafficking, weapons trafficking, prostitution, contract killings, extortion, kidnapping, money laundering, and *hawala*—an underground network of financiers who receive funds in one country then arrange for an associate in another country to pay the recipient. These business arenas and interests of terrorist groups intersect, providing opportunities for the two to cooperate, all the more so because both types of groups often operate in areas where law enforcement is weak and corrupting officials is possible.

While these criminal networks exist and operate across South Asia, they are particularly strong in large urban centers and commercial areas such as Mumbai and Karachi. Information regarding organized crime operations is more abundant in India than in Pakistan, largely because of limited press coverage and research on the issue in Pakistan. Political sensitivities in Pakistan regarding the connections of the government to organized crime and militant groups hinder this type of research. Journalists are pressured to avoid approaching the topic, facing harassment by police and intelligence agencies for excessive inquisitiveness.[7] In Karachi, Daniel Pearl, while researching the connections between Pakistan's militant groups and organized crime, was kidnapped and killed. As a result of the marked lack of data regarding crime in Pakistan, much of the data presented below reflect trends in Indian organized crime. However, as the groups are usually transnational and overlap in their business interests, the data illustrate many facets of organized crime that can be reflective of trends across South Asia. A closer look at specific cases of cooperation can reveal some of the methods used by these groups and highlight areas requiring further attention.

Over the past decade, South Asia has suffered from numerous terrorist attacks coordinated by a combination of individuals from both groups. Data from the investigations indicate that organized crime was consistently involved in some aspect of these attacks. This research summarizes three cases involving organized crime and terrorist groups working cooperatively, then gives an overview of the major business interests of Indian organized crime that are used to support these activities. The cases highlight some of the methods and opportunities criminal and terrorist networks utilize in India and Pakistan. The case of Dawood Ibrahim and the 1993 Mumbai Bombings, referred to earlier, illustrates how a criminal leader used his extensive criminal networks and finances to launch one of the largest terrorist attacks in the history of India, having become radicalized in response to attacks on Muslims. The case of Aftab Ansari describes how a criminal involved in kidnapping assisted in financing the 9/11 attacks through his terror connections. The Purulia Arms Drop Case suggests that criminals do not need to be ideologically inclined to assist terrorist groups; cooperation is often purely a business relationship.

Case I: Dawood Ibrahim and the 1993 Mumbai Bombings

The most powerful organized crime group in South Asia is currently the Dawood Gang (also known as D Company), led by Dawood Ibrahim. Dawood was designated a terrorist supporter by the United States in October of 2003 for his role in assisting al Qaeda through use of his routes, his role in assisting terrorist organizations such as Lashkar-e-Taiba, one of the largest

Pakistan-based anti-U.S. groups fighting in Kashmir, and for his role in terrorist attacks against India.[8] Although Dawood is an Indian Muslim, U.S. and Indian reports indicate that he resides in Pakistan and carries various Pakistani passports.[9] The Indian government has requested his extradition, but the Pakistani government has denied that he is in Pakistan.[10] The connections between his criminal networks and the terrorist groups based in South Asia are cause for international concern, as their interests spread far beyond the region.

Dawood, the architect of the 1993 Mumbai bombings, was first arrested for criminal activities in 1974. He developed his skills locally as a smuggler and was arrested several times over the following years. Over time, his gang incorporated and eliminated other local gangs and leaders, increasing Dawood's influence and wealth. In 1984, Dawood Ibrahim escaped to Dubai while on bail for murder and was followed there by other members of his gang. In recent years, Dawood moved to Karachi, Pakistan, although Dubai remains a major base for his operations, as well as for other syndicates. Nepal has also provided a critical access link for the syndicates. The Dawood Gang is one of South Asia's largest syndicates, with an estimated 4,000 to 5,000 members, over half of whom are from the Mumbai area.[11]

During the 1970s and 1980s, Dawood appeared to be relatively secular in his business interests. The profit motive remained the key factor in actions taken by his syndicate, and his group included large numbers of Hindu and Muslim gangsters. However, in 1992 religious tensions in India between Hindus and Muslims escalated, ultimately triggering large-scale violence that stirred religious divisions in the criminal underworld. Hindu nationalists destroyed the Babri Masjid, a historic mosque, on December 6, 1992. In the subsequent riots, hundreds of people died, though the numbers indicated that Muslims were most frequently targeted. The Srikrishna Commission Report conducted by the government of India noted that 900 people died, including 575 Muslims and 275 Hindus.[12] On March 12, 1993, Dawood responded by engineering the series of bomb blasts throughout Mumbai, avoiding predominantly Muslim areas. The targets included the Bombay Stock Exchange, Air India building, Shiv Sena (Hindu nationalist group) headquarters, gold market, and Plaza Cinema. His involvement was a surprise to law enforcement, as organized crime had not been directly involved in major terrorist attacks in the past. Vengeance for the violence against the Muslim community, combined with a desire to court the support of the Indian Muslim community, may have been the motivating factors for Dawood's involvement in the bombings, which killed 257.

The serial bombings of Mumbai in 1993 implicated several organized crime figures and their networks. In preparation for the attacks, Dawood Ibrahim and Tiger Memon (Ibrahim Mushtaq Abdul Razak Memon) recruited operatives for weapons training in the hinterlands of Pakistan and procured weapons and explosives. The operatives were sent first to Dubai, then onwards to Pakistan with new identities and false passports. The authorities in Dubai supplied the recruits with transit visas. Upon arrival in Pakistan, the recruits trained in the use of the AK-56, hand grenades, rocket launchers, and RDX (rapid detonating explosives) to be used in revenge for the mass violence against Muslims.[13] Shipments of the weaponry to be used in the actual attacks came in through ports near Mumbai, assisted by corrupt officials. In the investigations following the attacks, 1,034 kilograms of RDX was seized by Mumbai police in a warehouse and another 2,380 kilograms in a nearby creek, in addition to 459 grenades subsequently found to be manufactured in Pakistan, and 63 AK-56 rifles.[14] Collusion between terrorists and criminals was only possible as a result of cooperation by Pakistani officials and the corruption of various Indian agencies.

The Mumbai blasts caused a splintering of the Dawood Gang. Various members of the syndicate, including a Hindu criminal known as Chhota Rajan (Rajendra Sadashiv Nikhalje), rejected the March 1993 bomb blasts, calling them antinational. Chhota Rajan then formed an opposing group with other former members of the gang. Although Dawood still retains the support of many Hindu gangsters, the 1993 bombings changed the nature of his support base significantly and solidified his status as a protector of Muslim interests.

After September 11, Dawood surfaced again for his connections to the terrorist networks. Reports indicate that al Qaeda and Taliban leaders enlisted Dawood's aid in escaping from Afghanistan.[15] Dawood's smuggling routes through the region proved to be invaluable for individuals attempting to avoid detection. The Indian government has also stated that Dawood has used his networks to provide logistical support for Lashkar-e-Taiba's activities in Gujarat, Maharashtra, and Hyderabad.[16]

There is speculation that Dawood is moving some of his operations from the UAE to Saudi Arabia, as he has made repeated visits to that country in 2003. The authorities in the UAE have moved closer to India, signing an extradition treaty with India in 2003 and deporting wanted individuals. The UAE's increased cooperation with both India and the United States in turning over criminals and terrorists has made Dubai a less attractive base for Dawood's operations in the past year.

The Dawood Gang's ability to launch a massive terrorist attack on Mumbai, using tons of explosives and massive amounts of firepower, indicates that organized crime in South Asia is extremely capable of using its criminal networks for terrorist ends. Furthermore, criminal groups may have—or acquire, in this case, as retribution—ideological as well as business reasons for supporting terrorist activities.

Case II: Aftab Ansari

A well-known kidnapper and weapons smuggler, Aftab Ansari, provides an example of criminal financial assistance to terrorist undertakings. Based in Dubai, Ansari was primarily a criminal but developed links with terrorist financier Sayed Omar Sheikh from shared time in prison together in the 1990s.[17] Sheikh had been known for the prior kidnapping of British and Americans in order to obtain the release of Islamic militants held by India.[18] In 1999, Ansari was released from prison and left for Pakistan, where he was issued a Pakistani passport.[19] The same year, both Sheikh and Maulana Masood Azhar, leader of the Pakistan-based terrorist group Jaish-e-Mohammed, were released in December in exchange for hostages from the Indian Airlines flight that was hijacked to Afghanistan. Ansari and Sheikh came to an agreement that Ansari would provide recruits for training in Jaish-e-Mohammed and Lashkar-e-Taiba training camps in Pakistan, while Sheikh would make his terrorist networks available to assist Ansari's criminal activities.[20]

In August 2001, Ansari kidnapped an Indian shoe manufacturer, Partha Roy Burman, for $830,000 in ransom.[21] According to a trail of Hindi email intercepted by the Indian authorities, on August 11, Ansari then sent $100,000 to Sayed Omar Sheikh via Dubai. Sheikh is believed to have then sent the money to Mohammed Atta, a 9/11 hijacker.[22] In exchange for the money, Sheikh agreed to give training and weapons to the kidnappers. Later, Sayed Omar Sheikh and Aftab Ansari continued to cooperate, conducting the attack on American Center in Calcutta in January of 2002.[23] Sheikh was also believed to be involved in the Daniel Pearl kidnapping along with Khalid Shaikh Mohammed.[24]

In February 2002, Ansari was arrested in Dubai and admitted to funding terrorism through kidnappings for ransom, drugs, and arms. He also admitted ties to Sayed Omar Sheikh.

The case of Aftab Ansari reveals the possibility that individuals involved in organized crime activities may adopt or be converted to the ideological leanings of terrorists through prison contact and other association. In addition, his ability and intent to transfer funds in support of the September 11 hijacking indicates the international reach and efficiency of these operations. The linkages between organized crime and terrorist networks easily transcend the boundaries of the country in which the networks are based.

Case III: Purulia Arms Drop Case

The Purulia Arms Drop Case illustrates the transnational nature and vast scale of organized crime support for terrorist activities. In December of 1995, an Antonov 26 aircraft dropped over 300 AK-47/56 rifles, 20,545 rounds of ammunition, Dragnov sniper weapons, rocket launchers, and night vision devices into a village named Purulia in West Bengal, India. It was discovered that the Russian aircraft was bought from Latvia for $2 million and chartered by a Hong Kong-based company with the weapons picked up from Bulgaria.[25] The plane first flew to Pakistan and Bangladesh before entering India. The man suspected of leading the weapons deal is

Danish. A mixture of British, Latvian, and Indian nationals was found guilty in the case. The weapons were ultimately being procured by a religious cult in India known as Anand Marg, to be used in political revolt against the ruling communist party in the state of West Bengal. However, other than the man accused from Denmark, the individuals involved in the weapons deal were not all followers of the religious group.

This case illustrates a more familiar and tactical point: how organized crime can come to the assistance of terrorist organizations without sharing the ideological beliefs or goals of the organization. In the context of post-9/11 terrorist networks, it is clear that weapons dealers do not necessarily need to be ideologically allied with the terrorist groups that they are assisting. In effect, terrorist groups may be outsourcing much of the logistical and supply issues to affiliated organized crime networks. The result is an organization that may at times have more members of organized crime involved than committed terrorists. Despite the division of labor between the two networks, the ultimate outcome of creating mass terror remains unchanged.

THE BUSINESS OF TERRORIST LOGISTICS

Weapons selling is a prominent example, but the business interests of organized crime in South Asia include arms trafficking, drug trafficking, construction and real estate investments, extortion, prostitution, money laundering, and *hawala* transactions. Joint criminal and terrorist enterprises as described above are supported by a variety of businesses. The illegal investments of organized crime networks provide profits for the criminal organizations, as well as adequate funding for the procurement of weaponry and training for terrorist groups.

The criminal interests in arms and ammunition trafficking is a particular concern. Criminal groups involved in selling weapons may be particularly likely to cooperate with terrorists. Other criminal groups—providing prostitution or organs, for instance—often are in the business of providing illicit goods to consumers who may otherwise not be criminals. However, a portion of the proceeds from these businesses may be diverted toward supporting terrorist groups, as even these criminal arenas are dominated by large multinational criminal enterprises.

Small arms are brought into South Asia from the west, through Afghanistan and Pakistan, and from the east, originating in China. A large quantity of small arms entered the South Asian region with the advent of the war in Afghanistan in the 1980s, and then more arms were brought in with the most recent conflict in the country. The AK-47 and AK-57 have been popular weapons for their ease of use, low cost, and ready availability.[26]

South Asia is a critical transit region for drug trafficking of narcotics and other psychotropic drugs. Conveniently located between the Golden Triangle and the Golden Crescent, much of Asia's drug trade traverses South Asia.

Traffickers send narcotics from Afghanistan to Pakistan and through south India to the ocean and on to destinations in Europe and Russia. Pakistani traffickers also play an important role in financing and organizing of heroin produced in Afghanistan.[27] Heroin and other drugs are being transferred from Southeast Asia and Myanmar through India to points west. In addition, India is the world's largest legal producer of opium for pharmaceutical purposes.[28]

A small part of this licit production is diverted to be sold abroad illegally by organized crime, although the majority of diverted opium is used locally.[29] Various terrorist and extremist groups have been able to profit directly from this illicit trade in substances, using the profits from drug sales for the purchase of weapons. Militants in Afghanistan have long relied upon drug profits to assist them in funding weapons procurement and general financial support. The Liberation Tigers of Tamil Eelam is believed to use profits from drug trafficking to fund their activities and weapons procurement, as are various insurgent groups in India's northeast. The Dawood syndicate is also heavily involved in drug trafficking and has conducted terrorist attacks with the assistance of drug routes and funding.

The construction and real estate industry form another extremely profitable business venture for organized crime groups. The crime syndicates have played a role in forcibly vacating properties, settling property disputes, providing protection against other gangs, and providing loans. The Dawood syndicate, similar to other organized crime groups, has also expanded into legitimate businesses that remain convenient for money laundering purposes. Dawood owns shopping plazas, hotels, and other real estate in Pakistan and is believed to have large interests in the Pakistan stock market. He is also believed to have multiple hotels and businesses in Dubai. In 2003–2004, members of the Dawood Gang and several Mumbai civic officials were arrested in India for assisting in the gang's plan to construct the Sara and Sahara Shopping Centers on government land opposite the office of the police commissioner of Mumbai.[30] A dozen of Dawood's properties were confiscated after he absconded in the wake of the 1993 Mumbai bombings. However, he is known to hold many more under the names of others. The group launders vast quantities of money by purchasing old buildings and converting them into multiplex shopping centers.

The syndicates have also been able to profit from Bollywood—India's center of movie production in Mumbai—particularly by providing finance for films over the years and engaging in extortion. Criminals also played a role in recovering money for financiers from producers after the failure of films at the box office. As a result, several high profile killings of Bollywood personalities have taken place in recent years, including the murders of music producer Gulshan Kumar and film producer Mukesh Duggal.

Prostitution in South Asia is dominated by criminal syndicates, and the numbers of prostitutes in or trafficked from the region run into millions.

Prostitutes are smuggled into India from Nepal and Bangladesh. An unknown but large number of young girls are sent and sold to Arab countries each year, and small boys are also sold to the Arab states as camel racers. Dubai remains a popular destination and transfer point for the prostitution organized by South Asian criminal networks. These smuggling routes used for the illegal trafficking of humans could also be used effectively as routes for terror groups.

The criminal syndicates and terrorist networks also benefit from conducting *hawala* transactions, which arose from the weakness of the banking system, particularly in rural areas, and is based upon trust. *Hawala* exchange is common throughout South Asia and the Middle East and is not exclusive to Muslim communities. The Dawood and Chhota Rajan Gangs dominate the *hawala* network to and from India. The scale of *hawala* transfers is unknown, as these transactions cannot be traced easily. As a result, *hawala* has been useful for transmitting illegal proceeds from criminal activity and terrorist groups. Since September 11, *hawala* has come under intense scrutiny for the role that it plays in the funding of terrorist groups.

IMPLICATIONS

The boundaries between organized crime and terrorist groups in South Asia are blurring. Some of the connections between the two are primarily tactical, when criminal groups, especially those involved in weapons trafficking, make their wares available to terrorist groups. Organized crime groups provide substantial support to terrorist operations across South Asia as well as other parts of the world, operating under the cover of their other illicit businesses. Yet some of the blurring is longer term. Various members of South Asian criminal syndicates have come to adopt the ideologies or religious (especially Islamic) fervor of terrorists. And entire gangs, such as the Dawood Gang, have become more motivated by ethnic or ideological motives, especially in reaction to sharpening ethnic tensions or particular attacks on the Muslim community. As a result, the two phenomena need to be assessed together in combating both, and especially in the war on terror.

Improved judicial systems and fairer outcomes are critically important in addressing the problem of organized crime in South Asia and its support to terrorist networks. However, the needed reforms are considerably more sweeping for Pakistan than for India. The Indian government would benefit from law enforcement training, anticorruption initiatives, and streamlined judicial procedures. By contrast, Pakistan must undertake fundamental reforms of the political system in order to be effective.

In particular, Pakistan requires high-level political reforms and judicial reforms that strengthen the constitution and agencies against high-level corruption. The centralized and authoritarian system there does not allow for effective implementation of the rule of law, and it may permit collusion between high-level government officials and crime or terrorist groups. The example of A.Q. Khan's nuclear sales network provides a case study for such high-level corruption in the Pakistani system.

As the Khan case indicates, appropriate agencies may not be able to exert authority in cases involving people with high-level connections. Past and perhaps some continuing support from Pakistani intelligence or army of militant groups provides semilegal cover for operatives working for terrorist and criminal organizations. Until the judiciary is able to work independently, it will be difficult for Pakistan to root out criminal and terror groups operating there. Reforms should focus on isolating the judiciary from political influences. In recent years, President Pervez Musharraf was easily able to implement changes to the Pakistani constitution in order to validate his presidency. This type of political interference with constitutional and judicial procedure sets a precedent for further political manipulation of the legal system and should be protested by the international community. Currently, the U.S. provides some equipment, supplies, and training to Pakistani law enforcement agencies for combating the narcotics trade. Assistance is also provided to improve Pakistan's border security through surveillance equipment, communications equipment, vehicles, and aircraft. However, without fundamental changes to the political system, these tactical measures will be of limited effectiveness. The international community will need to assist Pakistan in undertaking political and legal reforms in order to address these issues.

The Indian judicial system also needs assistance to counter the strength of these criminal syndicates, though the problem there is less severe. Currently, several factors combine to the advantage of the syndicates. Bail is too easily available, and the pressuring of witnesses is all too common. Moreover, the criminals sometimes receive protection from politicians, bureaucrats, law enforcement agencies, and the judiciary, who may fear reprisal or benefit from these corrupt connections. Moreover, both Hindu nationalist parties and radical Muslim organizations contract the services of gangs and criminals for starting riots and political assassinations.

To address the issue of political corruption and its corrosive effect upon judicial proceedings, the Indian government needs to allow free access to information and increase transparency. Although transparency and the right to information are guaranteed by the Indian constitution, the freedom of information act has not yet been enacted by the central government. Implementation of freedom of information would allow citizens to understand the actions of bureaucrats and law enforcement authorities and provide a powerful tool for the people against corruption. Implementation of a law similar to the U.S. Racketeer Influenced and Corrupt Organizations Act (RICO) could also have a serious impact against organized crime in India. In the United States, citizens who have been harmed financially or otherwise by organized crime activity are empowered to file a civil suit under RICO.

Successful suits award the individual three times the amount of damages, as well as legal fees. This act dramatically increased the number of claims that could be brought against organized crime groups and enabled citizens to take initiative in combating crime.

U.S. law enforcement training and assistance could also help strengthen the Indian judicial system and law enforcement. Currently, the United States provides some assistance for improving customs enforcement, narcotics intelligence infrastructure, and enhanced laboratory facilities. Expanded assistance for equipment procurement, training for police officers in investigation techniques, and training in methods of effectively presenting evidence in court could be further areas of cooperation.

Terrorist groups will be able to continue operations as long as they can acquire the needed weaponry, financing, and personnel. Closing this access is difficult but crucial. Both groups rely upon weak law enforcement and corruption in order to be effective in their logistics and operations. In addition to military cooperation to interdict terrorists operating in ungoverned areas, much more attention needs to be paid to promoting the rule of law, combating corruption, and improving judicial proceedings. Police capabilities in urban areas need to be much improved if they are to locate and disrupt criminal networks. Many suspects wanted in connection with terrorism or organized crime can be intercepted by improving law and order in general. International cooperation on extradition laws and agreements must also be strengthened, so that criminals cannot easily elude arrest by fleeing the country.

For the analytic community, further research must be done to understand the links between organized crime and terrorist networks internationally. It is likely that international criminal syndicates were involved in providing the logistical requirements for the recent Madrid bombings, as well as in the Pakistani nuclear transfers to Libya and North Korea. Investigating these and other examples of linkages between terrorists and criminals could begin to improve measures to deal with both.

The linkages between the criminal and terror groups allow terror networks to expand and undertake large attacks internationally by leveraging criminal sources, money, and transit routes. Identifying the overlaps between the two networks—both tactical and more enduring—is critical to ending the financial and supply lines that support both sets of groups. Underestimating their bonds could prove disastrous.

NOTES

1. Louise I. Shelley, "The Nexus of Organized International Criminals and Terrorism," *International Annals of Criminology* 1, no. 2, (2002), 85–92.

2. Raymond Bonner and Craig S. Smith, "Pakistani Said to Have Given Libya Uranium," *The New York Times*, February 21, 2004; Seymour M. Hersh, "The

Deal: Why Is Washington Going Easy on Pakistan's Nuclear Black Marketers?" *The New Yorker*, March 8, 2004.

3. Paul Watson and Mubashir Zaidi, "Death of N. Korean Woman Offer Clues to Pakistani Nuclear Deals," *Los Angeles Times*, March 1, 2004.

4. Eileen Ng, "Libyan Nuclear Workers Trained in Malaysia: Official," Agence France Presse, May 29, 2004.

5. Raymond Bonner, "Multinational Network Aided Pakistan's Nuclear Help to Libya," *The International Herald Tribune*, February 23, 2004.

6. Reme Ahmad, "Probe Shows Reach of Nuclear Black Market; It Uncovers Web of Deceit Involving Experts from Various Countries and Clears Local Company of Wrongdoing," *The Straits Times*, February 21, 2004.

7. Husain Haqqani, "Trying to Create a New Pakistan," *The New York Times*, February 13, 2002.

8. Other significant Indian crime syndicates include the Chhota Rajan Gang, Arun Gawali Gang, and Amar Naik Gang.

9. "India Renews Demand for Dawood's Extradition," *The Times of India*, January 10, 2004.

10. "Dawood Not in Pak, Not Its National," The Press Trust of India, November 11, 2003.

11. Interviews of Indian law enforcement officials conducted by author, New Delhi and Mumbai, India, December 2003.

12. S. Hussain Zaidi, *Black Friday: The True Story of the Bombay Bomb Blasts* (New Delhi: Penguin Books, 2002), 19. Other estimates note that well over 1,000 people died in this violence.

13. Ibid.

14. Indian Central Bureau of Investigation Data; Zaidi.

15. Raj Chengappa with Sheela Raval and Anil Padmanabhan, "War on Terror: Getting Dawood," *India Today*, November 3, 2003.

16. "Dawood-Dossier," The Press Trust of India, October 17, 2003.

17. Celia W. Dugger, "India Says Man in Attack on U.S. Site Has Terror Tie," *The New York Times*, February 17, 2002.

18. Dave Goldiner, "Former Hostage Recalls Horror," *Daily News* (New York), February 9, 2002.

19. Praveen Swami, "The Arrest of Aftab Ansari," *Frontline* 19, no. 4 (February 16–March 1, 2002).

20. Ibid.

21. "Fear of Ansari's Flight Prevails," *The Statesman* (India), March 25, 2004.

22. Paul Watson and Sidhartha Barua, "Worlds of Extremism and Crime Collide in Indian Jail," *The Los Angeles Times*, February 8, 2002.

23. "Aftab Ansari Admits to Masterminding Kolkata Shootout," Redriff on the Net February 11, 2002 accessed at http://www.rediff.com/news/2002/feb/11usis.htm.

24. Watson and Barua, "Worlds of Extremism and Crime Collide in Indian Jail."

25. Sanjiv Kumar Upadhyay, "Crime in India," *Work Product of the 116th International Training Course: Resource Material Series No. 58* (Tokyo: United Nations Asia and Far East Institute, December 2001), 197.

26. Interview of senior Indian officials conducted by author, New Delhi, India, December 2003.

27. Bureau for International Narcotics and Law Enforcement Affairs, *International Narcotics Control Strategy Report 2003*, March 2004, accessed at http://www.state.gov/p/inl/rls/nrcrpt/2003/.

28. U.S. Drug Enforcement Administration, *Drug Intelligence Brief: India Country Brief*, May 2002, accessed at www.usdoj.gov/dea/pubs/intel/02022/02022.html.

29. United Nations, *Report of the International Narcotics Control Board for 2003*, accessed at http://www.incb.org/incb/en/annual_report_2003.html, 61–65.

30. "Mumbai Civic Body Officials Arrested in Mafia Probe," Indo-Asian News Service, January 27, 2004.

CHAPTER 12

Weak States and Porous Borders: Smuggling Along the Andean Ridge

Richard L. Millett

Illegal trafficking has a long, if not exactly honorable history in South America. Defying or simply ignoring state authority, especially in outlying regions, has never had any particular stigma attached to it. It is an activity that involves all levels of society, from elite families and powerful officials to common laborers and peasants. No area of the continent has been immune from this practice, though a few nations, such as Chile (largely because of its geographical isolation) have been less impacted. While smuggling remains an issue throughout South America, the focus of international attention has increasingly concentrated on two areas: the Andean Ridge from Venezuela through Bolivia, and the tri-border region of Paraguay, Argentina, and Brazil.

No regional economy has been more impacted by and dependent on smuggling than that of Paraguay. Its location between South America's two traditional powers, Argentina and Brazil, made it a haven for smugglers of all sorts of contraband, notably alcohol and cigarettes. In recent years, stolen cars, narcotics, appliances, and weapons have joined this list. The Paraguayan city of Ciudad del Este, located at the junction of these three nations, has become a haven for illicit traders, transnational criminals, and individuals connected to insurgent and terrorist groups such as Hezbollah and Colombia's illegal armed groups.[1] While this has made the region a subject of growing international concern, especially in the United States, the nature, volume, and negative impact of illicit trafficking flowing through this area is dwarfed by that along the Andean Ridge.

South America's Andean Ridge runs from Venezuela in the north through Colombia, Ecuador, Peru, and Bolivia to Chile. Chile is separated from its northern neighbors by the Atacama desert, the world's driest, and from

Argentina to the east by the Andes highest peaks. This fact, combined with its location at the continent's extreme south, takes it out of virtually all international smuggling routes. It neither produces nor refines major quantities of illegal narcotics, and its relatively prosperous society means that smuggling people north is not a major problem. Both the strength of its military and the lack of violent civil conflicts make it a virtual nonplayer in global arms trafficking. These conditions, however, do not apply to the rest of the region, which constitute the focus of this chapter.

Smuggling from Venezuela through Bolivia has long been a major activity. Historically, the major items were alcohol, tobacco, and, in more recent decades, electronics. These activities were facilitated by several historical factors. While governments in both the colonial and national periods were highly centralized, they rarely found it worth the cost or effort to attempt to exert effective control over outlying areas. Both the Andes and the interior jungles constituted virtually impassable barriers. The high-altitude location of capitols in Colombia, Ecuador, and Bolivia (combined with extremely rugged terrain) provided barriers against internal migration and promoted local autonomy. Colombia, the only nation in the region with ports on both the Atlantic and Pacific Oceans, was so internally isolated that until the development of aviation it was quicker to travel from coast to coast by going across the isthmus of Panama rather than using any land route. Until 1907, many of Colombia's states issued their own postage stamps because of the difficulty in procuring supplies from Bogota.

Ecuador was sharply divided between the traditional political elite, concentrated in the highlands around Quito, and a commercial elite centered on the port of Guayaquil. Internal divisions in Bolivia, reflecting topography, ethnicity, and external linkages, were always great and have grown in recent decades, producing a separatist movement around the lowland city of Santa Cruz. Peru's coastal capitol at Lima was always far removed from the reality of life among the indigenous peoples on the lofty *altiplano*. In Venezuela, the petroleum boom reduced, but by no means eliminated, long-standing rivalries between its Caribbean lowlands and the interior.

Ethnic divisions both reflected and exacerbated geographic separation. In Ecuador, Peru, and Bolivia, the bulk of the highland population clung to their indigenous language and culture, while Europeanized elites dominated politics, the military, and commerce. International borders meant little to the indigenous peoples who felt more in common with indigenous groups in neighboring countries than with national governing elites. In Colombia and, to a lesser extent, Venezuela, populations of African descent along the coasts felt discriminated against in both economic and political spheres.

All of this undermined the effectiveness of central control, facilitated the power of local strongmen (*caciques*), and made smuggling both easy and acceptable. Until at least the 1960s, dealing with smuggling was rarely a priority for national governments. It was more of a nuisance than a menace and had limited impact on either national politics or international relations. Government interest in and control over outlying areas was often low at best. These "ungoverned spaces" were out of control, but they were also out of touch, having little if any impact on the major concerns of central governments.

A variety of factors combined to alter this situation radically. Global communications, the proliferation of air transportation, population growth that spurred settlement of frontier areas, and, ultimately, a globalized economy (with the accompanying fall of traditional trade barriers) all meant that areas long out of control were no longer out of touch. Instead, they became prime areas for mounting campaigns against governments and also were increasingly attractive for operations by transnational criminal groups. The rapid growth in scope and power of these criminal networks greatly exacerbated the problem, making illegal activities in frontier areas a major source of international concerns.[2]

The nature of products being smuggled was also transformed, producing a symbiotic effect. As smuggling became more lucrative and more violent, the attractiveness of these "lawless areas" for a variety of illegal armed groups grew. As these areas became dominated by and dependent on illegal trafficking, their resistance to central authority intensified. Events soon began to spiral out of control.

Along the Andean Ridge, narcotics trafficking quickly occupied a central position in the rapidly expanding trafficking networks. In the 1960s and early 1970s, most of this was in marijuana, with Colombia's isolated Guajira Peninsula being a major production center. But by the late 1970s, U.S. consumption patterns were increasingly moving to cocaine. A Drug Enforcement Agency study at the end of 1979 showed that Colombia had become the major center for cocaine processing and trafficking, though most of the raw coca product was still produced in Peru and Bolivia.[3] Cocaine trafficking not only proved much more lucrative than the marijuana trade, but it also quickly generated much more concern in the consuming nations, notably the United States.

Andean trafficking networks spread steadily in the 1980s and 1990s, involving more and more countries and creating venues that were also utilized by arms traffickers and people smugglers. In the 1980s, a prominent Colombian explained the situation quite succinctly, stating that much of the profits from narcotics went into arms trafficking, and the arms were divided into three parts: One part the traffickers gave to Colombia's guerrillas as a protection payoff; the second part the traffickers gave to paramilitary groups to kill guerrillas; and the third part they kept to themselves to kill everybody. This was a recipe for national disaster, and the dire consequences rapidly became evident. Violence mounted and the size and strength of the illegal armed groups, notably two major Marxist insurgent forces—the FARC (*Fuerzas Armadas Revolucionarias de Colombia*) and the ELN (*Ejército de*

Liberación Nacional)—and the right-wing paramilitary AUC (*Autodefensas Unidas de Colombia*) grew steadily. Violence, long confined to the "ungoverned spaces," began to spread throughout the nation, exacting a growing toll of innocent civilians as well as those on all sides of the conflict.[4] At the same time, the heads of the major narcotics cartels, notably in the cities of Medellin and Cali, became nationally prominent figures.[5]

In the 1980s and into the 1990s, coca was largely grown in Bolivia and Peru and then transported to Colombia for refining and distribution. The bulk of this went through Peru, making the Colombian Amazon port of Leticia a key transit center. Some coca went by river, some overland, a growing amount by small- and medium-sized aircraft using hundreds of isolated and unsupervised landing strips. Government efforts to counter this trade were largely ineffective. Former Colombian cabinet member and Ambassador to the Organization of American States (OAS) Fernando Cepeda Ulloa cited the weakness of the legal system and the "tolerance of criminal conduct," a "growing belief in the invincibility of the drug barons," and the "lack of an effective international anti-drugs strategy" as major factors in the growth of narcotics trafficking.[6] In addition, Dr. Cepeda notes that while traffickers "have little regard for national sovereignty," governments are compelled to respect borders, national laws, and jurisdictions.[7]

In the face of the accelerating growth in narcotics trafficking, regional states often lacked the will, the resources, and the power to confront the traffickers effectively. Whether in isolated frontier areas, such as Peru's Upper Hualaga Valley or Colombia's Putumayo, or in sprawling urban barrios overwhelmed by poverty and violence, there was neither faith in nor support for government efforts to counter the rising power of the narcotics cartels. The police were usually seen as corrupt and inept, the judicial system as serving only the interests of the rich and powerful, and the narcotics issue as a problem of the consumer nations. The popular perception of the administration of justice was succinctly summed up by the auxiliary Bishop of Ayacucho, Peru. When the Bishop was asked about taking a case to court, he stated, "Absolutely not. I couldn't afford to buy the decision."

By the start of the 1990s, Colombia, Peru, and Bolivia faced a proliferation of states within the state, areas where not only the state lacked authority, but also effective rule was in the hands of violent insurgent groups, private paramilitary forces, or organized criminal gangs. The problem was not a failure of law enforcement but a spreading culture of lawlessness. In more and more areas, there was no heritage of respect for the administration of justice and no incentive to obey laws, especially those related to illegal trafficking. Government officials that were present in these "ungoverned spaces" often faced the choice of *plata ó plomo*, silver or lead. Either take a payoff for ignoring (if not directly *facilitating* trafficking) or take the lead bullet for yourself and your family. Given the state's inability to enforce laws or protect individuals, this was rarely a difficult choice.

From the sanctuaries, a web of trafficking networks spread throughout neighboring countries, into the Caribbean, then to the United States, and, over time, increasingly to Europe. The routes used to transport coca paste from Peru and Bolivia to Colombia for refining into cocaine and then from Colombia to the consuming world were complemented by an overlapping, but not identical network used to import weapons and chemicals used in the refining process. Much of the transport was done in light aircraft, but river boats, trucks, mules, and even on occasion railroads played a role. On the high seas, everything from modern container ships to rusty small freighters, to fishing boats, to small "go-fast" craft were utilized.[8]

Such a lucrative enterprise rapidly attracted a variety of participants. The FARC, AUC, and, to a lesser extent, the ELN in Colombia, and *Sendero Luminoso* in Peru all profited from the narcotics trade. In Colombia, bloody clashes between the FARC, the AUC, and the ELN were fought over control of producing areas and trafficking routes. *Sendero Luminoso* was less directly involved but did levy heavy taxes on coca production and defended the growers against government eradication efforts.[9]

A variety of international criminal organizations ranging from Italian, American, and even Albanian mafias to the Jamaican posses and North American street gangs became linked to and competed for the profits from illegal trafficking from the Andean Ridge. Of special importance were the activities of Mexican and Russian organized crime. The Mexicans became major rivals to the Colombian cartels for control over trafficking routes and distribution networks, their involvement facilitated by the relative success of Colombian-U.S. efforts to break up the Medellin and Cali cartels.[10] Russian organized crime became a much more important player after the breakup of the Soviet Union, especially in arms trafficking and money laundering.

It was not only overtly criminal organizations that profited from the network of illegal trafficking, but also police and military forces were riddled with corruption. The situation was perhaps at its worst in Peru during the 1990s: Revelations of blatant corruption by President Alberto Fujimori's intelligence chief and close confidant, Vladimiro Montesinos, led to the arrest of 18 generals and dozens of other high-ranking officials charged with a variety of offenses, including taking bribes from narcotics traffickers and supplying weapons to the FARC in Colombia.[11] Not all of this came as a surprise to American officials, with one Special Forces colonel noting, "We know as a fact that the Peruvian Army get payments for letting traffickers use airstrips."[12]

Smuggling and corruption go hand in hand throughout the region. With the establishment of elected civilian governments and the consequent increase in media freedom and assertiveness, corrupt officials find the risk of public exposure much greater. Unfortunately, the combination of the vast amounts of money involved and the credibility of the traffickers threats has ensured that there is always another crop of officials ready to be corrupted when their predecessors' actions are discovered.

Efforts to disrupt trafficking networks and curb coca production have met with mixed success at best. In the 1990s, growing pressure on crops in Bolivia and Peru led to a large-scale transfer of coca growing to Colombia. In recent years, eradication campaigns in Colombia have produced a resurgence of cultivation in Bolivia and Peru. A similar pattern has been followed in efforts to disrupt transit routes, with traffickers moving from air to sea to land routes as efforts at interdiction focus on one or the other. This has been aptly described as the *balloon phenomena*. When the balloon is squeezed at one end, it simply tends to bulge out at the other. Meanwhile, efforts to disrupt production led to charges of environmental destruction, health hazards, and human rights violations, especially among poor rural families. This, in turn, has contributed to a growing political crisis in much of the region, most notably in Ecuador and Bolivia.

While cocaine has largely replaced marijuana as the preferred and most lucrative smuggled crop, it is by no means the only item involved in narcotics trafficking. Most heroin and other opium poppy derivatives are produced and trafficked in the Middle East and Asia. Significant amounts come from Mexico. But there has always been some production on the Andean ridge, with most of the refining done in Colombia. Recently there are indications that this is increasing.[13] Amphetamines and Ecstasy are also produced and trafficked in Colombia and, to a lesser extent, Venezuela. Seizures of amphetamines peaked in the early 1990s, while Ecstasy production grew more in recent years.[14] Cocaine, however, clearly remains the dominant product in narcotics trafficking, a position it has occupied for a quarter of a century.

Narcotics trafficking and arms smuggling along the Andean Ridge are closely interlocked. Groups involved in narcotics also are the leading traffickers in armaments and much of the money used for arms purchases is generated by the narcotics trade. Colombia, with its ongoing multiple-actor civil conflict, is the primary destination for the bulk of the illicit arms trade. Peru, Ecuador, and Venezuela have all served as sources of arms smuggled into Colombia, but the majority of the trade comes from nations outside the Andean Ridge.

In 2003, Kim Cragin and Bruce Hoffman of the RAND Corporation completed an extensive study on "Arms Trafficking and Colombia." They found a "rapid and relatively free flow of small arms into Colombia," due to the nation's porous borders, a government presence that was "essentially nonexistent in southern Colombia,[15]" and easy access to both Caribbean and Pacific ports. Arms smuggling was not only destined for the illegal armed groups but also for private citizens convinced that the state was unable to protect them.

Arms usually arrive in relatively small shipments from Central America, where huge stockpiles remain from the civil conflicts of the 1980s and 1990s. While it supplied few weapons directly, Panama was the primary transshipment point.[16] A particularly notable case, which involved an unusually large quantity of arms, took place in November 2001. A Panamanian registered ship, the *Otterlou*, delivered nearly 3,000 AK-47 rifles and up to 5 million rounds of ammunition to AUC paramilitaries at the small Pacific port of Turbo, near the Panamanian border. The arms originated in Nicaragua and were ostensibly being shipped to Panama's National Police (the Public Force).[17] Arrangements were made through Israeli arms dealers operating out of Guatemala and Panama, with the assistance of contacts in Mexico.

This transaction generated a detailed investigation by the Organization of American States since it represented a violation of the Inter-American Convention Against the Illicit Manufacturing of and Trafficking in Firearms, Ammunition, Explosives and Other Related Material. While finding no evidence of direct Panamanian involvement, the final OAS report left unanswered questions about where the false purchase order for Panama's Public Force originated. It strongly criticized Nicaraguan officials, detailed the criminal actions of the Israeli arms brokers and their associates, and noted that "several Colombian customs agents were likely accomplices of or were bribed by the AUC."[18]

This incident underscores the complexity of the arms trade flowing into Colombia, highlights the multiplicity of actors involved, and illustrates the critical role of Central America in many transactions. But by no means all weapons smuggling originates in that region. Most of Colombia's neighbors are involved to a greater or lesser extent. Florida, as well as Panama, is a center for such transactions.[19] Smaller Caribbean nations, such as Antigua and Suriname, have been involved. Even the Russian mafia has found Andean Ridge arms trafficking, along with narcotics and people smuggling, a potentially profitable enterprise.[20]

Colombia's neighbors all present special problems. Panama is the greatest source with most weapons, along with chemicals for cocaine production, traveling by sea. But small quantities also go by land through the Darien Gap. Brazil is less directly involved, and there has been little evidence of high-level government involvement. But small planes coming from Brazil, or flying over from Suriname, have been a major source of weapons.[21] Much of the arms trade passing through Brazil originates in the tri-border area with Paraguay and Argentina. Brazil's introduction of a sophisticated radar system in the Amazon Basin may have worked to reduce this, but the traffic has simply shifted to other, more open frontiers.

The situation along Colombia's borders with Peru and Ecuador is more complex. Some of the arms used by the FARC came directly from Peruvian military stockpiles, especially during the administration of President Fujimori. The largest shipment involved a complex set of actors purchasing assault rifles from Jordan, ostensibly for the Peruvian military, then air-dropping them from a Ukrainian Boeing 707 into the jungle where they were retrieved by the FARC.[22] As details from this transaction surfaced, it led to the imprisonment of a large number of current and former Peruvian generals and ultimately helped bring down Fujimori's intelligence chief and confidant, Vladimiro Montesinos.[23]

Ecuador was also a significant source of arms supplies for the FARC, but the trail of corruption never reached as high as it did in Peru. These arms flowed over the border in small quantities, facilitated by the lack of government control over remote border areas and the dependence of communities in the area on dealings with Colombia's illegal armed groups. In 2002, the Bush administration criticized Ecuador for providing "a strategic conduit for arms, munitions, and explosives destined for Colombian armed groups," and the following year relations with Colombia were strained when a missile from Ecuador was used in an effort to murder a Colombian union leader.[24]

Ecuador has also been a source of the propane cylinders that the FARC converts into deadly, though highly inaccurate missiles used in indiscriminate attacks on populated areas.[25] While both Ecuador and Colombia have increased efforts to seal the border, the trade in arms, munitions, explosives, and the deadly propane cylinders continues to flow with regularity.

The involvement of Venezuela in providing arms and other supplies to Colombia's insurgents is the most controversial and generates significant tensions between the two nations. In part this stems from long-standing rivalries and territorial disputes between the two nations, in part from Venezuela's President Chavez' ideological affinity for the FARC and ELN, and in part from the long tradition of smuggling across their mutual border. Some weapons found in guerrilla hands have been traced back to the Venezuelan military. Most of the arms trafficked are probably exchanged for cocaine, again establishing the close linkage between narcotics and arms trafficking. Charges of high-level Venezuelan complicity in arms trafficking abound, definitive evidence is much scarcer.[26]

The intricate, multinational web of arms trafficking into and through the Andean Ridge reflects the global problem of controlling small arms. Similar to narcotics trafficking patterns, this trade has proved highly resilient and adaptive, easily able to shift routes in response to interdiction efforts and never lacking an abundant supply of dealers willing to sell and violent groups with abundant cash resources seeking to buy. An OAS study concluded that nearly 45,000 weapons enter Colombia illegally each year. In response, in March 2004 Colombian President Alvaro Uribe made an impassioned plea for greater international cooperation in halting the flow of arms into Colombia, noting that "more than 90 percent of the crime in Colombia" was committed with arms that entered the country illegally.[27] To date this plea has had little apparent effect.

Human smuggling is also a growing regional concern. The United States remains the preferred destination for most of those who turn to criminal organizations for migration, but it is by no means the only one. While the majority of undocumented immigrants heading north from Andean nations are natives of those nations, there is also a thriving trade in individuals from China and the Indian subcontinent. This is especially true in the case of Ecuador and Peru, but even Venezuela has been involved. Most go by sea to Central America or Mexico, then by land to the United States.[28] In an effort to counteract such smuggling, the United States has utilized a "Forward Operating Location" in Manta, Ecuador, to intercept vessels taking people north. This has led to charges that American vessels have sunk numerous Ecuadorian fishing vessels and violated Ecuadorian territorial waters.[29]

In addition to the United States, Europe (notably Spain), Japan, and Venezuela have been major migrant trafficking destinations. Much of this involves the worst types of abuses, sexual exploitation of women, especially minors, and forced labor. Migrants may also be used to smuggle narcotics, often placed in condoms which they are forced to swallow. The Department of State's Trafficking in Persons Report for 2005 details many of these abuses and cites Bolivia, Peru, Ecuador, Colombia, and Venezuela as playing significant roles in this trade. In most cases, unregulated borders are listed as a major factor in such trafficking, along with lax enforcement and, at least by implication, official corruption.

The report cites Colombian estimates that over 45,000 of its nationals are "engaged in prostitution overseas," some in neighboring nations, others as far away as Spain, Japan, and Hong Kong. Women and children from throughout the region (including the Dominican Republic and Guyana) are trafficked through Venezuela, and Venezuelan children are reportedly abducted for the sex trade in mining areas in Guyana and for forced service with the guerrillas in Colombia. While enforcement efforts are generally seen as inadequate, the report does cite a 2004 joint Peruvian-Ecuadorian operation that broke up a thriving human smuggling operation from Peru into Ecuador.[30]

Narcotics, arms, and people are the most important and most lucrative illegal trafficking operations along the Andean Ridge, but they are by no means the only ones. The longtime trade in smuggling alcohol and cigarettes continues virtually unabated. In 2000, a group of Colombian state governments filed suit against Philip Morris and British American tobacco in U.S. courts, charging them with conspiring to smuggle cigarettes and depriving the state governments of major tax revenues.[31]

Wildlife and pre-Columbian artifacts are also regularly smuggled. Some of the wildlife, unfortunately, are used as vehicles for narcotics smuggling, and narcotics traffickers at times exchange cocaine for endangered species.[32] This has reached potentially devastating levels in parts of the Amazon Basin and in Ecuador's Galapagos Islands.[33]

Stolen cars are also smuggled. Some come into Peru and Bolivia via Paraguay, which steals them from Brazil and Argentina. A more significant route runs from Venezuela into Colombia.[34] Coupled with this is a thriving business in smuggling gasoline from Venezuela into Colombia and Brazil. This is a product of the Venezuelan government's high subsidy of gasoline, making its price there less than bottled water. Despite efforts of governments on all sides of the borders to crack down, estimates of the amounts smuggled run up to 50,000 liters daily. Taxes on the trade have provided a major source of income for the AUC.[35]

The array and scope of illegal trafficking along most of the Andean Ridge both contributes to and is symptomatic of deeper problems. These include the historic failure of states to control frontier areas, deep ethnic divisions, serious interstate issues (between Colombia and Venezuela, Ecuador and Peru, Bolivia and Chile), weak judicial systems with little or no public credibility, and a generalized failure of traditional political elites. By most criteria, Bolivia fits the definition of a failing state.[36] Ecuador is not far behind and Peru has grave internal problems. Colombia has gained ground against the illegal armed groups, but the nation is still plagued by violence, poverty, and weak state structures. In Venezuela, the failure of the traditional parties has opened the door to the populist rule of President Chavez, polarizing society and producing growing tensions with Colombia and the United States.[37]

With the possible exception of Venezuela, each of these states is resource-starved, especially when confronted by the massive finances available to organized crime and illegal armed groups. Corruption is a major issue in every nation, contributing to a spreading culture of lawlessness, cynicism, and political apathy. Internal narcotics consumption is growing, talented professionals join the poor in seeking to migrate, and investors, both foreign and domestic, view the region with an increasingly wary eye.

Efforts to combat the web of illegal trafficking often result in damaging the environment or threatening the livelihood of poor farmers.[38] This, in turn, provides constant ammunition for populist politicians, such as Chavez and Bolivia's Evo Morales, and leads to a chorus of criticism of government actions from international nongovernmental organizations.

On a global scale, terrorism and trafficking in narcotics, arms, and people are increasingly linked. Fortunately, to date the worst aspects of this have largely escaped Latin America. The potential, however, is clearly present, a reality underscored by revelations of Irish Republican Army ties to Colombia's FARC.[39] Should there ever be a direct link between Andean Ridge trafficking and a terrorist incident outside the region, especially one in the United States, the economic and political effects would likely be catastrophic.

Illegal trafficking along the Andean Ridge is nothing new, and it is unlikely to decline significantly, much less go away, in the foreseeable future. The challenge to the region's nations and to the broader international community is to work together to limit its deleterious effects, strengthen threatened democratic institutions, and provide alternative paths to economic progress and personal security for the bulk of the population. The task is daunting, but the risks of failure are greater still.

NOTES

1. For information on the tri-border region, see *Terrorist and Organized Crime Groups in the Tri-Border Area (TBA) of South America*, report prepared by the Federal Research Division, Library of Congress, July 2003. For a Latin American view, see Mariano Cesar Bartolome, "*Amenazas a la seguridad de los Estados: La triple Frontera como 'area gris' el el cono sur Americano*," paper presented at *Terrorismo: Vulnerabilidades en el Nuevo Escenario Internacional* conference, Buenos Aires, November, 2001.

2. For a discussion of the growing importance of these areas, see Julio A. Cirino and Silvana Elizondo, "Hemispheric Security and Lawless Areas" (Buenos Aires: Center for Hemispheric Studies Alexis de Tocqueville, October, 2002).

3. Paul Eddy with Hugo Sabogal and Sara Walden, *The Cocaine Wars* (New York: Norton, 1988), 46–49.

4. For details on the violence in Colombia in the 1990s, see *Violence in Colombia, 1990–2000: Waging War and Negotiating Peace*, ed. Charles Berquist, Ricardo Penaranda, and Gonzalo Sanchez G. (Wilmington, DE: Scholarly Resources, 2001).

5. The rapid rise of these figures is documented in Guy Gugliotta and Jeff Leen, *Kings of Cocaine* (New York: Simon & Schuster, 1989).

6. Fernando Cepeda Ulloa, "Introduction," in *Latin America and the Multinational Drug Trade*, ed. Elizabeth Joyce and Carlos Malamud (London: Institute of Latin American Studies, University of London, 1998), 3–5.

7. Ibid., 7.

8. For a description of the routes and varied modes of transportation used, see U.S. Department of Justice, Drug Enforcement Administration, *The NNICC Report, 1996: The Supply of Illicit Drugs to the United States*, 11–27.

9. The nature and extent of Sendero's involvement in the drug trade remains a matter of dispute. For a more limited view, see Simon Strong, *Shining Path: Terror and Revolution in Peru* (New York: Random House–Times Books, 1992), 96–124. See also David Scott Palmer, "Peru, the Drug Business, and Shining Path: Between Scylla and Charybdis," *Journal of Interamerican Studies and World Affairs*, vol. 34 (Fall 1992), 65–88.

10. For a colorful description of some of this effort, see Mark Bowden, *Killing Pablo: The Hunt for the World's Greatest Outlaw* (New York: Penguin Books, 1992).

11. Anthony Faiiola, "U.S. Allies in Drug War in Disgrace," *The Washington Post*, May 10, 2001. Also see Coleta A. Youngers and Eileen Rosin, "Drug War Paradoxes: The U.S. Government and Peru's Vladimiro Montesinos," *WOLA Drug War Monitor*, July 2004.

12. Peter Andreas, "Profits, Poverty, and Illegality: The Logic of Drug Corruption," *NACLA Report on the Americas*, 27, no 3 (November-December 1993), 26.

13. Laura Crimaldi and O'Ryan Johnson, "Heroin's Journey Traces Coke Trail: Colombia Joins Trade," *Boston Herald*, September 14, 2005. Carol Cratty, "DEA: Artwork furniture used to smuggle heroin," CNN.com, December 8, 2005.

14. United Nations Office on Drugs and Crime (Vienna), *Ecstasy and Amphetamines: Global Survey, 2003* (New York: United Nations, 2003), 28.

15. Kim Cragin and Bruce Hoffman, *Arms Trafficking in Colombia* (Santa Monica, CA: RAND, 2003), xvi–xvii.

16. Ibid., xvii.

17. Kathia Martinez, "OAS Report Blames Nicaragua for Gun Deal," Associated Press, January 21, 2003.

18. Organization of American States (OAS), Report of the General Secretariat of the Organization of American States on the diversion of Nicaraguan arms to the United Self Defense Forces of Colombia (Washington, DC: OAS, January 6, 2003), 1–17.

19. For an example of Florida's role, see "Pipe break leaked clue to arms smuggling," *St. Petersburg Times*, August 21, 2004, accessed at www.spstimes.com/2004/08/21/news_pf/State/Pipe_break_leaked_clu.shtml.

20. Sue Lackey with Michael Moran, "Russian Mob trading arms for cocaine with Colombian Rebels," MSNBC News, November 17, 2004, accessed at www.msnbc.com/id/3340035/.

21. Cragin and Hoffman, xx. In 2001, the leader of the paramilitary AUC publicly complained that he had arranged the shipment of Chinese-made weapons from Suriname, but once they arrived in Brazil, "the FARC outbid him for the shipment." See Nick Rosen, "Colombia conflict highlights impact of global small arms trade," Associated Press, July 9, 2001, accessed at www.nisat.org/blackmarket/latin america&caribbean/south america/colombia2.

22. Kathi Austin, *Arms Trafficking: Closing the Net* (Washington, DC: The Fund for Peace, June 15, 2001), 12–18.

23. Faiola.

24. Nicholas Moss, "Ecuador 'failing' on arms and immigrants," *Financial Times*, May 31, 2002. "*Militar ecuatoriano llega a Colombia para analizar cohete usado en atentado a lider gremial*," *El Tiempo* (Bogota), October 16, 2003.

25. Richard L. Millett, *Colombia's Conflicts: The Spillover Effects of a Wider War* (Carlisle, PA: Strategic Studies Institute, U.S. Army War College, October 2002), 16.

26. Cragin and Hoffman, 28. Steven Dudley, "Colombian Rebels Widening Reach," *Miami Herald*, July 17, 2005.

27. "Colombia asks world to stop arming Marxist rebels," Reuters, March 9, 2004.

28. The author became aware of this in El Salvador in the 1990s, when local newspapers reported large numbers of dead "Hindus" washing up on the coast. The author traced this story to a Peruvian smuggling ship that had gone aground off the coast and dumped its cargo of Asian migrants in order to escape. For a more recent case, see "Boats with illegal immigrants sinks in Pacific, more than 100 people feared dead," Associated Press, August 17, 2005.

29. Tom Barry, *Pushing Our Borders Out*, IRC Americas Program Policy Brief, February 17, 2005, available at americas.irc-online.org/briefs/2005/0502immigration_body.html.

30. U.S. Department of State, *Trafficking in Persons Report*, July 2005, available at www.state.gov/g/tip/rls/tiprpt/2005.

31. See "BAT faces punitive racketeering charges over Colombian cigarette smuggling," press release, September 21, 2000, available at www.ash.org.uk/html/press/000921.html; and Maud S Beelman et al., "How smuggling helps lure generations of new smokers," *The Guardian*, January 31, 2000.

32. Adam M. Roberts, "The Trade in Drugs and Wildlife," *Animals Agenda* 16, no. 5 (November-December 1996), 34–35.

33. Charles Arthur, "Smuggling spells disaster for Galapagos isles," *The Independent*, February 20, 2004, accessed at http://news.independent.co.uk/world/environment/story.jsp?story=492803.

34. "*Por falsas 'gangas' muchos colombianos estan comprando carros que han sido robados en Venezuela*," *El Tiempo* (Bogota), October 1, 2005.

35. Mike Ceasar, "Life in the Land Where Filling Up an SUV Costs $3," *Christian Science Monitor*, September 28, 2005. See also "*Analaisis: El combustible gobierna la frontera Colombo-venezolana*," *El Tiempo* (Bogota), August 8, 2003. Mike Ceasar, "Even with Gas at 4 cents Per Litre, Venezuelans Still Complain," *Globe and Mail* (Toronto), October 31, 2005.

36. Peter DeShazo, "Bolivia's Deepening Crisis," *Center for Strategic and International Studies Hemisphere Focus* 13, no. 4 (December 8, 2005).

37. For a more detailed view of the political, social, and economic problems of the region, see Russell Crandall, Guadalupe Paz, and Riordan Roett, eds., *The Andes in Focus: Security, Democracy, and Economic Reforms*, (Boulder, CO: Lynne Rienner, 2005).

38. See, for example, Lloyd R. Lewis III, *Peru, Coca Trade, and Environment*, TED Case Studies Number 437 (Washington, DC: American University, January 1998), available at www.american.edu/TED/perucoca.htm; and John Otis, "War on Drugs may doom jungle towns," *Houston Chronicle*, November 28, 2004.

39. Thomas Davidson, "Terrorism and Human Smuggling Rings in South and Central America," *Terrorism Monitor* 3, no. 22 (November 17, 2005). Federal Research Division, Library of Congress, *The Nexus among Terrorists, Narcotics traffickers, Weapons Proliferators and Organized Crime Networks in Western Europe* (Washington, DC: Library of Congress, December 2002), 6–8.

CHAPTER 13

Smuggling and the Caribbean: Tainting Paradise throughout History

James L. Zackrison

One hot, sweltering day late in July of 1995, the crew of the U.S. Coast Guard *Bravo* spotted a fishing boat about 780 nautical miles west of Peru. A file search revealed that the boat was owned by a corporation on the list of suspected drug smugglers, so orders were given to detain the Panamanian-flagged fishing boat. A request to board and inspect was approved by the Panamanian government, and a party was dispatched to carry out the orders. They found almost no fishing gear on board, no fish, not even ice to keep fish fresh on board, even though the master stated that they had been fishing heavily over the past week.

This boat, the *Nataly*, had departed from Balboa, Panama, in mid July with a 10-man crew of Colombians, whose objective was not to fish but to smuggle cocaine hidden in a compartment welded to the inside of a waste oil tank. The cocaine was to be delivered somewhere along the Pacific coast of Mexico, the United States, or Canada. In the end, they arrived at their destination when the *Nataly* was towed to San Diego for further investigation by the Drug Enforcement Agency (DEA) and U.S. Customs officials. It proved to be a record arrest when more compartments were found, in all yielding 24,325.5 pounds of cocaine packaged, with green and gold stickers labeled "HHH" in 3-inch high numbers. The haul was estimated to be worth $143 million to the street-level retailers. Analysis of the ship's document revealed that it belonged to Pesquera Azteca, S.A., a Panamanian-based company that had probably contracted with the Vikingos shipyard in Cartagena, Colombia, to install the hidden smuggling compartments. The master had been paid $3,000 in advance for his service and was promised another $1,000 and an airline ticket to a destination of his choice to deliver the goods. His cabin contained a wealth of documentation on this and previous smuggling

TABLE 13.1
List of Locations Used by the *Nataly* to Smuggle Cocaine

Belize	Cat Island, Little Salvador Island
Colombia	Isla Malpelo, Cartagena, Buenaventura, Isla Gorgona, Barranquilla, Cabo de la Vela, Rio Magdalena
Dominican Republic	Monte Cristo
Ecuador	Guayaquil, Galapagos Islands
Haiti	Ile de la Tortue, Port au Prince
Honduras	Punta Herrero to Cabo Gracias a Dios
Panama	Puerto Cristobal
Puerto Rico	Bahia de Mayaguez
Suriname	Paramaribo
Trinidad and Tobago	Port of Spain
Turks and Caicos	Acklins Island
United States	Vermillion Bay, Louisiana

operations, a global positioning system (GPS) instrument with 19 locations recorded over the past 3 months, plus written instructions, frequencies to be used at various times, addresses, and charts where he had plotted hundreds of navigation lines.[1]

There are precious few examples of smuggling in the Caribbean; most cases involve goods clandestinely taken from one part of the world to another, transiting the Caribbean en route. The *Nataly* case perfectly exemplifies the situation throughout the six centuries in which smugglers have exploited the region, having spent a lot of time clandestinely ferrying cocaine from Colombia to the United States along either the Pacific coast of Mexico, through the Gulf of Mexico, along the Caribbean routes, or skirting the edge of the Atlantic Ocean.

INTRODUCTION

Most smugglers move goods through the Caribbean with almost complete impunity, using the myriad hidden bays, rivers, unmapped islands, ports, or open seas to hide or mask such activities from authorities. They do not limit themselves to the Caribbean, though theoretically it is possible to do so. Most transit the region, stopping at various destinations to drop off or pick up goods. Transiting from the Caribbean to the Pacific has been relatively simple since the Panama Canal was completed in 1914, though instances of smugglers crossing the Panamanian Isthmus overland date to the sixteenth century. One enterprising corporation set up a network of warehouses, forts, ports, and mule caravans based in the town of Natá and challenged the colonial government for over 30 years. It took a military operation combining militias from as far away as Costa Rica to eradicate the network, and the subsequent investigation implicated over 200 men

TABLE 13.2
Charts Found on the *Nataly*

Panama	Nombre de Dios to Punta Brava,
	Punta San Juan to Cabo Cadera,
	Panama to Punta Piña
Colombia	Punta Canoas to Magdalena River
	Punta San Bernardo to Punta Barux
	Port of Cartagena
	Punta Charambira to Punta Coquito
	Bahia de Buenaventura
Chile	Valparaíso to Islas Diego Ramírez
Costa Rica	Cabo Matapalo to Morro de Puercos
Cuba	Crooked Island passage to Cabo Maisi
Dominican Republic	Monte Cristo to Cabo Frances Viejo
Ecuador	Mexico to Ecuador
United States	North Pacific Ocean
	Straights of Florida
	Mississippi River to Rio Grande
Mexico	North Pacific Ocean, Mexico to Ecuador
Peru	Golfo Dulce to Bahia de Paita
Puerto Rico	Virgin Passage, Sonda de Vieques
South America	Panama to Cabo de Hornos
	East Pacific Islands
	Isla del Cano to Isla La Plata
Venezuela	Puerto Cabello to Rio Orinoco
	Gulf of Paria
	Gulf of Venezeula
	Gulf of Paria to Moroni river
Virgin Islands	Virgin Gorda to St. Thomas

representing almost all the merchant houses and government offices in the colony.

There are exceptions. For instance, when the British government allowed all its citizens to emigrate from the colonies in the 1930s, many West Indians took advantage of the law. Family links were established between the Caribbean and Europe, beginning a clandestine shipment of marijuana, hashish, and heroin, providing the new immigrant communities with all the comforts of their former homes.[2] Marijuana is cultivated primarily in Belize and Jamaica and exported within the region to the Bahamas, Guyana, Trinidad and Tobago, and smaller states in the Eastern Caribbean. Surplus production is exported outside of the region.[3]

Smuggling groups use a complicated network of methods and routes to transit the Caribbean without detection. Where pirates and smugglers once sailed on brigantines and pirogues, today there are thousands of miles of remote shorelines with secluded points where go-fast boats or low-observables transfer illicit goods to and from mother ships in international waters. Often, drugs are dropped from small airplanes at predetermined locations, where boats can rendezvous and continue the trip northward. These tactics are not new, as the archives in London and Seville demonstrate. The South Sea Company in the mid-1700s pioneered the use of a legal galleon arriving in Spanish ports and offloading its licensed 600 tons of goods. But at night, the *Royal George*'s holds would be replenished by smaller ships, so that by the end of the trade fair the company could profit from the sale of over 1,200 tons of goods.[4] Today's smugglers specialize to keep up with changing technology and tactics, often subcontracting for specific routes, such as transporting cocaine from airdrop areas near the Bay Islands in Honduras to northern Mexico or inserting cash into banks and change houses along the Texas border areas for later electronic movement to safer locations.

In the process, these myriad methods and routes not only work together to move illicit goods but also leave in their wake a trail of corruption and lawlessness. According to Anthony Bryan, "The most conspicuous threat to internal law and order in the Caribbean comes from the traffic in narcotics and the strong possibility that it might lead to the emergence of 'narco-democracies' in the region."[5] Most island nations pay some lip service to the problem of smuggling but acknowledge that the problems are the corruption and violence that accompany the clandestine movement of proscribed goods between the United States, Europe, and the South American production areas. Most of the population opposes its government's cooperation with the U.S. interdiction efforts, on account of the perceived violation to national sovereignty. Interestingly, the suborning efforts of the traffickers are not seen as an intrusion on the region's sovereignty, despite being an undue external pressure to change domestic governance.

Since the 1970s, the products of choice for Caribbean smugglers have become illegal drugs and people, moving them into the United States or to Europe from Latin America, taking money and weapons on the return trip. This chapter provides a broad overview of smuggling and trafficking through the region, describes some of the attempts to reduce the flow of illegal groups, and provides analysis on the effectiveness of these efforts.

HISTORY

The volume of products being smuggled and the profits available from the business are impressive. The DEA estimated that $60 billion in drug and organized crime proceeds are laundered through the Caribbean every year. In 2002, about 145 tons of cocaine available in the United States flowed through the Caribbean corridor.[6]

Smuggling in the Caribbean began when the Spanish empire first imposed regulations on the movement of people and goods into the region in 1497. Those regulations failed to stop either the *piratas luteranos* (as the Spaniards called them) or the "private trade" (as the English called it)—or even the Spanish colonists themselves from using the services of the smugglers to evade onerous taxes and prohibitions. Throughout history, such illicit commerce has evolved into what many refer to as a culture of smuggling, an ambivalence toward national or international regulations or laws that affects the very survival of many of the region's governments.

It is interesting to compare the routes and hiding places used by smugglers during the past five centuries, noting how little these have changed over time. All have taken advantage either of the lack of effective government presence or of tolerant government attitudes, moving rapidly as policy and enforcement changed. Early on this meant pirate havens in Tortuga Island in what is today Haiti. Later, as English, Dutch, and French governments sponsored or took possession of the hideouts, this meant small islands on the periphery of the Spanish holdings, such as Barbados, Guadeloupe, St. Vincent, Curaçao, Providence Island, or Roatan. As these governments solidified control through diplomatic treaties, the smugglers moved with the governments to larger holdings in Jamaica, Haiti, Louisiana, Trinidad, Bermuda, Virginia, and New York. Today, these same places are being used by smugglers, moving the same types of products: people, tobacco, clothes, animals, drugs, weapons, and money. The destination of the goods in most cases has changed, as the Spanish empire gave way to British commercial control, and later to the influence and proximity of the United States. Some products being moved reflect changes in technology, as do the vehicles being used to move them, to include electronics and cars moved on self-powered ships or aircraft, increasing the speed at which the goods are moved to market.

GEOGRAPHY

Anyone who has vacationed in the Caribbean knows why the region is so well suited for smuggling: small islands, great climate, little industry or agriculture, and a high level of movement of people (mostly tourists)—a virtual paradise for relaxation. Unfortunately, this relaxation also permeates much of the attention to rules or laws, as underfunded governments attempt to maintain a semblance of order. The geography seems to have been planned for smuggling operations between the three major land masses of North and South America and Europe. The Bahamas alone has over 700 islands and cays, with hundreds of places to hide and never be detected. All the islands straddle three major sea lines of communication (SLOCs) connecting the Panama Canal, the South Atlantic, and the North Atlantic to the Gulf of Mexico. There are thousands of ships and millions of tons of goods transported in all directions.[7] Air routes crisscross the region unimpeded by ocean currents, national boundaries, though occasionally the weather forces a deviation to land for the safety of the crew and passengers.

ROUTES

The case of the *Nataly* demonstrates the variety of routes used by the drug smugglers. It also demonstrates that it is almost impossible to analyze smuggling in the Caribbean only, as smugglers do not often pay attention to the analytical boundaries of historians and criminologists. Since the days of the Spanish empire, smuggling networks have operated throughout the region, crossing borders and landmasses between the Caribbean, Atlantic, and Pacific with impunity, choosing routes according to risk or whim.

Routes reflect the goods moved therein and react to countermeasures and market change. Early smuggling (1520s–1630s) began in Europe and moved goods into the areas populated by Europeans: from Spain, England, Holland, and France to the islands of Cuba, Hispaniola, Puerto Rico, and the mainland regions of New Spain (Mexico and Central America), Tierra Firme (Panama, Colombia), and the Main (Colombia, Venezuela).[8] Most smugglers during this time took their wares directly to the markets, or to bays or islands nearby, making contact discreetly before exchanging goods. Bolder merchants, or those wealthy enough to suborn government officials, used the Spanish fleets to carry goods to the Americas, either off register or registered inaccurately (a tactic known today as the false manifest).

Later, during the seventeenth, eighteenth, and into the nineteenth centuries, the routes evolved to reflect changes in national holdings and commercial patterns. As Spain increasingly emphasized the areas of the empire that produced treasure (New Spain and Peru), the peripheral areas increased in size, allowing England to take over Jamaica, Barbados, the Bahamas, St. Thomas, St. Kitts, Anguilla, Trinidad and Tobago; Holland took over Curaçao, Bonaire, Aruba, Saba, and St. Maarten; and France occupied Haiti, Louisiana, and Guadeloupe. Smuggling routes changed as merchants were allowed to ship goods legally from their home countries to the colonies. The smuggling routes were thus shortened to the navigation between Kingston, Jamaica, and Cuba, or from Curaçao to Caracas. North American colonial participation in the illicit trade grew during this period, competing with fellow Englishmen in Jamaica and Barbados. Thus, the smuggling became more concentrated in the Caribbean region.

A new development reflected changes in Spanish policy as well. Foreign merchants were able, through a commercial house in Spain, to ship goods for sale in the Americas. Many shipped more goods than they reported: in some cases as high as 95 percent of the goods on a given ship had not been registered or paid import duties.[9] The return trip also reflected this new tactic, as silver shipments from Peru and New Spain reached similar percentages of illegality. A second development was the Spanish policy of contracting with foreigners for slaves. Contractors and subcontractors shipped their human cargo from Africa to the *entrepôt* ports in Guadeloupe, Curaçao, Barbados, and Jamaica, and then on to the Spanish markets. The *asiento* (government contract) agreement included a clause allowing the merchants to carry a specified volume of clothes and foodstuffs, theoretically to care for the human cargo, but this was always used as a pretext for smuggling. In fact, many of the South Sea Company's slave ships carried only a few slaves, as the income from selling the clothes and foodstuffs was much more profitable, in part because of the severe restrictions imposed from Madrid (and often ignored in the Americas). A third development was the consolidation of the smuggling by large companies, such as the Dutch West India Company or the English Royal Africa Company. The creation of these monopolistic giants reduced the number of small merchants, taking larger shares of the easily saturated markets in the Americas.

During the national period (after the colonies achieved their independence from Spain), most of the smuggling routes remained the same. The only change was that government officials who had participated wholeheartedly in subverting Spanish trade regulations now ignored the prohibitive power of the national governments. Merchants who had ignored Spanish law now ignored the prohibitions imposed on an increasing flow of goods (primarily silver) from the new republics toward Europe. Britain especially was an avid participant, using the Royal Navy to overwhelm the national forces and safely carry silver back to London or Bristol.[10]

During the twentieth century, much of the smuggling involved moving goods produced in Europe and the United States to Central and South America, responding to protectionist commercial policy. The flow of goods remained the same, moving west and south through the Caribbean, with money flowing north and east. As these protectionist policies were abandoned, so too was the trade in smuggled goods.

PROHIBITION

After the Harrison Act of 1914 and the constitutional amendment prohibiting alcoholic beverages, yet another development took place as smugglers sought to fill the demand for drugs and alcohol now considered illegal to own or use. This transformed the smuggler into a trafficker and greatly increased the risk of serious penalty for failure (for example, getting caught). This changed the nature of smuggling in general, reversing the flow of goods. Most destinations were now in the United States and Europe for drugs and to South America for the money.

On January 17, 1920, the implementation of the Volstead Act (the 18th amendment to the U.S. Constitution) launched one of the greatest periods of smuggling in American history. Canadian whisky suppliers, aware that the law would do little to reduce the demand for alcoholic drinks, rushed cargos to the Bahamas. Within a year this smuggling route carried over 100,000 cases of whisky per week. Prior to Prohibition, the Bahamas normally imported £15,000 worth of wine and spirits per year (1918 figures). In

1922, the figure was £1,028,000. Of note, the Caribbean bases were merely stopping-off points as the smuggling took the whiskey from the Canadian production centers to the islands of St. Pierre and Miquelon in Newfoundland, and from there to various southern states after touching at one or two of the Bahamas islands. In 1926, an agreement with the British government allowed the U.S. Coast Guard to inspect ships in the Bahamas, which slowed the traffic somewhat by seizing 330 ships during the next year.[11]

PRODUCTS

The products smuggled through the Caribbean always reflect government restrictions imposed in the destination countries. Spain attempted to restrict all goods, allowing only Spanish goods shipped on Spanish ships by Spanish merchants to Spanish colonies. Thus, as insufficient Spanish goods were provided, foreign smugglers provided whatever the market requested, from foodstuffs to furniture. The primary demand was for cloth and clothes, but any manufactured product shipped found a buyer.

North American colonies entered the market by underbidding competitors to provide wheat to almost all Spanish ports. Interestingly, even during wartime the demand for wheat was such that any ship carrying it was given license to enter Spanish ports. During the War of Jenkins' Ear (1739–1745), Jamaican ships carried wheat from Virginia to Cartagena, knowing that much of it was converted to biscuit supplied to the Spanish navy to patrol against the Royal Navy. Profit outweighed nationalism to the point where many smugglers carried between a third to half of its load in wheat, the rest loaded with other contraband goods that sold for a higher profit.[12]

Smuggling in the other direction involved primarily the silver and gold used to pay for the European goods, though colonial products provided the bulk of the volume shipped. Therefore, ships used silver and gold as ballast and loaded the cargo holds with dye woods, hides, tobacco, medicines, cacao (for making chocolate), and spices native to the Americas (cinnamon and pepper mostly). As Spanish taxes on silver increased in the mid-1500s, Spanish merchants began smuggling their silver onto the foreign ships, paying a commission for bills of exchange delivered to families or agents in Madrid and Seville. The treasure fleets returning to Seville also carried a high volume of silver off register, though the risk of confiscation upon arrival was high. The Spanish kings' frequent confiscation, even of legally owned and shipped treasure, merely encouraged merchants to use foreigners to ensure their profits arrived intact.

Main stopping points for trafficking goods and drugs into the United States include Jamaica, the Bahamas, the Dominican Republic, and Haiti, though probably every island in the Caribbean has at one point been used in some way or another by the traffickers. Other popular stopping points include Trinidad and Tobago, Curaçao, Bonaire, Cuba, and many of the

Lesser Antilles.[13] Geography is a major contributor to the ease of smuggling operations (for example, Trinidad and Tobago provides an international border beyond which Venezuelan police forces chasing smugglers down the Orinoco River cannot cross).

The Bahamas have always been a haven for smuggling, and especially so during the past 50 years. The former English colony has 29 islands and 661 cays only 60 miles from Florida. The national jurisdiction covers over 250,000 miles of ocean in which boats can hide with ease and impunity. By the end of the 1970s, entire fleets of speedboats lining up to offload drugs from mother ships were the norm. Local residents often became involved as day laborers or lookouts. In 1979, police commander Lawrence Major stopped a small plane and found 247 pounds of cocaine worth $2 billion; he later found a supply of marijuana on Black Rock (Grand Bahama Island) 6 feet high and more than 2 miles long. One attempt to stop a drug transshipment led to a flotilla of 15 speedboats chasing the DEA and national police with machinegun fire. Police have been ordered to stand guard while drugs are transferred from aircraft to go-fast boats. Central Bank shipments of cash to Bimini during 1978–1983 totaled $31 million—but none of it could be linked to legitimate businesses on the island.[14]

Early in the 1980s, smugglers used fishing boats and coastal freighters as mother ships, with speedboats to offload the goods close to shore. Interdiction was low and had little effect on the volume of smuggling. In 1982, the South Florida Task Group had some early successes, and the smugglers switched to aircraft drops to high-speed boats. In 1986, the U.S. military became involved, bringing in more intelligence assets, such as the Joint Task Force-4 in Key West.[15] Smugglers moved away from south Florida and the Bahamas, increasingly using Puerto Rico and Lesser Antilles as their primary route. They began using smaller aircraft with GPS and high-tech communications gear to coordinate operations. The U.S. Coast Guard designed new radar to help find these smaller ships. The Mona and Anegada passages are now monitored heavily. In the 1990s, the multinational counterdrug operations began, with cooperation of U.S., Dutch, British, and other local governments. Indeed, there was a change in attitude in the governments of Central America, as transit smugglers began exploiting local populations and a growing consumption problem ensued.[16]

One of the primary products smuggled through the Caribbean is money. All the products shipped clandestinely have to be paid for, and the proceeds need to be moved illegally to distance them from the initial activity. This process is primarily done electronically after the initial placement of cash into the banking system and generally involves moving through accounts all over the world. But the Caribbean is a haven for offshore banking, in part because it is close to the United States, has an excellent communication system, has a large English-speaking population, and hosts a large population of expatriates managing such systems while enjoying the environment of paradise. There are a plethora of legal systems linked variously to the former colonial powers, little cooperation among the many nations—none of which effectively confronts an extremely flexible and maneuverable system of crime.[17] Perhaps the best climate for laundering money is the banking system provided in the Cayman Islands, where an estimated $3 to $10 billion per year in specifically criminal money moves with ease. In 1968, a Mutual Legal Assistance Treaty was signed between the Cayman Island government and the United States for criminal matters. Unfortunately, this treaty has proved grossly insufficient, as it only relates to drug money. Security Exchange Commission and Internal Revenue Service crimes were exempted, and complaints are handled through "letters rogatory" on the basis of "comity" (deference and mutual respect rather than obligation). In this way the Caymans sought treatment as sovereign equals in issues relating to the country's main industry—banking.[18]

Cocaine is smuggled through what is known as the "transit zone," basically any route used between the production centers in Colombia, Brazil, Peru, Bolivia, and Venezuela, and the consumption zones in North America and Europe. In the English-speaking Caribbean, the major transit zone includes Antigua and Barbuda, Dominica, Grenada, St. Kitts and Nevis, St. Lucia, St. Vincent and the Grenadines, Anguilla, Monserrat, and the British Virgin Islands. Major shipments transit the Greater Antilles, using Cuba, Haiti, and the Dominican Republic as springboards to penetrate Puerto Rico or the continental United States.[19]

The drug smuggling business brings with it many problems for the transit zone countries, political instability and corruption being two of the largest and most intractable. But other smuggling is attracted to the well-established routes as well. For instance, an inquiry commissioned by Prime Minister Vere Bird, Sr., in the early 1990s revealed that a large cache of Israeli-made weapons and ammunition were being shipped to the Colombian Medellín Cartel, using Antiguan defense force cover, involving Israelis, Panamanians, and Colombians, as well as high-level Antiguan officials. Cultivation of marijuana on St. Kitts and Nevis attracts cocaine smugglers, who seek to use the clandestine links already established by the locals, sending go-fast boats through the national waters of nearby Guadeloupe, St. Martin, Anguilla, Monserrat, the British Virgin Islands, and Puerto Rico for protection. St. Vincent and the Grenadines have attracted the attention of Colombian drug mafias for decades, forging links to the political leadership. St. Vincent's program to license ships under flag of convenience laws makes it almost impossible to trace crimes to the ship owners, further attracting smugglers who need to move cocaine, weapons, and money without discovery.[20] Haiti is an easy target for organized crime because of the poor governance there that produces rampant poverty, corruption, weak police, and faltering democratic institutions. It is no surprise that in this environment U.S. law

TABLE 13.3
Drug Seizures in Kilograms (2002)

Country	Marijuana	Cocaine	Hash Oil	Heroin
Antigua and Barbuda	211.50	51.40		
Bahamas	11.46	2.45		
Barbados	690.00	47.00		
Dominican Republic	1,700.00	1,100.00		
Grenada	357.00	77.00		
Jamaica	26,630.00	3,390.00	497.00	
Netherlands Antilles	3,372.00	1,047.00		72.00
St. Lucia	230.00	152.00		
St. Vincent and the Grenadines	7,400.00	13.20		
Trinidad and Tobago	772.00			14.50

Source: U.S. Drug Enforcement Agency, *The Drug Threat in the Caribbean: A Threat Assessment,* DEA–03014 (Washington, DC: September 2003), accessed at www.dea.gov.

enforcement operations interdicted over 4 tons of cocaine en route between Haiti and Miami in 2002.

Cuba presents a different problem for both the smuggler and law enforcer. Political differences with most of the region have produced an environment in which the black market and clandestine economic activity thrives, albeit at a higher risk than elsewhere. This risk is ameliorated by the government's declining budget, the island's decaying infrastructure, and continual fuel shortages, which produce spotty counterdrug cooperation.[21]

LESSONS LEARNED

Lessons learned from drug interdiction operations in the Caribbean include:

- No individual factor accounts for the successes of the operation.
- The combination of mode and route shifts are forced on the smugglers to make them vulnerable.
- Successes in air interdiction force smugglers to use ships.
- Pacific routes are used for larger loads.
- Intelligence is critical to successful operations.
- The interaction of government agencies and foreign governments helps increase success.[22]

Many academic studies have been made on the effect of smuggling on governance in the region. Anthony Bryan, for example, posits a series of

TABLE 13.4
Preferred Products, Routes, and Methods

Country	Production	Trans-ship	Go-fast	Container	Air Freight or Drop	Hidden Compartment	Destination	Money Laundering	Comment
Aruba		X		X	X		Europe		Low-price cocaine indicates easy availability
Bahamas		X	X	X	X	X	United States		Aircraft overfly Cuba for protection
Barbados		X	X	X			United States, Canada, Europe	X	Important international banking center, use of cruise ships
Cayman Islands		X						X	Occasional smuggling, mostly offshore banking center
Cuba		X					Europe		
Dominican Republic		X	X	X			United States, Puerto Rico	X	Illegal migration overlaps drug smuggling via Mona Passage, overland from Haiti
French Guyana		X				X	Europe, United States		Brazil, Venezuela to Europe
Grenada		X		X		X	United States		Brazil, Venezuela, Colombia to United States
Haiti		X	X	X	X	X	United States Panama	X	Cocaine overland to Dominican Republic, by sea to United States; money in bulk to Panama

Country					Primary destination		Comments
Jamaica	X	X		X	United States, Europe	X	Major producer of marijuana and hash oil to Europe; links South American smugglers with Bahamas insertion specialists
Dutch Antilles	X	X	X			X	Banking ties to the Netherlands, proximity to Puerto Rico (150 miles)
Puerto Rico	X	X	X	X	United States	X	Money laundering through Casas de Cambio
St. Lucia	X				United States, Lesser Antilles		Marijuana, body-carry or ingestion by couriers
St. Vincent and the Grenadines	X		X		Lesser Antilles	X	Major marijuana producer, sells citizenship, front companies
Suriname	X	X		X	Europe	X	From Brazil, Venezuela to Amsterdam
Trinidad and Tobago	X	X	X		United States		Pirogue shipping from Venezuela, 7 miles away
Turks and Caicos	X			X		X	Proximity to United States attracts smugglers

Source: U.S. Drug Enforcement Agency, *The Drug Threat in the Caribbean: A Threat Assessment*, DEA-03014 (Washington, DC: September 2003), accessed at www.dea.gov.

recommendations to improve U.S. foreign policy in the region in hopes of improving the economic and political climate, which would result in a better chance of reducing the flow of drugs through the region.[23] Bryan's list reads:

- Promote trade liberalization (North American Free Trade Agreement) to enhance regional prosperity.
- Provide technical assistance to implement such economic reforms in order to combat drug trade, political corruption, and money laundering.
- Provide technical assistance to enhance law enforcement and cooperative security, as well as to strengthen democracy and human rights.
- Increase close cooperation in security issues.
- Include other players in the region (for example, Great Britain, Canada, France, and the Netherlands).
- Increase dialogue to ensure a peaceful transition to democracy in Haiti and Cuba.

These recommendations are based on the idea that smuggling results from the incentives provided when government policies ignore natural forces of the market. Prohibitions and high taxation are the worst offenders; restrictions on usage are a close second. But this analysis conveniently ignores the fact that most of today's smuggling involves illegal, highly addictive drugs that produce profit margins of over 95 percent. Increasing the economic performance in Jamaica by 2 to 3 percent, for example, will not wean the posses from profitability. Likewise, reducing unemployment in Trinidad and Tobago by even as much as 5 percent will not reduce that nation's geographical importance as an outlet for Colombian cocaine shipped down the Orinoco River. Only reducing the supply and demand of illegal drugs will reduce this type of smuggling.

In terms of law enforcement, it appears that the lack of a coherent anti-smuggling plan reduces the chance of success of any efforts to stop smuggling. The common comparison to a balloon is appropriate in relation to specific antismuggling tactics. Enforcing one tactic on one side of the balloon only results in a bulge at another point—and pushing on two or three points at a time produces the same result. Only by deflating the balloon entirely can the problem be solved. A corollary would be that overall increases in security should reduce smuggling, a theory supported by the fact that after the terrorist attacks in New York and Washington, DC, on September 11, drug smuggling across the border with Mexico dropped by about 80 percent because of the perception that security had been increased. There was no similar decrease in drug smuggling through the Caribbean, though illegal immigration did drop significantly, because of the same perception.[24]

Other lessons learned include:

- Smugglers disregard the law; all use corruption to succeed. Thus, smuggling leads to corruption in the government forces.

- Smugglers are criminals; all resort to violence at some point in order to enforce contracts or to threaten antismuggling efforts.
- Smuggling of one product leads to smuggling of other products.

The best lesson for today's government leaders is that they can ignore history at their own peril. Smuggling is not a new phenomenon in the Caribbean or elsewhere, and neither are the efforts to stop it. The decision to restrict the market system is a political one, made by political leaders either as a reflection of societal values or a governing philosophy of protecting individuals from themselves. Thus, any effort to stop smuggling must likewise be a political decision. When done in concert with society, it is theoretically possible to stop smuggling, but history records no such coincidence to prove the hypothesis. What is true is that law enforcement cannot hope to succeed without adequate strategic guidance from political leaders. This fact has been proved over and over throughout the history of smuggling in the Caribbean.

CONCLUSIONS

An analysis of the *Nataly* case demonstrates the flexible nature of smuggling. The ship was probably chosen because it fit the profile of a myriad other boats found throughout the Caribbean. It was used whenever a platform was required to move goods clandestinely or wherever the master could find a job suitable to his skills. That meant crossing the Panama Canal occasionally, though apparently it spent most of its time sailing throughout the Caribbean islands. Its point of departure was usually the Magdalena region of Colombia or the eastern coastline of Venezuela. It sailed along the northern coastlines of the greater Antilles, delivering drugs to either Florida or Louisiana.

The *Nataly* experience typifies smuggling over time, as people seek to sell goods in spite of government impositions and restrictions. These businesses are flexible to the extreme, reacting to government action in order to protect their illicit incomes. The example of the switch in routes from Mexico to the Caribbean following President Bill Clinton's antidrug policy directive in 1993 is illustrative: Within 3 months, the percentage of cocaine shipped along each route was reversed. Prior to the change in strategy, 80 percent of the cocaine entered the United States through Mexico; afterwards, 80 percent was shipped along the Caribbean routes. Immense and immediate changes are possible when smugglers are confronted by changing government strategies. The smugglers succeeded, too, as there was no net drop in the volume of cocaine sold in the United States.[25]

The culture of smuggling that permeates the Caribbean brings serious problems to the governments and societies of the region. Among these are political insecurity and instability brought through corruption and loss of law and order; military security as arms traffickers violate territorial control and increase the possibility of terrorism; economic insecurity resulting from capital flight and declining tourism; social concerns arising from an increased use of drugs and the crime surrounding such problems; ecological insecurity as the drug mafias create pollution, erosion, and desertification because of their operational methods; and, finally, crime brought by the corruption and political violence.

NOTES

1. The data for this case was found in archives of the Office of the Historian, U.S. Coast Guard Headquarters, Washington, DC, in the files entitled "Law Enforcement."

2. Neville Williams, *Contraband Cargoes: Seven Centuries of Smuggling* (London: Longmans, Green and Company, 1959), 263.

3. Baytoram Ramharack, "Drug trafficking and money laundering in the Caribbean 'mini'-states and dependent territories: The U.S. response," *Round Table*, issue 335 (July 1995), 319–332.

4. Vera Lee Brown, "The South Sea Company and Contraband Trade," *American Historical Review* 31, no. 4 (July 1926), 662–678.

5. Anthony Bryan, "The New Clinton Administration and the Caribbean: Trade, Security and Regional Politics," *Journal of InterAmerican Studies and World Affairs* 39, no. 1 (Spring 1997), 106.

6. U.S. Drug Enforcement Agency, *The Drug Threat in the Caribbean: A Threat Assessment*, DEA–03014 (Washington, DC: September 2003), accessed at www.dea.gov.

7. The Panama Canal alone sees almost 12,000 ships per year, transporting nearly 1 million tons per day. "Panama Canal Turns 90," Canal News, August 16, 2004, available at www.pancanal.com/eng/cgi-bin/news/boletin.cgi?submit=Consulta&item=143.

8. There are many studies on this subject, such as Héctor R. Feliciano Ramos, *El Contrabando Inglés en el Caribe y el Golfo de México (1748–1778)*, El V Centenario del Descubrimiento de América, vol. 10 (Sevilla: Publicaciones de la Excma. Diputación Provincial de Sevilla, 1990); Clarence Henry Haring, *Trade and Navigation Between Spain and the Indies in the Time of the Hapsburgs*, Harvard Economic Studies, vol. 19 (Cambridge, MA: Harvard University Press, 1918); and Jean O. McLachlan, *Trade and Peace with Old Spain, 1667–1750: A Study of the Influence of Commerce on Anglo-Spanish Diplomacy in the First Half of the Eighteenth Century* (New York: Octogon Books, 1974).

9. Enriqueta Vila Vilar, *"Las ferias de Portobelo: Apariencia y realidad del comercio con Indias,"* Anuario de Estudios Americanos, vol. 39 (Sevilla: Publicaciones de la Excma. Diputación Provincial de Sevilla, 1982).

10. See John Mayo, "Consuls and Silver Contraband on Mexico's West Coast in the Era of Santa Anna," *Journal of Latin American Studies* 19, no. 2 (November 1987), 389–411.

11. Williams, 247–253.

12. See Lance Grahn, *The Political Economy of Smuggling: Regional Informal Economies in Early Bourbon New Granada* (Boulder, CO: Westview Press, 1997).

13. Reuters Report, March 1, 2003.

14. Bruce Bullington, "A Smuggler's Paradise: Cocaine Trafficking through the Bahamas," in *War on Drugs: Studies in the Failure of U.S. Narcotics Policy*, ed. Alfred W. McCoy and Alan A. Block (Boulder, CO: Westview Press, 1992), 214–219.

15. The Posse Comitatus Act of 1878, 18 U.S.C. 1385, prohibits the use of U.S. military assets in law enforcement operations. The U.S. Navy and Marine Corps are proscribed from direct participation by Department of Defense policy.

16. Christopher Tomney and Joseph Di Renzo III, "Countering High Tech Drug Smugglers," *Proceedings* (July 1996), 59–61.

17. Anthony P. Maingot, "Dirty Money," *Freedom Review* 26, no. 4 (July/August 1995), 5–11.

18. Ibid.

19. Ramharack.

20. Ibid.

21. Reuters Report, March 1, 2003.

22. Office of National Drug Control Policy (ONDCP), White House Drug Policy Director McCaffrey and United States Interdiction Coordinator Kramek Release Details on Special Maritime Drug Interdiction Operations Within the Last 11 Weeks (Washington, DC: ONDCP Public Affairs Office, November 14, 1996).

23. Bryan, 113.

24. Patricia Kine, "Smugglers Don't Miss a Beat," *Navy Times* 51, no. 2 (October 2001), 56.

25. James L. Zackrison, "North America," *Strategic Assessment 1997: Flashpoints and Force Structure* (Washington, DC: National Defense University Press, 1997), 80.

CHAPTER 14

The Rise and Diversification of Human Smuggling and Trafficking into the United States

Louise I. Shelley

The majority of new residents arriving in the United States enter the country illegally. Legal migration and guest worker programs satisfy only part of the demand for cheap labor in the United States. Therefore, millions of individuals who enter the United States illegally find employment. The majority of illegal entries into the United States are people arriving from Latin America. But illegal immigrants are drawn from all over the world. Millions enter illegally by crossing the U.S.-Mexican border and, to a far lesser extent, the U.S.-Canadian border. As controls have increased on the southern border, illegal migrants increasingly use human smugglers to facilitate their crossing. A large and sophisticated industry has grown to meet the demand that can draw on the smuggling base of the narcotics traffickers.[1]

The contemporary American reality of migration to the United States recalls that of an earlier period of U.S. history. From the time of the Nation's founding, individuals could enter as slaves and indentured servants. Such entry is now forbidden. Recent prosecutions and revelations by human rights and legal aid groups, however, reveal the enormity of human exploitation in the United States as hundreds of thousands are in forced labor, indentured servitude, and are enslaved in prostitution, domestic service, and as laborers.[2] Congress has responded to these revelations by passing the Trafficking in Persons Act in 2000 and creating numerous programs to address contemporary slavery in the United States. In contrast, the limited number of criminal cases against human smugglers and traffickers in the United States reveals the ineffectiveness of the government to address this massive problem of human smuggling and trafficking through the criminal justice system.[3]

Current illegal immigration into the United States strongly resembles the structure of early migration in the seventeenth, eighteenth, and early nineteenth centuries. The fundamental difference is that in this earlier period of U.S. history, individuals *could* legally enter the territory that is now the United States as slaves or indentured servants. This was not an infrequent occurrence as approximately 120,000 indentured servants came to Maryland and Virginia in the seventeenth century representing a majority of the immigrant laborers. They assumed a substantial role in these states' economies.[4] The practice of indentured servants endured on a lesser scale in subsequent centuries and was only outlawed at the same time as slavery.

The United States, in contrast with Western Europe, has less human trafficking, and a greater proportion of its illegal migrants are smuggled. This balance may be changing in Western Europe as enormous numbers of Africans are trying to enter there using the services of smugglers.[5] The higher economic growth rate of the United States, its openness to foreigners, and its capacity to absorb both legal and illegal migrants stand in sharp contrast to the experience of Western Europe. The different U.S. perspective on migration helps explain the long-term American tolerance of human smuggling that has allowed approximately 10.5 million illegal immigrants to reside in the United States with little intervention by the authorities.[6]

Addressing the rise of smuggling has not been a top governmental priority until 2006, when President George W. Bush visited the U.S.-Mexican border and the Border Patrol Academy seeking greater vigilance in policing American borders.[7] This contrasts sharply with Western Europe where the smuggling issue has been a central concern of Europeans since the late 1990s. This is a consequence of a strong sense of national identity, the anti-immigrant backlash, and the coupling of transnational crime with illegal migration.[8]

During the twentieth century, the illegal movement of individuals into the United States was once largely facilitated by *coyotes*, small-scale entrepreneurs who helped temporary workers and immigrants cross the U.S.-Mexican border.[9] Increasingly, the individual facilitator has been replaced by the crime group. Many Mexicans were once able to enter the United States without "professional assistance"; however, that situation is now rare. With increased border enforcement, more illegal aliens from Mexico rely on professional smugglers, or *polleros*, and pay more to enter the country. The International Organization for Migration estimated in 1999 that 70 percent of illegal aliens from Mexico used professional smugglers to assist them crossing the border.[10] Immigration and Customs Enforcement estimates that this percentage has risen since then.[11] The farther the individual has to travel to enter the United States illegally, the more likely the smuggled individual will utilize the services of a crime group. Chinese and other Asians, as well as individuals from the former Soviet Union, often arrive having paid smugglers significant sums to enter the United States.[12]

America presently faces competing objectives—security and economic growth. The rise of security concerns post–September 11 has tightened controls on the borders. But, at the same time, the demand for cheap and available labor has resulted in a consistent demand for immigrant laborers, even if they are not legal. Therefore, while there has been an increasing drive by many sectors of American society to limit illegal migration and to address human trafficking, there is also little action by government to penalize employers who employ smuggled aliens or trafficked people. The Federal Government, through its *Trafficking in Persons Report*, ranks other countries on their capacity to address the problem of human smuggling, but a realistic appraisal of the United States would reveal an absence of its own political will or allocation of resources to address the trafficking and smuggling problem seriously.

FORCES MOTIVATING SMUGGLING AND TRAFFICKING

The incentive for the massive illegal population movement derives from the grave economic and political situations in many parts of the world. Since the 1980s and the collapse of the Soviet Union, there has been a rise of regional conflicts. Many of these conflicts have occurred in Latin America, which is a primary source of illegal immigrants to the United States. Conflicts in Colombia, El Salvador, and southern Mexico are just some of the more important to affect the region. Many caught in these political conflicts enter the United States illegally because they face a long struggle and often little chance of obtaining political asylum.

Contributing to this large-scale illicit movement of people is the widening economic disparity between the developed and the transitional developing economies. Economic growth is confined almost entirely to the developed world, whereas population growth is confined to the developing world. Therefore, every year the gap between the resources available per capita in the developed and developing world grows.[13] Aggravating the absence of capital in the developing world is the globalization of corruption that has permitted elites in developing and transitional countries to steal state resources and transfer this money to offshore havens and Western banking centers.

Globalization, according to the Center for Global Development, has been particularly hard on women, who have suffered disproportionately in the economic dislocations that have accompanied globalization. Therefore, women and children are disproportionately victims of the slavery observed in the United States as they are trafficked into prostitution and enslaved as domestic workers.

The rise of a global market has contributed to dramatic increases in cross-border movement of people and goods. Contrary to the popular notion that free trade is conducive to a more open and transparent environment, this is not the case with regard to illicit commodities.[14] In recent years, since the enactment of the North American Free Trade Agreement, there has been a rise in illicit trade and population movement across the southern and northern borders of the United States, as the illicit movement has been hidden within the larger licit movement of people and goods.

The demand for low-cost labor and the existence of individuals willing to engage in menial labor means that there is work for most of those who enter the United States illegally. The illegal workers are employed in every region of the United States, including parts that were once almost entirely homogeneous, such as the upper Midwest. Economic opportunities for illegal workers throughout the United States have led to the proliferation of smuggling networks delivering workers to many regions of the country.

People seeking greater political freedom and economic opportunities are trafficked and smuggled into the United States by land, sea, and air from many regions of the world.[15] Estimates by the Pew Hispanic Center in 2004 suggest that approximately 10.3 million people are residing in the United States illegally, of which 80 to 85 percent of the undocumented population are of Mexican origin.[16] That number would be even larger if approximately 1 million individuals were not detained at the border each year. The vast majority of these illegal entrants are made to leave voluntarily.[17] Therefore, approximately 3 percent of those residing in the United States are residing illegally.

THE BUSINESS OF HUMAN SMUGGLING AND TRAFFICKING

The 1990s have seen an enormous rise in transnational organized crime. Most major transnational organized crime groups are based in the developing and transitional countries. Many of them make enormous profits by moving their commodities between their home bases and the affluent markets of the developed world. The most lucrative of their illicit activities is the international drug trade, which is estimated by the United Nations at $500 billion annually and is thought to represent 2 percent of the world's economy.[18] Intense law enforcement, military, and intelligence resources are currently deployed against the drug traffickers. While this has not curtailed the drug trade, it has increased the risks for drug traffickers, which in turn has reduced profits.

Most organized criminals, as rational actors, make conscious business decisions. Facing increasing risks of detection and severe punishment in the drug trade, many have chosen to enter into the area of human smuggling and trafficking. Others, according to the United Nations, have diversified their activities into the trafficking arena.[19] Facilitating the phenomenal growth of this sector is the fact that trafficking and smuggling in human beings is rarely prosecuted. Despite intense efforts to increase trafficking prosecutions, the

U.S. Department of State has identified less than 8,000 cases worldwide, in contrast to the tens of thousands of cases generated in relation to drug trafficking.[20]

The number of cases of human trafficking and smuggling prosecuted in the United States annually is minimal, with well under the 500 total and a small number of convictions annually.[21] Unlike the drug trade, the risks of detection are low, as are the risks of incarceration and asset forfeiture. Under these conditions, it is hardly surprising that human smuggling and trafficking is one of the fastest growing forms of organized crime. Several years ago, it was estimated that human smuggling generated over $6 billion in profits annually, while current estimates are $9 billion or higher.[22] Certain crime rings in Mexico that smuggle individuals to the United States are thought to generate over a billion dollars annually. The Mexican government estimates that the 15 to 20 smuggling groups operating in Sonora alone smuggle an average of 840,000 people a year, netting nearly $1.3 billion dollars annually.[23]

TRAFFICKERS

The smugglers and traffickers of people into the United States are enormously diverse. They range the gambit from diplomats and employees of multinational organizations who traffic a young woman for domestic labor to the large organizations of Asia that specialize in human smuggling and trafficking. There is every size of organization in between the family business and the multinational criminal organization. The high social status of some human traffickers contrasts sharply with that of drug traffickers who originate primarily from poorer families or criminal environments such as *triad* (Chinese organized crime) or mafia families. In Baja California, there is increasing use of children as smugglers.[24] Women assume a larger role in this form of transnational crime than others; they serve as recruiters, madams, and even kingpins of major smuggling operations. The prosecution of Sister Ping for smuggling large numbers of Chinese aliens and of Rimma Fetissova for running a large-scale prostitution ring in Los Angeles with trafficked women are illustrative of this point.[25]

The profitability of human smuggling and trafficking results in groups that have no prior history of involvement in trafficking moving into this activity. Illustrative of this is the recent involvement of U.S. motorcycle gangs in the kidnapping of smuggled aliens.[26] These gangs have historically engaged in extortion, drug trafficking, and many forms of contraband trade, but they are also now active in human trafficking. MS-13 gang members have diversified their crime activities to include human smuggling.[27] Deported members of the gang now operate on the Mexican-Guatemalan border in the state of Chiapas, where they have established a smuggling operation for persons, drugs, and weapons. MS-13 also has used the cargo railroad that departs from the border city of Tapachula to transport its smuggled cargo to northern Mexico. Some have also implicated the gang in the coercion of smuggled aliens into their criminal enterprises.[28]

Moving people distances requires significant logistical planning and expense. The discovery of large tunnels constructed along the U.S.-Mexican border that can smuggle both people and drugs points to the enormous investment in infrastructure made by the smugglers on the southern U.S. border.[29] Smuggling groups can also move people en masse in buses, trucks, or boats across the border. Some cross on foot and then walk hundreds of miles through the desert. Hundreds die each year of starvation and dehydration, having been deceived or abandoned by their traffickers.[30]

Other crime groups that do not enjoy such proximity to the United States engage in elaborate procedures to gain entry for those they seek to smuggle. These include the production of false documents such as fictitious letters of invitation and job offers.[31] Traffickers and smugglers may find other ways for their clients to enter the United States, such as setting up travel agencies or entering into collusive relationships with agencies that can provide clients tourist visas. In other cases, such as the White Lace prostitution ring in Los Angeles, the traffickers secured places for the women on visiting delegations of sports groups, charities, and religious organizations.

In other cases, crime groups manage to penetrate the visa issuance process for the United States. In the 1990s, the Immigration and Naturalization Service investigated a young consular officer stationed in India who had been blackmailed by an Indian smuggling ring. He provided visas to the smuggling ring who, in turn, received large sums for their ability to move their clients to the United States.[32] In a later case, a trafficking network managed to place a member of its criminal organization in the visa section of the U.S. Embassy in Prague. Despite intense scrutiny over local national employees, the Czech criminal in the consular division issued numerous visas to the young women that his organization sought to traffic to the United States. The traffickers operated successfully for several years until one of their unwilling victims escaped. The subsequent criminal investigation led to the crime member in the visa section of the Czech embassy.[33]

SECURING RESIDENCE

Trafficking victims may enter the country on legal visas, but these visas rarely give them the right to reside for any extended period. Securing visas for long-term residence of trafficking victims is a significant challenge for human traffickers. A variety of methods are used by the traffickers, including the provision of false documents, retention of the services of visa mills, false marriages, and other subterfuges.

In the Los Angeles White Lace case, the prostitutes obtained visas as students from a language school. This particular language school was a visa mill. It did not ask questions of its prospective students, nor did it monitor their language class attendance. It is hardly then surprising that this school provided visas for two of the 9/11 hijackers, illustrating the fact that the service providers for transnational crime often intersect with the world of terrorists.[34]

Lawyers are also hired by smugglers and traffickers to obtain residence permits. The fees paid to the lawyers are often the largest cost to the traffickers. In one case investigated in the United States, a small New York law firm was engaged in visa fraud, concocting applications for permanent residence to aid an Indian smuggling operation. A more famous case involved a Harvard-educated lawyer, Robert Porges, and his wife, who gained $13 million from filing false political asylum claims for large numbers of Chinese smuggled to the United States by a Chinese crime ring.[35]

Traffickers and smugglers extract enormous sums from those they have moved long distances and those who cannot pay initially are forced into situations of indentured servitude or slavery. In some cases, the smugglers extract an initial fee from those smuggled into the United States and extract compensation from those trafficked after they enter the United States. As a result, they are paid subsistence wages working in construction, restaurants, as domestic servants, and in sweatshops. The largest number in this situation comes from China, but they are not unique in this status. A smaller group of individuals, estimated at approximately 17,500, are trafficked into the United States.[36] The presence of so many enslaved individuals in the United States is certainly a major human rights concern for this country, but it is not a situation without historical precedent in American history.[37]

Significant profits have been made by these smugglers and traffickers. A human smuggling operation into the Washington, DC, area entitled "Asian Cruise" by its law enforcement investigators accumulated profits of $60 million for the smugglers.[38] Sister Ping was recently sentenced to 35 years in prison for running a massive criminal smuggling operation that resulted in numerous fatalities and gained her enormous profits.[39] A pair of Uzbek professors in Texas prosecuted for the trafficking of two women from their home country netted over $400,000 during the year long period in which the women were sexually exploited.[40]

THE STATUS OF SMUGGLED AND TRAFFICKED INDIVIDUALS

Over 10 million individuals reside illegally in the United States, having entered the country illegally. All are illegal immigrants, and they share the same status under American law. American law, since the enactment of the Trafficking in Persons legislation, strictly differentiates between trafficking and smuggling, allowing individuals who have been trafficked into the United States protection by means of a t-visa if they agree to cooperate with law enforcement authorities in providing evidence against their traffickers. Other illegal migrants have violated American laws and are subject to deportation as illegal immigrants.

The situation of individuals residing in the United States illegally is determined not only by American law. As important for illegal immigrants may be their relationship with the person or group who facilitated their entry into the United States, a relationship that exists in approximately 70 percent of illegal entries into the United States. Although the relationships and obligations between the smuggler and trafficker are not legally recognized, they may prove to be the most important determinant of the illegal immigrants' life in the United States. Because so little effort has been made in the United States to break up human smuggling and trafficking groups, illegal immigrants' status is determined by their relationship with those that have brought them to the country.

Those who travel long distances pay so much that they may be indebted for years to their human smugglers. They therefore face a dual illegality: they are in the United States illegally and have an illegal debt to their smugglers. Whereas this debt may not be enforceable under law, it will be enforced by the smugglers. It is more real than any legally enforceable debt, and repayment may be sought from the family in China if payments are not made in the United States.

As a result of the power of smugglers and traffickers, all illegal immigrants do not enjoy the same status within the United States. Three groups can be identified depending on their status upon arrival: free laborers, indentured servants or in-debt bondage, and slaves. The latter two groups have an on-going relationship with those who brought them to the United States where coercion ensures compliance with the smugglers and traffickers wishes.

FREE ILLEGALS

The largest group of illicit immigrants is the free illegals. Most of these are Mexicans and Central Americans who enter the United States to satisfy the demand for low-paid laborers. In the Mexican case, the motivation is almost entirely economic, while in Central America there are often political reasons that accompany the quest for a better financial future. The vast majority of those who cross are young men or children brought by smugglers to join family members already residing in the United States, though there are instances of entire families crossing the border as units.

As mentioned earlier, the increasing use of professional smugglers and the increasing costs of being smuggled are creating problems for the smuggled themselves, who are free to move and work in the United States but are burdened by enormous debt. Illustrative of the problems faced by a smuggled illegal worker is the situation of a Mexican fruit picker in Florida after the terrible hurricanes of September 2004. With much of the citrus crop on the ground, he could not earn money as a fruit picker. But he could not return home because he owed $2,300 to the human smuggler who facilitated his entry into the United States. Without access to U.S. legal protections and unable to expect any action against his smuggler from corrupt Mexican law enforcement officials, he faced a personal and economic crisis.[41]

A great variety of criminal actors in Mexico facilitate the cross-border flows. Facing increasing competition, some Mexican smugglers provide a range of services apart from simple border crossings, including safe houses, transportation to a location within the United States, and links to employers. But most smuggling operations are not so personalized. Instead, they resemble a supermarket model of human smuggling, the business based on high volume and low cost. Large numbers of migrants are packed into trucks and boats to cross the border.[42] Organizations, through their intelligence capacity, are able to respond rapidly to changes in border surveillance by the border patrol.

Mexican smugglers market their services primarily by word-of-mouth advertising rather than the kinship networks that characterize Chinese smuggling. To succeed, the organizations must be able to provide logistical support for their transport networks, bribe officials on both sides of the border, and move their profits. Bribery is possible because family ties often link the smugglers and the border officials on both the U.S. and the Mexican sides of the border.[43] Approximately 108 to 120 smuggling rings are operating in Mexico employing at least 15,000 people. Servicing a clientele from Mexico and Central America, these diverse organizations operate in many regions of Mexico. The large organizations do not monopolize all of the trade. As a report by Mark Wuebbels for the Arizona Attorney General commented, "News sources from the Mexican media indicate that many smaller and less sophisticated operations have also proliferated. The size and sophistication of operations vary according to the Mexican state and nationality of the illegal migrant."[44]

Most Mexicans cross the border after paying their smugglers a one-time fee of several hundred to several thousand dollars. According to data of the Immigration and Naturalization Service, three individuals make it across the border for every one person detained.[45] Individuals who are not successful on the first try often have success during subsequent attempts.[46] The smuggling organizations appear to be distinct from drug organizations. Unlike the drug networks that control their commodities through their delivery and distribution in the United States, only some of the human smuggling operations provide services within the United States. There are, however, cases of coercion of Mexicans into different trafficking situations as will be discussed subsequently.

The free illegals may find work in a place and a locale of their choosing. But the conditions available to these individuals are often those that legal workers will not take. The work conditions are dangerous, the work is exhausting, and there is no medical aid or compensation in the case of an accident. Jennifer Gordon's *Suburban Sweatshops* provides vivid examples of the grave physical harm suffered by many illegal migrants who wind up severely injured in the emergency rooms of hospitals abandoned by their employers.[47]

INDENTURED SERVITUDE AND DEBT BONDAGE

The illegally smuggled Chinese are the largest group of individuals held in indentured servitude, or debt bondage, within the United States. Chinese must travel long distances and their entry into the United States may require many months in transit through multiple countries. The involvement of Chinese government officials demanding bribes combined with officials in transit countries in Latin America and the Caribbean compound the expense.[48] Due to this high cost, the Chinese human smugglers, or *snakeheads*, agree to receive a portion of their fee later through forced bondage in the destination country or through a system of "pay-as-you-go" at overseas staging points.

The control of the smuggling from recruitment through debt bondage allows for long-term profits. The business employs no middlemen, and the smugglers' costs are paid as they incur—bribes, transport, and safe houses. Therefore, the smugglers maximize profits by running an integrated business from start to finish. As the exploitation of the smuggled individual endures for several years, the business generates very high profits. This trade resembles legal trade from China that spans continents and results in significant investment capital for China.

Although many Chinese are clearly exploited and some die on their way to their intended destination, the number of deaths is not as high in Mexican smuggling, where the smuggler does not derive money from delivering the alien to a specific destination. Therefore, many more individuals from Latin America are abandoned en route because they have already paid their smuggling fee in advance. Moreover, there is a seemingly endless supply of individuals waiting to be smuggled from Mexico and Central America, and smugglers do not suffer much business loss if those smuggled die en route. In contrast, the Chinese smugglers have a long-term interest in wresting maximum profit from the men they have smuggled and depend on their survival to recruit the next generation that will purchase their services.

Some estimates suggest that as many as 400,000 Chinese have been smuggled by Chinese crime groups into the United States. This number is significant but many fewer than the free illegals who arrive having paid their smugglers in advance. The crime groups controlling most Chinese to U.S. human smuggling emanate primarily from Fukien province in southern China, although smuggling and trafficking from other regions of the country have been detected on a much smaller scale. The recent conviction of Sister Ping, who ran smuggling rings into the United States and Europe, indicates that these are not small freelance operations but rather large-scale organized business operations generating tens of millions in profits.[49] In the Washington, DC, area alone, over 400 restaurants and carryouts have been tied to the Chinese smuggling trade, and the number of smuggled Chinese into the capital is small compared to other locales, such as New York and San Francisco, where the domestic Chinese population is much larger. Ledgers of ship rosters confiscated from smugglers revealed that 90 to 95 percent of those trafficked are males, brought to work as laborers in restaurants, sweatshops, and other dangerous work situations.[50] With debts averaging as much as $50,000, they must remain as indentured servants for years to pay off such significant sums.

Most smuggled male migrants work long hours, often in dangerous or unpleasant conditions, and reside in miserable circumstances until they have paid off their debt. They work in sweatshops, restaurants, and construction. Serious health problems are often faced by these individuals as they have no or extremely limited access to health care. Some arrive in the United States with tuberculosis and other serious communicable diseases contracted on their long voyage to the United States often in the holds of ships.

In some cases the indentured servitude borders on slavery because enormous coercion can be applied to the trafficking victim who fails to meet payments to their smugglers. There have been cases of torture of those who are smuggled and even cases where those who have been smuggled have been killed.

Unlike in Italy and some other countries in Western Europe, the Chinese who serve their period of indentured servitude are freed from their obligations to their smugglers. The contracts between the smuggled and the smugglers are generally observed. This is true because the smugglers have a ready supply of new individuals to smuggle and can replace the "freed" workers. Furthermore, those who have been freed from their servitude in the United States often go on to be successful entrepreneurs who can then subsequently sponsor other family members.[51] This situation contrasts with the situation in some European countries where the difficulties in replacing smuggled laborers result in violations of the "contracts" between the smugglers and the smuggled who find themselves unable to free themselves from their period of servitude.[52]

TRAFFICKING: CONTEMPORARY SLAVERY

Citizens of many different countries find themselves enslaved in the United States—in factories and homes, as beggars, farm workers, and sex workers. The majority of those who are enslaved are female, but there are many identified cases of men being enslaved as beggars, agricultural workers and laborers. In a notorious case, several dozen deaf and mute Mexicans were trafficked to the United States and forced to beg in the New York area.[53]

The terms of the enslavement differ. In some cases, the individuals are locked up in a home, a factory, or a brothel and earn nothing. They are fed only enough to keep them alive and are deprived of adequate shelter or medical care. In other situations, the trafficked women actually earn some money but are subject to deception and coercion, thereby qualifying them as trafficking victims. The trafficking victims are not able to exit from their situation because of the violence or other threats that will be made against them or their families back home.

Many trafficking victims contract with smugglers to move them, ignorant of the fate that awaits them upon their arrival in the United States. They are deceived by these "human smugglers" who are in reality traffickers with no intention of abiding by the conditions that they offer to those they move. In other cases, the vulnerability of those who have been smuggled often results in their subsequently becoming a trafficking victim in the U.S. Estimates of a Midwest human rights group suggest that as many as one-quarter of the humans smuggled into the United States wind up being trafficked;[54] their smugglers turn on them, and they are vulnerable to exploitation by others and believe that they have no recourse to legal protection.

Those imported for sexual trafficking originate most often from Asia, the former Soviet Union, and more recently from Latin America. The women and minors brought in for this purpose in some cases enter the United States believing that they will work as prostitutes and then find themselves in a coerced situation. For others, the deception and the coercion are complete from the recruitment stage. In the Cadena case, for instance, minor Mexican girls were recruited from their families in the state of Veracruz. Their families were told that the girls would work in the United States as childcare providers and domestic servants. But the Cadena brothers who trafficked them always had different intentions. They made the girls and young women serve multiple clients in filthy trailers frequented by Mexican migrant workers.[55] In a prosecuted trafficking case in Alaska, a group of young women thought that they were coming to dance in a festival. But the deception of the traffickers was total as no dance festival existed. Upon arrival, without funds or passports, they were forced to work in a strip club until law enforcement discovered their existence.[56]

Trafficked victims are often confined within closed communities that make it hard to detect them. These can be immigrant communities where law enforcement cannot penetrate, the homes of foreign diplomats and employees of international organizations where domestic workers are enslaved, and on the private lands of farmers or the sweatshops of entrepreneurs.[57] A brothel in Chinatown, just a 5-minute walk from the headquarters of the Immigration and Naturalization Service in Washington, DC, chained its victims to the wall to prevent escape.[58] Many who are trafficked do not know English, lack education, and retain a fear of law enforcement from their home country. All of these conditions allow those who enslave them to retain control over their victims for extended periods of time. In one of the longest known cases, a Nigerian woman was enslaved by a Nigerian social worker in New York for 12 years before she escaped.[59]

Traffickers routinely confiscate the passports and the documents of the trafficked. Without these documents, the trafficked have no legal status. Loss of identity is the key to the dehumanization of the victim. It also has very practical implications. If the trafficking victims escape, they cannot prove their identity or citizenship, complicating any investigation of their status.

Newspaper advertisements and employment agencies in the United States are also conduits for trafficking. Stranded women in the United States have answered advertisements and fallen into a trafficking situation. Likewise, Russian-speaking employment agencies in New York do not bother to differentiate whether an individual is a legal or illegal immigrant. They place individuals in exploitative labor situations with inadequate pay and working hours, in violation of labor laws. Those ending up in these trafficked labor situations are not necessarily the uneducated. Research conducted among Kyrgyz, a Central Asian people from one of the poorest Soviet successor states, revealed that many of the educated elite from the country—now residing illegally in the United States—were in trafficked labor situations. They endured this situation because they could send home some money.[60]

Women trafficking victims may be forced to work in strip clubs and nightclubs, in brothels and even for "massage parlors."[61] Latin American and Chinese trafficked women most often are forced to work within their diaspora communities, whereas women trafficked from the former Soviet Union, Korea, and Thailand serve a more diverse clientele. Women forced into sexual slavery are informed by their smugglers that they have debts to work off, unlike the voluntarily incurred debts that many Asian immigrants owe their human smugglers. In an Atlanta-based case, 1,000 Thai women were identified as having been trafficked for the purposes of prostitution.[62] The figures for Asia are often underestimated because of the difficulties of law enforcement in penetrating Asian trafficking networks.

CONCLUSIONS

The United States in recent decades has seen an enormous growth of human smuggling and trafficking. Over 10 million people presently reside illegally in the United States. Approximately 7 million of these have entered the United States as a result of the actions of human smugglers and traffickers. This makes smuggling and trafficking one of the largest, most lucrative, and fastest growing forms of transnational crime in the United States. The individuals who are smuggled and trafficked into the United States come from every region of the world, although the largest share comes from neighboring Mexico.

The United States has long ignored the rise of human smuggling and trafficking. The Trafficking in Persons Act was passed only in 2000 after widespread mobilization in the late 1990s by the political right and left to introduce such legislation. But the much larger-scale problem of human smuggling has gotten much less attention even with the current concern about the rise in illegal migration to the United States. Much more attention is paid by the U.S. Government to crime groups that traffic drugs to the United States rather than to those who smuggle and traffic humans. The resources, intelligence, and failure to train enough law enforcement in the investigation of these cases mean that most individuals who exploit individuals entering the United States function with impunity.

While the United States is supposed to be the "land of the free," the presence of so many well-developed transnational crime groups means that many residing in the United States are *not* free. The failure to address this problem with adequate resources and political will means that the exploitation of individuals entering and residing in the United States continues on a dramatic scale denying the fundamental values of American society.

NOTES

1. 10News.com, "Agents Discover American-Mexican Tunnel Length of Eight Football Fields," January 27, 2006, available at www.officer.com/article/article.jsp?id=28273&siteSection=8.

2. This number is derived from totaling figures on trafficking victims, exploited Chinese labor, and estimates of extreme exploitation of some Latin American labor. For discussion of the phenomenon, see Peter Kwong, *Forbidden Workers Illegal Chinese Immigrants and American Labor* (New York: New Press, 1997); Jennifer Gordon, *Suburban Sweatshops The Fight for Immigrant Rights* (Cambridge, MA: Harvard University Press, 2005).

3. United Nations Office on Drugs and Crime (UNODC), *Trafficking in Person: Global Patterns*, April 2006, available at www.unodc.org/pdf/traffickinginpersons_report_2006ver2.pdf.

4. See U.S. Department of State, Victims of Trafficking and Violence Protection Act of 2000: *Trafficking in Persons Report*, June 2004, available at www.state.gov/g/tip/rls/tiprpt/2004/.

5. P. Smucker, "Sahara Town Booms with People Smuggling," *International Herald Tribune*, October 25, 2004, 2.

6. Mitra Kalita and S. Hsu Spencer, "Huge Backlogs, Delays Feared under Senate Immigration Plan," *The Washington Post*, July 24, 2006, A3.

7. Miko Holloran, "President Bush Visits Yuma Border," Arizona National Guard Public Affairs, May 19, 2006, available at www.az.ngb.army.mil/PublicAffairs/PAO%20Pages/Pres%20Bush%20Yuma%20Visit%20Article%20and%20Photos.htm.

8. Peter Andreas, *Border Games: Policing the U.S.-Mexico Divide* (Ithaca, NY: Cornell University Press, 2000); Kitty Calavita, *Immigrants at the Margins: Law,*

Race, and Exclusion in Southern Europe (Cambridge: Cambridge University Press, 2005).

9. Craig McGill, *Human Trafficking: Sex, Slaves, and Immigration* (London: Vision, 2004), 139.

10. Statistic from a 1999 International Organization for Migration study cited in James O. Finckenauer and Jennifer Schrock, "Human Trafficking: A Growing Criminal Market in the U.S.," International Center National Institute of Justice, available at www.ojp.usdoj.gov/nij/international/ht.html.

11. Mark Wuebbels, "Demystifying Human Smuggling Operations Along the Arizona-Mexico Border," available at www.american.edu/traccc/resources/publications/wuebbe01.pdf. Wuebbels cites Jeffrey S. Passel, "Unauthorized Migrants: Numbers and Characteristics," Background Briefing Prepared for Task Force on Immigration and America's Future (Washington, DC: Pew Hispanic Center, 2004), available at http://pewhispanic.org/files/reports/46.pdf.

12. James O. Finckenauer, "Russian Transnational Crime and Human Trafficking," in *Global Human Smuggling Comparative Perspectives*, ed. David Kyle and Rey Koslowski (Baltimore, MD: The Johns Hopkins University Press, 2001), 166–186.; Zai Liang and Wenzhen Ye, "From Fujian to New York: Understanding the New Chinese Immigration," in *Global Human Smuggling Comparative Perspectives*, 187–215.

13. Center for Global Development, Commitment to Development Index 2006, available at http://www.cgdev.org/rankingtherich/home.html.

14. Moisés Naím, *Illicit: How Smugglers, Traffickers and Copycats are Hijacking the Global Economy* (New York: Random House, 2005).

15. For a discussion of the entry points for illegal Chinese, see Ko-lin Chin, *Smuggled Chinese Clandestine Immigration to the United States* (Philadelphia, PA: Temple University Press, 1999), 49–93.

16. Wuebbels, citing Passel.

17. Donald Bartlett and James Steel, "Who Left the Door Open," *Time*, September 2004, 62; Wuebbels, 19.

18. United Nations International Drug Control Programme, *World Drug Report* (Oxford: Oxford University Press, 1997), 124.

19. UNODC, 68–70.

20. U.S. Department of State, Victims of Trafficking and Violence Protection Act of 2000: *Trafficking in Persons Report*, Part V.

21. UNODC, 98–99.

22. U.S. Department of State, Victims of Trafficking and Violence Protection Act of 2000: *Trafficking in Persons Report*.

23. Wuebbels, citing "INM Estimates 70,000 Illegal Migrants Trafficked Per Month; 15-20 Organized 'Pollero' Groups Operating in Sonora State," *El Imparcial*, April 25, 2004 ("Highlights: Mexico, Crime, Narcotics," FBIS Report LAP20040426000058, 28).

24. Wuebbels, citing "Police Capture 3 Alleged 'Polleros,' 3 Underage Migrants," *La Frontera*, August 2, 2005. ("Highlights: Mexico Crime and Narcotics," FBIS Report. LAP20050802000078, 37).

25. P.R. Keefe, "The Snakehead," *The New Yorker* (April 2006), 68–85; Los Angeles Police Department, New Release, "Operation *White Lace*," available at www.lapdonline.org/newsroom/news_view/21690.

26. Author interview with Lou DiBacco, U.S. Civil Rights Division, Department of Justice, 2004.

27. Statement of Chris Swecker, U.S. House of Representatives, Committee on Homeland Security, Subcommittee on Management, Integration, and Oversight, March 8, 2006; H. Abadinsky, *Organized Crime*, 7th ed. (Belmont, CA: Wadsworth, 2003), 4–18.

28. Wuebbels, 39.

29. John Pomfret, "Tunnel Found on Mexican Border," *The Washington Post*, January 27, 2006, A3.

30. U.S. Department of State, East Asia and the Pacific, "The Allure of Land Crossings Persists, Although Hundreds of Migrants Die Each Year," available at http://usinfo.state.gov/eap/Archive_Index/Land_Crossings.html.

31. Wuebbels, 39.

32. Author interview with Bob Trent of the Immigration and Naturalization Service (INS), 1999.

33. Jane Lii, "Two Czechs are Charged in Sex Ring Near Times Sq.," *The New York Times*, March 14, 1998, B2.

34. Based on author's interviews with investigator in December 2005 in Los Angeles.

35. Edward Epstein, "It's That Time Again: Lawmakers Revisit Daylight Saving," San Francisco Chronicle, April 9, 2005, final edition; Mark Hamblett, "Government Outlines Case Against Porges," *New York Law Journal*, September 27, 2000, 1.

36. Amy O'Neill-Richards, "International Trafficking in Women to the United States," April 2000, available at https://www.cia.gov/csi/monograph/women/trafficking.pdf. The number of 17,500 was provided in Ambassador John R. Miller's question and answer to the *Trafficking in Persons Report*. See Miller, "On-The-Record Briefing by Ambassador John R. Miller, Ambassador-at-Large for International Slavery," on Release of the *Sixth Annual Trafficking in Persons Report*, available at www.state.gov/r/pa/prs/ps/2006/67559.htm.

37. For an historical framework, see David Kyle and John Dale, "Smuggling the State Back: Agents of Human Smuggling Reconsidered," in *Global Human Smuggling Comparative Perspectives*, 29–54.

38. Author interviews with investigators of the Immigration and Naturalization Service, Arlington, VA, 2000.

39. U.S. Immigration and Customs Enforcement, "Sister Ping Sentenced to 35 years in Prison for Alien Smuggling, Hostage Taking, Money Laundering and Ransom Proceeds Conspiracy," March 16, 2006, available at http://www.ice.gov/pi/news/newsreleases/articles/060316newyork.htm.

40. Beatrix Siman Zakhari, "Legal Cases Prosecuted under the Victims of Trafficking and Violence Protection Act of 2000," in *Human Traffic and Transnational Crime: Eurasian and American Perspectives*, ed. Louise I. Shelley and Sally Stoecker (Lanham, MD: Rowman and Littlefield, 2004).

41. Jennifer Lee, "Lost Fruit in Central Florida Means Lost Jobs for Migrants," *The New York Times*, September 10, 2004, A22.

42. Louise I. Shelley, "The Unholy Trinity: Transnational crime, corruption, and terrorism," *Brown Journal of World Affairs*, 11, no. 2 (Winter/Spring 2005), 101–111.

43. John Pomfret, "Bribery at Border Worries Officials," *The Washington Post*, July 15, 2006, 1.

44. Wuebbels, 27.

45. Bartlett and Steel, 53.

46. Personal communication with Border Patrol Agents.

47. Gordon.

48. Kwong, 66; author interview with law enforcement officers investigating Chinese immigrant smuggling in Central America and the Caribbean, 1999 and 2000.

49. Willard Myers, "Of Qingqing, Qinshu, Guanxi, and Shetou," in *Human Smuggling: Chinese Migrant Trafficking and the Challenge to American's Immigrant Tradition*, ed. Paul Smith, (Washington, DC: Center for Strategic and International Studies, 1997), 128.

50. Author interviews with investigators of Asian Cruise case, 1999 and 2000.

51. Keefe.

52. Author interviews with Italian investigators of Chinese organized crime in Washington, DC, 2000.

53. Mirta Ojito, "For Deaf Mexicans, Freedom After Slavery and Detention," *The New York Times*, July 18, 1998.

54. Elissa Steglich, presentation at the 2006 Joint Area Centers Symposium entitled *Criminal Trafficking and Slavery: The Dark Side of Global and Regional Migration*, University of Illinois at Urbana-Champaign, Champaign, IL, February 23–25, 2006; Ojito.

55. Florida State University Center for the Advancement of Human Rights, *Florida Responds to Human Trafficking*, (2003), 37–62, available at www.cahr.fsu.edu/H%20-%20Chapter%202.pdf.

56. Zakhari.

57. Sarah Garland, "This Woman was Forced into Slavery... in the U.S.," *Marie Claire*, May 2006, 126–129.

58. Author interview with INS official in 2000, discussing a case he had worked on earlier in the 1990s.

59. Advocacy Net, News Bulletin 67, June 20, 2006.

60. Saltanat Sulaimanova, presentation to the Transnational Crime and Corruption Center at the American University, Washington, DC, April 12, 2006.

61. Zakhari; Florida State University Center for the Advancement of Human Rights; Garland.

62. Regan Ralph, Testimony before the Senate Committee on Foreign Relations Subcommittee on Near Eastern and South Asian Affairs, February 22, 2000, available at www.hrw.org/backgrounder/wrd/trafficking.htm.

CHAPTER 15

The Implications for U.S. National Security

Rhea Siers

In assessing the threat of transnational crime to the United States, there has been a traditional emphasis on the victims of crime: individuals, society, or businesses. The reality is that the broad spectrum of smuggling and trafficking crimes directly affects U.S. national security because of its impact on global stability and its destabilization of worldwide economic markets. We cannot continue to view smuggling and trafficking as impacting only their direct victims or solely as a law enforcement matter. We must also understand the threat to American strategic and domestic interests. While we emphasize nonstate actors in our current national security approach, we tend to focus on terrorist groups. The reality is precisely what Louise Shelley pointed out in August 2001:

> Transnational organized crime will be a defining issue of the 21st century for policymakers—as defining as the Cold War was for the 20th century and colonialism was for the 19th. No area of international affairs will remain untouched, as the social fabric and political and financial systems of many countries deteriorate under the increasing economic power of international organized crime groups.[1]

To understand the impact of transnational crime on the United States, we must review the causes for its global explosion. While globalization is touted as a boon to our economy, it brings with it technology and economic forces that feed crime and instability. The growing sophistication of criminal activities, along with the diversification of these global criminal enterprises and increasingly porous borders, poses a much deeper threat than traditional crime. As adaptable, sophisticated, and opportunistic organizations, criminal groups encompass an entire range of activities, from street-level drug trafficking to more corporate-level endeavors that can include human smuggling, environmental crime, bank fraud, and intellectual property crime.

In fact, these crimes are at the forefront of the threat to U.S. national security in what Moisés Naim describes as the "Five Wars of Globalization":

> The illegal trade in drugs, arms, intellectual property, people, and money is booming. Like the war on terrorism, the fight to control these illicit markets pits governments against agile, stateless, and resourceful networks empowered by globalization. Governments will continue to lose these wars until they adopt new strategies to deal with a larger, unprecedented struggle that now shapes the world as much as confrontations between nations-states once did.[2]

Clearly, smuggling, trafficking, and other forms of transnational crime have a deleterious impact on national and strategic interests. In 2000, a U.S. Government interagency group published a broad perspective of this threat and included three categories:

- "threats to Americans and their communities, which affect the lives, livelihood, and social welfare of U.S. citizens living in the United States and abroad
- "threats to American businesses and financial institutions, which affect U.S. trade, the competitiveness of U.S. products, and the U.S. interests in a stable worldwide financial system
- "threats to global security and stability, which affect the broader U.S. national security interest in promoting regional peace and democratic and free market systems, particularly in regions where outlaw regimes aspire to develop weapons of mass destruction or where U.S. forces may be deployed."[3]

While the threat has been recognized and, in some cases, acted upon by the U.S. Government, it is interesting to note that the National Security Council has not yet followed up on the 2000 Threat Assessment, although a reassessment was scheduled to be completed in 2006. Nor has the National Security Council revised the 1998 International Crime Control Strategy.[4]

It is clear that the depth of these threats assumes several factors. First, smuggling and trafficking crimes are multifaceted and complex, encompassing the initial or predicate crime and a series of supporting or secondary crimes such as money laundering. Secondly, the crimes themselves are not necessarily large-scale threats that are coercive but rather a series of crimes that often include some form of state or official complicity. Thirdly, the economic impact of the criminal threat is felt from the grassroots level (that is, by individuals and small businesses), but extends all the way to the international banking system, multinational corporations, and national and state budgets and tax systems. Finally, evidence continues to grow that terrorist groups are availing themselves of criminal methodologies and operations to finance their activities. This nexus is not a new development, but given our attention to terrorism since 9/11, it is part of the global war on terrorism that has not been fully developed strategically. Failed states do not occur in a political vacuum. Moreover, the role of criminal activity in destabilizing states, such as Somalia, cannot be underestimated in regard to creating havens or bases for terrorist activities.

SIGNIFICANT CRIMINAL THREATS TO NATIONAL SECURITY

The four greatest smuggling and trafficking threats to U.S. national security are nuclear/technical smuggling, drug trafficking, trafficking in persons, and intellectual property crime. In previous chapters, the authors provide details about the methodology behind these operations including enabling functions. This chapter discusses the considerable impact by each crime on U.S. strategic interests.

Nuclear/Technology Smuggling

Most observers would find this the most self-evident threat because of the possibility that nuclear materials or weapons could find their way to terrorist or insurgent groups and used directly against the United States or to destabilize a region. The threat from complete nuclear weapons is quite clear: consider the dreaded suitcase or dirty (a radiological dispersal device) bomb that some believe may be in al Qaeda's arsenal. Less well known are the threats from raw nuclear materials that could cause considerable environmental hazards either in the United States or abroad and components and technology that, with the proper training, could result in a useable weapon.

The example of A.Q. Khan, the Pakistani scientist considered one of the inventors of the Pakistani bomb, is particularly instructive in understanding U.S. concerns about the nuclear black market. By the 1990s, Khan was suspected of selling nuclear materials and blueprints to a variety of clients, including Iran, North Korea, and Libya—all clearly of significant concern for the United States. He employed a global network for these transactions, from Germany to Dubai and from China to South Asia.[5] Most important, he essentially provided one-stop shopping for his customers, offering parts and technical assistance, causing International Atomic Energy Agency head Mohammed El Baradei to label Khan's laboratories the "Wal-Mart of private-sector proliferation."[6] Clearly, Khan had upped the ante in the nonproliferation effort: Instead of piecing together their sources of materiel, plans, or engineering know-how, three states with interests endemic to the United States obtained their nuclear technology in a much more direct fashion. The arrest of Khan may have disrupted his network, but it provided a model for future nuclear trafficking and, of even greater concern, may drive the traffickers even further underground,[7] further complicating U.S. nonproliferation efforts.

Drug Trafficking

The trafficking of illegal drugs into the United States and its secondary crimes such as money laundering are a direct threat to economic, social, and political security. The corruption that dominates the drug trade overseas has also infiltrated the United States through corruption of law enforcement officials and others. The damage to society through drug-related crime is disheartening, and the deleterious impact on the health, safety, and well-being of our citizens is catastrophic. The ravages resulting from drug trafficking into the U.S. include:

- the explosion of the acquired immune deficiency syndrome/human immunodeficiency virus and the resulting overtaxing of our health systems, particularly those that serve the poor
- violent crime in significant portions of our cities that has spread to the suburbs and even rural areas through gang violence
- the premature deaths of thousands of U.S. citizens and even the exposure of babies to drug-induced dependencies and diseases.

All of these outcomes of drug trafficking undermine the fabric of American society, short-circuit economic recovery in urban and other areas, and divert important resources from strengthening society and health care.

While the social and economic impact of drug trafficking on the United States is well documented, we must also focus on the threat to global stability posed by the so-called narcoterrorists, such as the Armed Revolutionary Forces of Colombia (FARC), who merge their insurgencies or terrorism goals with the lucrative business of drugs. Once the FARC realized that their control over territories and the local peasant population was inherently linked to coca production, it moved to consolidate its control of coca cultivation and ultimately to cocaine trafficking.[8]

The drug profits amassed by FARC initially fueled its insurgency and, over time, became its raison d'être. While estimates differ on the FARC's profits from drug trafficking, a number of analysts place the number at between $75 and $100 million annually.[9] This is, in essence, a double strike at the United States: an insurgency or destabilizing force seeks to upset the global balance and finances itself with drug trafficking, which, in turn, has negative impacts on American society.

Another example of this dual impact on U.S. security is the Taliban. Given its orthodox Islamist theology, many doubt that the Taliban could actively engage in drug production and trafficking. However, given its financial needs, at least those that were not satisfied by al Qaeda and its control over areas where poppies were grown as well as its borders, it is probable that the Taliban reaped profits from drug cultivation and trafficking. The continuing question is whether al Qaeda was also complicit and profited from drug production, although the 9/11 Commission could find no evidence to support this claim.[10] The U.S. Government believes that Afghan-estimated poppy production figures clearly indicate that the Taliban was an active supporter of drug production; from 1996 through 2000, the tonnage of opium steadily increased.[11] Even if the connection between al Qaeda and heroin cannot be substantiated, the key is that the Taliban, the hosts for al Qaeda and sponsors of terrorism, continued to survive economically because of the active drug trade originating within its borders and used these financial resources to fight their opposition to the Northern Alliance.

Finally, we should recall that the March 11, 2004, Madrid train bombings, resulting in the killing of 191 victims, was the work of an al Qaeda subsidiary that financed itself through the sale of ecstasy and other illegal drugs. Even outside the realm of production, groups that threaten both the U.S. and global stability are financing themselves through drug trafficking. Given the relative small amount of money necessary to carry out a terrorist action (estimates of the Madrid bombings range from $15 to $25,000), even street-level drug trafficking becomes a major component of the threat to national security.

Human Trafficking and Smuggling

The smuggling of individuals into the United States and the trafficking of people without consent for labor and exploitation represent similar threats to U.S. national security. The war on terror has caused many to focus on the potential for terrorists to enter the country, using the same conduits employed by human smugglers and traffickers.[12] While the smuggling or illegal entry of terrorists is certainly a concern, it is also important to understand the serious harm resulting from the illegal entry of both consenting and nonconsenting individuals, including the role of organized crime. U.S. Government estimates indicate that 800,000 to 900,000 individuals are trafficked worldwide and that 17,500 to 18,500 are trafficked into the United States.[13] This is, in fact, the fastest growing of the trafficking and smuggling crimes, immensely profitable, and frequently ignored by officials.[14] The syndicates that engage in human trafficking and smuggling are involved in crimes ranging from forgery to money laundering to prostitution. The specific threats of human smuggling and trafficking are closely related to those of other transnational criminal activity:

- Economic security: undocumented cheap migrant labor brings with it tax avoidance and, in certain cases, unemployment for legal residents. The costs for enforcement and border control, including alien detention centers, significantly impact the Federal budget.

- Criminal activity: criminal organizations not only arrange for the initial entry of aliens but also may continue to profit off the labor and exploitation of the trafficked individuals for years, such as in the case of women smuggled into the country for prostitution rings. These criminal networks continue to expand and be used for other trafficking and smuggling, such as drugs and contraband. Clearly, this affects the safety of our existing communities and creates inhumane conditions for the victims of trafficking.

In her work on human trafficking and smuggling, Louise Shelley discusses the connection between this illegal trafficking with other forms of transnational crime as exemplified by the Ludwig Fainberg case. In this case, a Russian gangster owned a strip club in Miami that was populated by trafficked women. These women were also coerced into prostitution for the criminal clientele, which included Colombian drug cartel operatives. Fainberg negotiated the sale of Russian arms between corrupt officials in Russia, including military officers and the Colombians. Interestingly, while Fainberg was prosecuted for his arms dealing, he was not ultimately prosecuted for the crime of human trafficking.[15] Fainberg's arrest points to a recurrent theme: transnational crimes, especially smuggling and trafficking, often operate jointly, thus increasing the threat to national security and public safety.

Intellectual Property Crime

One area of trafficking and smuggling—fraudulent or phony goods—is an immensely lucrative criminal enterprise. As a former New York City Police commissioner remarked, "Counterfeiting has all the ideal traits of an ideal criminal enterprise."[16] How much money could be available through intellectual property crime (IPC)? Interpol estimates that the global trade in counterfeit goods is approximately $450 billion—nearly 7 percent of total global trade. Within Europe alone in 2001, approximately $95 million worth of counterfeit goods were seized, at a loss to business of about $2 billion. The Federal Bureau of Investigation (FBI) states that counterfeiting cost U.S. business between $200 and $250 billion per year,[17] clearly a substantial economic impact that also includes lost jobs for workers in legitimate businesses. Remarkably, law enforcement authorities believe that the profits from counterfeiting are similar to those in drug trafficking—an approximate return of 10 euros for every euro invested—an immense profit by any measure.

Another lucrative aspect is that the criminal penalties for IPC are relatively mild, especially when compared to drug laws. For example, in France, a conviction for selling counterfeit goods carries a maximum 2-year prison term and a 150,000 euro fine, while drug dealing brings a 10-year prison term and a 7.5 million euro fine. Minimal penalties, coupled with a lack of strong enforcement or attention by law enforcement, help make this a winner in any profit/risk ratio assessment. Furthermore, most consumers view this as a victimless crime. After all, consumers see only the final vendor—usually a street seller (sometimes an illegal alien who has been smuggled or trafficked into the country)—certainly not someone who appears to have connections to either terrorism or organized crime.[18]

One of the most striking examples of IPC and its threat to national security is found in the investigation of the first bombing of the World Trade Center. The FBI believes that the first bombing of the World Trade Center was financed by the sale of fake Nike and Olympic t-shirts by followers of Sheikh Omar Abdul Rahman who was convicted for plotting that bombing. The supporters of Abdul Rahman sold their wares from a textile shop on Broadway in Manhattan.[19]

In addition to the terrorist financing connection, the manufacture and distribution of fraudulent goods could have a very serious impact on the health and security of this country and others. Consider the fact that the counterfeit pharmaceutical industry is growing at a faster rate than the legitimate pharmaceutical business.[20] Even if terrorist or criminal groups do not directly participate in the manufacture of counterfeit drugs, their involvement in the supply chain merits serious consideration and concern. Even worse, the potential to adulterate or taint drugs is a national security nightmare waiting to happen. The phony pharmaceuticals industry is ideal for terrorist-criminal involvement, as terrorist groups are known for their extensive presence on the Internet and use of Web sites. A recent study by the risk management research firm Global Options determined that many of the online pharmacies using Canada in their names are actually based elsewhere, and in a number of cases, the origin of the drug's manufacture is unknown.[21]

Thus, while a number of IPC cases have demonstrated a threat to U.S. national security, the reality is that this transnational criminal activity will only increase and spread to other industries. From Hezbollah-connected criminals in the Tri-Border Area of South America,[22] there is little doubt that the appearance of these goods on U.S. soil is another example of dual impact, undermining the U.S. economy while providing significant income to criminal syndicates and terrorist groups.

DEADLY NEXUS: TERRORIST ENABLERS AND MORPHING ORGANIZATIONS

Much attention has been given to discussions of a so-called alliance between terrorist groups and criminal syndicates, which would seem the ultimate threat to U.S. national security. However, the reality is somewhat different: terrorist groups avail themselves of criminal methods, such as money laundering, front companies, and criminal activities, sometimes even using the same offshore money launderers or smuggling routes. The terrorists do not necessarily form an active alliance with organized crime, but there is clearly a nexus in their activities.[23]

Even without a clear joining of forces, the separate strengths of terrorist groups and transnational crime syndicates are powerful threats to national security. In his testimony to the House Committee on International Relations, the Drug Enforcement Agency (DEA) Chief of Operations, Michael Braun, noted that Arab drug trafficking organizations based in South America are funneling a significant amount of their profits into both Hezbollah and Hamas.[24] Smuggling and trafficking also has emboldened an important category of terrorists called enablers. Although not directly employed by terrorist groups, enablers funnel their profits to these groups through money laundering or so-called charities. The Tri-Border Area of South America, for instance, appears to host a diverse set of extreme Islamic group operatives and supporters. These groups include the Islamic Jihad as well as al-Muqawamah ("the Resistance"), an offshoot of Hezbollah with even stronger ties to Iran.[25]

Finally, there is the issue of terrorist groups that ultimately morph into criminal enterprises once their money-raising operations begin to take precedence over their "political" agenda. This was certainly the case with the infamous Abu Nidal Organization (ANO), which committed a host of terrorist attacks throughout the 1970s and 1980s. To a certain extent, Sabri-Al Banna (Abu Nidal) was the Osama bin Laden of his time. Beginning with a manifesto to attack Israel, the ANO organization built a diversified business, including gunrunning, extortion schemes, real estate and front companies, and even a coupon fraud scheme run by operatives in the United States.

While the basis of ANO had certainly morphed from the Palestinian revolution to a self-sustaining criminal syndicate, its threat to U.S. national security and to other Palestinian groups did not diminish. In fact, as its criminal business grew, it became more of a threat to its targets in Europe, the Middle East, and the United States. While the terrorist label certainly makes a more compelling case for national security, it should not obfuscate the clear threat posed by criminal activity, whether or not the attendant trafficking and smuggling is to underwrite a so-called political purpose. As we well know since 9/11, the lines between traditional law enforcement activities and counterterrorism have been blurred, just as the distinction between domestic and foreign affairs has diminished because of globalization.

POLICY IMPLICATIONS

The growing recognition of trafficking and smuggling is recognized in the March 2006 *National Security Strategy of the United States of America*:

> Many of the problems we face—from the threat of pandemic disease, to proliferation of weapons of mass destruction, to terrorism, to human trafficking,

to natural disasters—reach across borders. Effective multinational efforts are essential to solve these problems. Yet history has shown that only when we do our part will others do theirs. America will continue to lead.[26]

But is the recognition at the macrolevel carried through to government policy and operational leadership? Individual agencies and joint task forces have carried out aggressive campaigns against money laundering, nuclear smuggling, and other smuggling and trafficking crimes. The Federal Government framework was clarified in the 1998 International Crime Control Strategy issued by the National Security Council.[27] Recognizing the threat of trafficking and smuggling as well as transnational crime, the strategy set forth the basic goals for the U.S. Government, including the interdiction of trafficking and smuggling before such crime reaches American shores. Since the publication of that strategy and the International Crime Threat Assessment completed in 2000, the National Security Council has undertaken a review of the 1998 assessment and will decide whether to issue a new strategy. As noted previously, the NSC has not yet published or announced its findings.[28]

To challenge traffickers and smugglers, U.S. and foreign authorities must have a degree of agility as well as the ability to tackle the economic and social issues that form the basis for the rise of crime and provide substitutes for the loss in income from crime. As Kimberley Thachuk notes, "Economic assistance is needed to ease the domestic impact associated with the loss of illicit sources of foreign exchange in weak states."[29] We are now all too familiar with the pattern of weak states serving as hosts for terror and transnational crime. No U.S. strategy will succeed without recognizing that we must also battle smuggling and trafficking abroad by reviving financial institutions, restoring governmental, judicial, and law enforcement integrity, and short-circuiting corruption.

The threat is clear, and it targets our economic, political, and social systems. There can be no greater threat to our national security.

NOTES

1. Louise I. Shelley, "Crime Victimizes Both Society and Democracy," *Global Issues* 6, no. 2 (August 2001), available at http://usinfo.state.gov/journals/itgic/0801/ijge/gj06.htm.

2. Moisés Naim, "Five Wars of Globalization," *Foreign Policy*, January/February 2003, available at www.foreignpolicy.com/story/cms.php?story_id=2.

3. U.S. Government Interagency Working Group, *International Crime Threat Assessment*, December 2000, available at www.fas.org/irp/threat/pub45270index.html.

4. John R. Wagley, "Transnational Organized Crime: Principal Threats and U.S. Responses," Congressional Research Service, March 20, 2006, 4.

5. "A.Q. Khan," GlobalSecurity.org, available at www.globalsecurity.org/wmd/world/pakistan/khan.htm.

6. Esther Pan, "Non-proliferation: The Pakistan Network," Council on Foreign Relations, February 12, 2004, available at www.cfr.org/publication/7751/nonproliferation.html.

7. Ibid.

8. Alain Labrousse, "The FARC and the Taliban's Connection to Drugs," *Journal of Drug Issues* (Winter 2005), 172, 177.

9. Ibid., 178

10. National Commission on Terrorist Attacks, *The 9/11 Commission Report: Final Report of the National Commission on Terrorist Attacks Upon the United States* (New York: W.W. Norton, 2004), 19.

11. Asa Hutchinson, "International Drug Trafficking and Terrorism," testimony before the Senate Judiciary Committee Subcommittee on Technology, Terrorism, and Government Information, Washington, DC, March 13, 2002, available at www.state.gov/p/inl/rls/rm/2002/9239.htm.

12. Remarks by John P. Torres before the House Judiciary Subcommittee on Immigration, Border Security, and Claims, Washington, DC, May 18, 2004, available at http://usinfo.state.gov/eap/Archive/2004/Jul/14-1985.html.

13. "Fact Sheet: Distinctions Between Human Smuggling and Trafficking," The Human Smuggling and Trafficking Center, Department of Justice, January 2005, 1, available at www.usdoj.gov/crt/crim/smuggling_trafficking_facts.pdf.

14. Louise I. Shelley, "Trafficking and Smuggling in Human Beings," presentation to the George C. Marshall European Center for Security Studies, May 2001.

15. Ibid.

16. Remarks by Raymond W. Kelly, February 1, 2005, quoted in Ronald Brownlow, "Sales of Fake Goods May Finance Terror, Police Commissioner Says," *Columbia Journalism News*, February 1, 2004.

17. Ronald Noble, "The Links Between Intellectual Property Crime and Terrorist Financing," testimony before the House Committee on International Relations, Washington, DC, July 16, 2003, available at www.interpol.org/Public/ICPO/speeches/SG20030716.asp.

18. Ibid.

19. See Brownlow.

20. See Graham Satchwell, *21st Century Health Care Terrorism: The Perils of International Drug Counterfeiting* (San Francisco: Pacific Research Institute, September 2005), available at www.pacificresearch.org/pub/sab/health/2005/Graham_Satchwell.pdf. Projected growth to 2010: counterfeit drug sales—13% annually; legitimate pharmaceutical commerce—7.5%.

21. Global Options, Inc., *An Analysis of Terrorist Threats to the American Medical Supply* (Gaithersburg, MD: Signature Book Printing, 2003), available at www.globaloptions.com/booktext2003.pdf.

22. The area where Paraguay, Argentina, and Brazil meet, which is a well-known haven for smugglers and other criminals.

23. See Louise I. Shelley, "The Nexus of Organized Criminals and Terrorism," available at www.american.edu/traccc/resources/publications/shelle51.pdf.

24. Michael Braun, "Counternarcotics Strategy in Latin America," testimony before the House Committee on International Relations, Subcommittee on the Western Hemisphere, Washington, DC, March 30, 2006, available at www.house.gov/international_relations/109/bra033006.pdf.

25. See The Library of Congress, Federal Research Division, *Terrorist and Organized Crime Groups in the Tri-Border Area (TBA) of South America*, July 2003, available at www.loc.gov/rr/frd/pdf-files/TerrOrgCrime_TBA.pdf.

26. The White House, "Introduction," *The National Security Strategy of the United States of America* (Washington, DC: The White House, March 2006), available at www.whitehouse.gov/nsc/nss/2006/intro.html.

27. See National Security Council, "International Crime Control Strategy," available at http://clinton2.nara.gov/WH/EOP/NSC/html/documents/iccs-frm.html.

28. Wagley, 4.

29. Kimberley L. Thachuk, *Terrorism's Financial Lifeline: Can It Be Severed?* Strategic Forum 191 (Washington, DC: National Defense University Press, May 2002), available at http://www.ndu.edu/inss/strforum/SF191/SF191.pdf.

INDEX

An "n" after a page number denotes a note on that page; a "t" after a page number denotes a table on that page.

About the Editor
and Contributors

Kimberley L. Thachuk is the Assistant Director of the Transformation Short Course Program and a Senior Fellow at the Center for Technology and National Security Policy at the National Defense University. She was previously a Visiting Professor in the Security Policy Studies Program of the Elliott School of International Affairs at The George Washington University where she directed the Transnational Threats Concentration. Her research is mainly on Transnational Threats to national security, including organized crime and terrorism, drug, human, and arms trafficking, alien smuggling, smuggling of weapons of mass destruction, cyber threats, and health and environmental threats. She holds a Multidisciplinary PhD in Criminology/Political Science/Latin American Studies from Simon Fraser University, Canada.

Esther A. Bacon is a Supervisory Intelligence Analyst in the Federal Bureau of Investigation. Prior to joining the FBI, Ms. Bacon was a Research Analyst in the Institute for National Strategic Studies at the National Defense University. She holds a bachelor of science from Boston University and a master of arts from New York University. Both degrees are in political science and international relations.

Spike Bowman is a Senior Research Fellow in the Center for Technology and National Security Policy at the National Defense University. Prior to this appointment, he was Director of the Intelligence Issues Group at the Federal Bureau of Investigation. He received his Juris Doctor from the University of Idaho and holds a master of laws degree with highest honors from The George Washington University.

Svante E. Cornell is Research Director of the Central Asia–Caucasus Institute and Silk Road Studies Program, a joint transatlantic research and policy center affiliated with The Johns Hopkins University–SAIS and Uppsala University.

Audra K. Grant is a Political Scientist with the RAND Corporation. Before joining RAND in 2004, she worked as a Policy Analyst for the U.S. Department of State, Bureau of Intelligence. She is also Assistant Professor at Alkhawayn University in Ifrane, Morocco, where she teaches courses related to Middle East politics and American foreign policy. She holds a PhD in political science from the University of Wisconsin-Milwaukee. In 2003, she was awarded the Franklin Award for expanding the State Department's Middle East research program after September 11.

André D. Hollis is a vice president of the Van Scoyoc Associates, Inc., and focuses on homeland security, homeland defense, and transnational threats. He graduated from Princeton University and earned a Distinguished Military Graduate Commission in the U.S. Army. He also earned his Juris doctorate from the University of Virginia School of Law.

Rollie Lal is a Political Scientist at the RAND Corporation. She is the author of *Understanding China and India: Security Implications for the United States and the World* (Praeger Security International, 2006) and *Central Asia and Its Neighbors: Security and Commerce at the Crossroads* (RAND, 2006). She holds a BA in economics from the University of Maryland, an MA in strategic studies, and a PhD in international relations from The Johns Hopkins School of Advanced International Studies.

Francis T. Miko is a Specialist in International Relations in the Congressional Research Service at the Library of Congress.

Richard L. Millett is a Senior Advisor for Latin America at Political Risk Services and Research Associate in the Center for International Studies at the University of Missouri–St. Louis. He has published widely, and his articles have appeared in *Foreign Policy*, *The Wilson Quarterly*, and *The New Republic*. He received his undergraduate degree from Harvard University and his master's and doctoral degrees from the University of New Mexico.

Boris O. Saavedra, Brigadier General, Venezuelan Air Force (Ret), is the Liaison Officer between the Center of Hemispheric Defense Studies at the National Defense University and the Inter-American Defense College. General Saavedra received a BS in science and military arts from the Venezuelan Air Force Academy and a master's degree in international policy and practice from The George Washington University. He has published articles in the areas of transnational security issues, terrorism, civil-military relations, education, management, and strategic planning.

Louise I. Shelley is founding director of TraCCC (www.american.edu/traccc) and a leading expert on transnational crime and terrorism with a particular focus on the former Soviet Union. She is a professor in the School of International Service at the American University. She is the recipient of fellowships from the John Simon Guggenheim Memorial Foundation, National Endowment for the Humanities, International Research and Exchanges Board, Kennan Institute, and Fulbright Program and received a grant from the John D. and Catherine T. MacArthur Foundation to establish Russian organized crime study centers that are still functioning over a decade later.

Rhea Siers is a member of the adjunct faculty in the Elliott School of International Affairs and a Senior Fellow of the Homeland Security Policy Institute, both at The George Washington University.

David Smigielski is an Analyst at the Central Intelligence Agency. He has worked on national security issues in the nonprofit and private sectors and spent 2 years working on nonproliferation and nuclear security issues at the Washington, DC-based Russian-American Nuclear Security Advisory Council. Mr. Smigielski holds a master's degree from the George Washington University's Elliott School of International Affairs and a bachelor's degree in political science from Eastern Michigan University.

Anny Wong is a Political Scientist at the RAND Corporation. Her research covers science and technology policy, international development, international relations with a focus on East and Southeast Asia, U.S. Army security cooperation, and performance measurement. Since 2000, she has also been a contributing author to the Freedom House annual report, *Freedom in the World*, a survey of political freedom and civil liberties around the world. She received her PhD in Political Science from the University of Hawaii at Manoa.

James L. Zackrison is a lecturer for International Strategic Studies Association conferences, and has most recently presented papers on the involvement of gangs in smuggling and how smuggling finances terror networks worldwide. He was formerly a senior Latin America analyst for the U.S. Navy, where he specialized in producing analysis on geopolitics, naval capabilities, doctrine and strategy, terrorism, and drug trafficking. He holds master's degrees in Latin American history and national security studies from Loma Linda University and the California State University and is working on a doctorate in history at St. Antony's College at Oxford University.

DATE DUE

Demco, Inc. 38-293